My Life in High Heels

My Life in High Heels

Loni Anderson

with Larkin Warren

William Morrow and Company, Inc.
New York

The authors gratefully acknowledge permission to use the following:

Quote from *Designing Women* courtesy Linda Bloodworth-Thomason

I WON'T SEND ROSES
Music and lyrics by Jerry Herman
© JERRY HERMAN
All rights controlled by JERRYCO MUSIC CO.
Exclusive Agent: Edwin H. Morris & Company, a division of
MPL COMMUNICATIONS, INC.
All Rights Reserved

It is the policy of William Morrow and Company, Inc., and its imprints and affiliates, recognizing the importance of preserving what has been written, to print the books we publish on acid-free paper, and we exert our best efforts to that end.

Library of Congress Cataloging-in-Publication Data

Anderson, Loni, 1945–
    My life in high heels / by Loni Anderson, with Larkin Warren.
      p. cm.
    ISBN 0-688-14272-9
    1. Anderson, Loni, 1945–   . 2. Actors—United States—Biography.
I. Warren, Larkin. II. Title.
PN2287.A59A3 1995
791.45'028'092—dc20
[B]   95-24197
                                                                                      CIP

Printed in the United States of America

5   7   9   10   8   6   4

BOOK DESIGN BY SUSAN HOOD

This book is dedicated with great love to the circle of my life—
to my parents, with gratitude, and to all the loved ones who came
before them; to my sister and my friends, and all the extended
family they bring with them; to my children and grandchildren,
in celebration; and to all the loved ones who will come after

December 5, 1994—just three short weeks before Christmas, and the last place I wanted to be was sitting in a small courtroom in Los Angeles. Although the streets outside didn't look remotely like the snow-covered ones of my Minnesota childhood, they were decorated with all the signs of the season, providing a bittersweet contrast to what was going on in this room.

My divorce from Burt Reynolds had been final for some months, and so, I had hoped, was all the wrangling about property, custody, child support, visitation—all the heartbreaking details that any couple deals with when their dream of a life together goes sour. It was not my first encounter with sorrow and disappointment, and I had long ago learned that the only way to get on with life is just to *do* it. And yet we kept coming back into rooms like this one, with judges, lawyers, and accountants, all of them negotiating, arguing, and objecting, while the family at the heart of this (and we were a family, no matter how splintered) tried to muddle through. Each day contained something that required attention and emotional energy—children, grandchildren, birthdays, holidays—yet everything kept coming back to this. It didn't help that every step of the way was accompanied by camera crews, reporters, and an inevitable two-minute sound bite on that night's *Hard Copy* or *Inside Edition*.

I tried to concentrate on what was being said, tried to listen closely to the man in the witness chair. If anyone had told me a decade ago that this was where he and I would end up, I would not have believed it—because this time, I had promised myself, was the keeper. This time I'm sticking until we're both too old to get out of our rocking chairs and too toothless to argue about it. We had been through so much before we were actually married, it was almost incomprehensible that tougher times lay ahead. I guess there's something oddly comforting about that kind of naïveté—and if a woman can't have it on her wedding day, then what's the point of getting married at all?

Burt seemed to be having a hard time on the witness stand. The lawyers (one of whom, I admit, was mine) were dancing rings around him. He didn't know his net worth, he said. He didn't know where the millions had gone these past few months. He was sorry he couldn't keep his promises. His eyes behind his glasses looked uncertain and confused.

It was hard to see in him the funny, romantic dazzler who had swept me off my feet, the one who had flown me from one end of the country to the other just so we could spend our first New Year's Eve together. And what a night it had been: champagne, lovemaking, a slow dance au naturel on a terrace under the Florida stars—a dizzying sense that from that moment on, nothing would ever again be the same.

I wasn't a child when I fell in love with Burt Reynolds. I had been married and divorced twice; I had raised a daughter; I had a successful television career, my own house, my own car, my own life. I had heard the gossip—his temper, his moodiness, and the long roster of other women, the ones he had loved, the ones he had left. But when I looked at him, I didn't see the cowboy, the charmer, the Peck's bad boy of Hollywood. Instead I saw a man who reminded me of my dad, strong and masterful, someone who could make me laugh, keep me safe, be my friend. A true partner, to share my life and the people and things I loved.

We were together nearly twelve years. I wouldn't have married him—or adopted a son with him—if I hadn't expected us to be together the rest of our lives. We'd had our battles, God knows, but I always believed that the biggest battle was the one we fought together—the drug addiction and terrible depression that had interrupted and nearly ended his career. Over and over, I thought we had won it. But as anyone who has been in that kind of battle knows, it's never over. The only weapon you have with addiction is truth—and in our lives, truth had become a casualty a long time ago.

As I sat in that courtroom, a wave of real sadness rolled over me, the kind I had struggled to keep under control for more than a year. I didn't recognize the man I'd been married to anymore. He had crawled so far inside himself that there was no reaching him. Once, I might've crawled in after him and dragged him out. But no more.

I tried to distract myself with a list of things to do—or, more realistically, a list of things undone. I hadn't finished the Christmas cards, I hadn't finished the Christmas shopping. I hadn't yet wielded one single cookie cutter, hadn't had a consultation with Santa. I was distracted and irritated, and a certain six-year-old was getting pretty cranky about it.

After his rambling testimony, Burt stepped down and walked the short distance to his own table, his own chair, his own lawyer. It was a walk that took him past where I was sitting, and as he approached, I tensed up. When our eyes met, he paused, for just a moment. "Honey," he whispered down to me, "please make them stop this now. Don't let them humiliate me anymore." And then he walked past me.

I sat back in my chair, stunned. Excuse me? *Honey?* Don't *let* them? Hey, this divorce was never *my* idea. Scenes from the past eighteen months went racing through my memory like a bad video on fast-forward. Who served whom with divorce papers and a one-way plane ticket out of Florida? Who gave an interview to the *National Enquirer,* accusing me of sleeping around? Who posed for *Enquirer* pictures in a hot tub with another woman?—a woman, it turned out, who had been in the background for years, a woman who'd been waiting for my husband in a hotel room a few blocks from where I sat beaming with pride the night Burt won his Emmy for *Evening Shade.* Who was it, I wanted to ask him, had brought our lives crashing down around our feet? Not me, *honey*.

For a breathless moment or two, it was all I could do to keep from picking up a piece of furniture—a chair, say—and hurling it at someone's head. His, maybe. But furniture-hurling has never been my style. And we were beyond the point where that kind of anger could have done any good. Besides, we still had to get past those reporters standing outside the courtroom. And then we still had to come back the next day and try to settle this. In the meantime I wanted only to go home for dinner, to the big house filled with light and love, where the littlest inhabitant just wanted to talk about Santa Claus.

I took a deep breath, sat up as straight as I could, and said to myself, Loni, let it go. *Just let it go.*

My Life in High Heels

"When all is said and done, the only thing that counts is what is true, and truly felt. And how we treated one another."

—Julia Sugarbaker, *Designing Women*

Chapter 1

Of all the romantic stories in novels and fairy tales and movies, here's my favorite one: My parents fell in love at first sight. Well, at least my mother did. Maxine Kallin was just fourteen when she saw Klaydon Anderson in the hallway of her high school in St. Paul. He was the new kid, a senior whose family had just moved from Iowa. And if anybody typified a young girl's dream of "tall, dark, and handsome," he did. As Maxine watched him walk past her and on down the hall, she turned to her girlfriend and said firmly, "That's the man I'm going to marry."

My mother was probably every potential mother-in-law's nightmare. She had long legs, red hair and flashing brown eyes, and a figure that stopped traffic, and she registered an unashamed "10" on the Serious Flirt Scale. She even flirted with the school principal—heck, that's how she got through school, she told us later, laughing merrily while she told tales on herself. She had a wonderful sense of humor and fun, and she loved to dance, to go places and have good times. And her dearest wish in life was to find a boy she could adore, marry him, have babies, and live happily ever after.

Dad didn't actually meet Mom until after he'd graduated. When she was a senior, she went one evening—with a date—to a local dance club where all their friends congregated. My unsuspecting future dad walked in with a pal of his, a boy who had always been after Maxine to go out with him but whom she couldn't stand. Fearless when she wanted something, she marched right up to them and got her introduction to Klaydon, whom everybody back then called Gat. And then she asked him to dance.

"I don't dance," he told her.

"Well, I just *love* to dance," she retorted, and steered him out onto the floor. Where they proceeded to dance and dance and dance.

When her date finally came up to claim the wayward Maxine, he was not a happy man. "Excuse me, but you're with me," he huffed.

My straitlaced, proper dad was mortified. Horning in on another guy's date wasn't his way of doing things. "Oh, I'm so sorry," he stammered to his dance partner. "I didn't know you were here with someone. My apologies. And to the gentleman, too." Mom just glared at her date.

At the end of the evening, she went up to Gat and handed him a piece of paper. "Here's my telephone number," she said. "Call me sometime, and I'll teach you to dance."

My dad just shook his head and said to his friend, "I think I better stay away from that one. I could really get to like her—and I think she's trouble."

But he did call her, of course, and they did go out. They dated for almost three months before he even kissed her. I was just a little girl when I first heard this story, and this detail didn't square with what I knew of fairy tales. "But, Daddy," I asked, "why didn't you kiss her?"

"Because I knew that she was the one. And I knew if I kissed her, I wouldn't be able to stop."

One night, exasperated, my mom just put her face right smack up to his, and, Dad said, "I just had to kiss it." That settled the matter for both of them.

When World War II broke out, Dad left college and joined the navy, going into officer candidate school. While he was still in training, in a breaking-the-rules move that was completely uncharacteristic of the kind of person he was, he went AWOL to see Maxine. As punishment he was tossed out of OCS and ended up an enlisted man, stationed in Memphis, waiting for what he knew would ultimately be a transfer to the Philippines.

"Marry me before you go," wrote the determined Maxine to her sweetheart, "or I won't be here when you get back."

So he sent for her, and they were married on November 13, 1943, the day after he turned twenty-one. His parents—my Grampa Carl and Gramma Sally—were horrified. They had wanted him to marry his childhood sweetheart, Ardith; in fact, my grandmother called my mother Ardith for years afterward. After it stopped being painful, it got to be funny.

The new Mrs. Anderson stayed in Memphis for more than a year, praying each night with her husband, both of them on their knees, for a baby, a son whose name, they'd decided, would be Gary. But there was no baby. Mom came home to Minnesota to see her family, and while she was there, her husband was transferred to San Diego, a preliminary to being shipped out to the Pacific. Grampa Carl felt bad for her, so he gave her the train fare to go to San Diego for a three-day farewell weekend.

There, their prayers were finally answered—she came home pregnant—and then he went off to war in the Pacific. He was a radioman in a bomb squadron. I have all his journals and pictures and their letters to each other. It's a devastating and moving record of my dad's experience of the war.

The son my parents had hoped for was, instead, me. Dad had wanted to name me Leilani, after a name he'd heard in the islands. He liked the musicality of it, he said, but he thought I'd probably take a lot of teasing for the first syllable and so settled for Loni Kaye. Sometimes he would sing "Sweet Leilani, heavenly flower . . ." and promise that someday he would take us to Hawaii, which he had loved.

My little sister, Andrea, came along three years later. We lived in Roseville, a suburb of St. Paul. After the war, Dad sold furniture for a while, and he made a pretty good living at it. But my grandfather, who owned his own chemical company, had always wanted his only son to come into the business with him.

Dad went back to night school, became a chemist, and joined the company, and years later it finally became his own. It was environmental chemistry, all about water, noise, and air pollution—he was way ahead of his time, I think. After he sold the company to a big national conglomerate, he stayed on as a district manager, running a five-state area.

My mother had achieved her dream—being Andy's wife (he'd become Andy in the navy) and being our mother. It was her job, and she took it very, very seriously. We used to joke that we lived in the kind of house where, if you got up in the middle of the night for a glass of water, when you came back into the room, your bed had been made.

And no matter how much Mom had scrubbed and vacuumed during the day, she looked like Donna Reed when Dad came home from work at night. Dinner was ready, waiting warm in the oven, and she was all dressed up and gorgeous, in high heels, fresh makeup, the works. I would watch as she chose a pair of earrings out of the little velvet jewelry box that played "Star Dust," patted some Chanel No. 5 on her wrists, and got ready for him to come through the door. He took her in his arms and gave her a backbend kiss just about every night. Then they'd have cocktails and hors d'oeuvres, and Andrea and I were dismissed until dinner. It was their time together. We would try to be patient, reading or playing in our room, but after a while we'd kind of wander into the living room, and there they'd be, her on his lap, cooing and kissing.

"Are we going to have dinner soon?" we'd ask, and Mom would giggle.

"Oh, Andy," she'd say, "we forgot about the girls!"

She was so crazy about him; sometimes after he left for work, she would go into the closet and inhale the scent of his clothes—his shirts, his sportcoats.

After we were put to bed at night, we could hear them singing to each other while they cleaned up the kitchen. They sang all the forties songs and danced around the living room. One night I woke up in the middle of the night and heard them singing in their bedroom, harmonizing to "It's Been a Long, Long Time."

"Kiss me once, then kiss me twice, then kiss me once again . . ."

But they fought, too, and they were noisy about it. Never anything violent or physical, never slamming out the door or "I'm going home to mother" or anything like that. But they were both stubborn, strong-willed people, and they weren't reluctant to stand toe-to-toe and argue.

And then they'd make up. Passionately. I used to think, gosh, maybe that's the point. Because whatever they were, my parents were passionate. About each other, about us—they had huge fights about us, about how we were to be raised, about what was good for us. But they always worked it out. I don't remember being scared of the fights, because whatever was going on between them, it wasn't scary. It was just the way they were.

And they always, each of them, had a place, a role. Dad would sit in his chair, with his feet up, watching television, and he'd say, "Mackie, I'd like a beer." And she would immediately jump up and go get it. And I'd think, what, he can't walk? Why does she do that?

And then ten minutes later, Mom might say, "Oh, Andy, I'm out of cigarettes." And Dad would *fly* right out of that chair, go jump into the car, and head for the corner store to get her cigarettes!

From the time I was little, I watched them closely, trying to figure out the secret of what was between them, and how, because of that secret, everything in our lives seemed to fall into an orderly pattern. He did the yard work, she did the laundry; she cleaned the house, he took out the trash. He made the money, she stayed home. And they both cooked. I didn't need to wait until the eighties and "The New Man" to see a man who was comfortable in the kitchen; I had that from my earliest childhood.

Mom was not a morning person, so Dad made breakfast. I mean, if you got a box of cold cereal from my mother while she was in her morning haze, having her coffee and cigarettes, you were lucky. Instead, there would be my dad, whistling, singing, an eggs-and-bacon, everybody-happy kind of man. How he did that every morning I can remember, I will never know. Because boy, could he drink. They both could. And did.

It was the kind of drinking everybody did back then, I think, and it wasn't confined to Saturday night. Maybe you had a martini or two for lunch and cocktails before dinner, and then you had drinks or wine with dinner, and then you had after-dinner drinks, and then you went to bed. They both smoked heavily, three, maybe four packs of cigarettes a day each. And they went out every Friday and Saturday night and danced and partied until all hours.

Some people remember their parents as being stuffy or old. I remember mine as having a complete blast together most of the time. They even had plans for what they were going to do after Andrea and I grew up and moved out. They would have a restaurant. It would be called, they told us, grinning, the KlayMax Klub!

Our family social life centered to a great degree on our church, Resurrection Lutheran. My parents were elders in the church, and they taught catechism and the youth group. Dad made popcorn for the Saturday movies, and they were both chaperons at the dances. So, no matter how much of a ruckus they might've raised on Saturday night, we were all at church on Sunday morning. When I was in junior high school, I started teaching Sunday school, and I taught it all through high school.

One time, when Andrea and I weren't babies anymore, Mom decided she wanted to get a job, in a dress shop. So she did that for a while, and pretty successfully, too. But when they offered her a job as manager, that was it for Dad.

"I want you here during the day for the girls," he said, "and when I come home, I want you to be here for me." So that was it for her, too. She said OK, no more job. It wasn't even a fight. Her life was about Andy and what he wanted, and if he wanted her home, well, that was fine with her.

We all felt like that about him. He was really revered, among their friends and in his business community. He won all kinds of trophies and awards, from the chamber of commerce, from his colleagues. The best this, the top that. He was as handsome as she was gorgeous—black hair, strong blue eyes, a solid six feet tall. As he grew older, he got more imposing and began to look like the movie version of a Mafia don. I adored him; he was my hero. From the very beginning, he and I had the kind of talks . . . well, there was very little I wouldn't tell him. From the time I was a little girl, he took me fishing with him, taught me how to bait a hook, gut a fish. I felt like his buddy, his pal.

With my mother, my relationship wasn't quite so cozy, especially as I became an adolescent. She'd say, "Why can't you be like so-and-so?" She wasn't talking about my grades, either, because I always got terrific grades. But she didn't care if I failed everything, as long as I was more outgoing. More fun. More like her.

She wanted me to be a cheerleader in school, and to be in the drama club. I was in the school choir instead. She and my grandmother were teaching me to sew (my dad called Mom "Maxini Kallini and her Sewing Machini")—because it was practical, Mom said, but I loved to sit at the machine for hours, playing with fabric, inventing costumes, using up the "good" thread. I painted and drew, taking my sketchbook everywhere. I loved to sit alone and read—fairy tales when I was little, then mysteries, then the classics, and anything I could get my hands on in the school library. I had consumed the whole Nancy Drew series by the time I was fifteen, read *Gone with the Wind* before I ever saw the movie, and sobbed over Somerset Maugham's *Of Human Bondage* the summer I was sixteen. But that was a waste of time, Mom said— they were having a dance somewhere, why wasn't I at it? College wasn't a big part of her plan for me. She talked about how important it was that I "make a good match." Like she did.

But I didn't want to do what she did. She was always so flirtatious, so outrageous. She'd have a few drinks, and she'd be twirling and dancing and laughing, the life of the party, and I'd think, why can't she be like everybody else's mother? When I think of her now, I see her in a big picture hat, leaning on her elbows, with a cigarette in one hand. She'd wave her hands while she talked, and all of a sudden, *zzztt*, there would be a tiny cigarette hole burned into the hat brim. To me, my father was like a romantic knight out of one of my books, but Mom was like . . . well, not like I wanted to be.

I wanted to be classy. Elegant. Grace Kelly elegant. I listened to opera, I watched ballet on television. I didn't necessarily want to *do* opera or ballet, but there was something about them that thrilled me. "Turn that stuff down," everybody would say.

I loved pretty clothes from the very beginning. One Christmas my cousins were all bragging about the toys they got, but all I could talk about was my patent leather shoes. The minute I took them out of the box, I hugged them and hugged them and couldn't put them down. I even wanted to take them to bed with me.

I never wanted to get dirty—so I simply didn't. I could play outside all day, climb trees, build forts, and never get a spot on me. I could go fishing with Dad, bait the line, catch a fish, gut it, and pack it in the cooler, all while wearing a little ruffled sunsuit and a flower in my hair.

And I was such a goody two shoes. Miss Perfect. You weren't allowed to swear in front of me, heaven forbid. If you uttered a four-letter word in my presence, well, I'd just never speak to you again. I never swore at all, until one night in high school, my boyfriend Tony locked the car doors and threatened to keep tickling me until I said "shit." It was about three minutes before curfew when I finally gave in, spat out the word, and then sprinted for the front door.

Later, in my twenties, spurred on by another boyfriend (he had accused me of not knowing how to get mad), I stood in front of the mirror glaring at myself until I finally said, "*Fuck* it!"— and then saw my dad standing out in the hallway behind me. When our eyes met, we both started laughing helplessly. But that moment took years to get to, and it wasn't repeated soon.

I got my first kiss at twelve—and rushed right into the house to brush my teeth. And if a boy tried to get away with more than a kiss, well, that was it, he was out the door. I broke up with guys just for suggesting the possibility of going any further. In fact, years later my sister said to me, "You had so many boyfriends, I thought you were promiscuous. But it was because you kept banishing them!"

I lectured to my friends, too, judging everyone by my own

standards and usually finding them wanting. It was all about per-fection—not about achieving it, like the saints spent their lives trying to do, but about already *having* it. My way was the perfect way. It's little wonder they called me "conceited" in high school.

My little sister was different. Being perfect was of no interest whatsoever to her. She was a tomboy, she got into scrapes, she hardly ever did what she was told—in short, she never tried to fit anybody else's idea of what her "role" should be. I was the sweet one, and Andrea was the rowdy one. At least, "sweet" was the word all my relatives used. "Loni is so sweet," they'd say approvingly. "But that Andrea, she's something else again."

And she was a handful. Mom used to joke, "We would've had more children, but for Andrea. And if she had been the first, she would've been the only." My dad called her Ornerya; draw a line in the dirt, stand back, and count the seconds before Andrea would go over it.

She literally *did* cross a line once. She crawled out into the middle of the street when she was about eighteen months old. I wasn't quite five, and I stood right there like a dutiful statue and watched her do it. Because we had been told: Stay in the yard. Andrea had all her little cars lined up, pushing them up and down the white line. And I couldn't move. Finally I ran inside in a panic and told my mother the baby was out in the street. Mom was appropriately horror-struck and snatched her up in a heart-beat. I couldn't understand why *I* was scolded.

I started performing when I was still pretty little. Mom said I sang before I talked, sitting in my high chair and singing the popular postwar songs I heard on the radio. My first "public" performance, I guess, was the Christmas I was four. One of the department stores in St. Paul had a Christmas carol sing-along for all the kids who were in the store that day with their parents. I was standing in the crowd of little kids belting 'em out for all I was worth, and all of a sudden somebody said, "Hey, you, little girl. Come on up here, you can really sing." And I went right up onstage and starting singing like I knew what I was doing. My version of "Rudolph the Red-Nosed Reindeer" (no threat to Gene Autry's) was piped through the entire store. Thank goodness there's no tape of *that* in anybody's archives.

When my parents were out, and my grandparents would baby-sit, I'd sneak out of bed and down the hall when they were watching TV. Their chairs faced the television, so I could scooch down behind them and watch the wonderful variety shows of the fifties. I had no idea then, of course, that I was watching the "Golden Age" of television. I just knew that I liked Sid Caesar's *Your Show of Shows,* I liked Milton Berle. I liked the pretty girls in the long gowns who sang, I liked the dancers, I even liked the pie-in-the-face stuff. I liked it all. I loved listening to George Burns and Gracie Allen, the smart silliness of their marriage. He'd roll his eyes at something she had said, and you just knew he adored her.

And somewhere in there, I decided that although I fantasized about the ballet and opera, what I wanted to *be* was funny. W. C. Fields, Laurel and Hardy, the Marx Brothers. Slapstick made me roar, and as I grew older, I got all the jokes. When I'd watch with my dad, though, sometimes I pretended that I didn't—because it wouldn't have been ladylike to get some of those jokes, and I knew it. How, I pondered, could I want to be Grace Kelly *and* Gracie Allen?

When I was about six or seven years old, I saw some old movie on television where the leading lady, who played an actress, had a big library—the kind with a sliding ladder—and a big marble staircase that came sweeping down into the foyer. We lived in a little rented cracker-box house then, just like every other house on the street. And I said to my mother, "When I grow up, I'm going to be an actress. And I'm going to have a house just like that, with a marble staircase and a two-story library full of books, and you'll need a ladder to get to them all."

She just shook her head. "I don't like it when you talk like that, honey. It's like you think you're too good for everybody else," she said. "When you grow up, you'll probably live like Bea." Bea was the young woman who lived behind us; she was so pretty that all the men on the block watched her on Sundays when she mowed the lawn. "You'll have a nice little house like this one, and you'll be lucky if you have a really nice husband like hers, or a nice man like Daddy."

I didn't say anything else. She was wrong, I thought. She just had to be wrong.

From about first grade on, I organized plays in the neighborhood. We'd put on shows in the garage and charge nickels and dimes for them. Andrea was in them, too—we both sang and danced. Years later she played the lead in the musical *The Boy Friend* in high school, and I thought she was wonderful, talented and beautiful. But it wasn't what she wanted to do, so she didn't pursue it. I think we were very lucky that way. We never had much sibling rivalry; in fact, we've never even had an argument. And once I got a little braver about crossing lines, I became quite fierce about protecting her at school and on the playground (and she did get into a few face-offs!). She was my first real girlfriend.

Everybody told me from my childhood that I was pretty (everybody but my mom and dad, who didn't want me to get a swelled head), but I'm not sure I believed them. I had dark eyes, black hair, and olive skin in a family—in a state!—that was populated mostly by blue-eyed, fair-skinned, blond people. We were German, Norwegian, and Swedish (*Scandahoovian,* Dad said); everybody else in the family got the Norse genes, and I got the dark eyes, square jaw, and prominent cheekbones of some long-ago Slavic ancestor.

I understood early about ancestors and heredity and the "someplace else" where families had their beginnings. My father's German grandparents came through Ellis Island. My great-grandmother died just before I was born, and for a while we lived with my paternal grandparents, Carl and Sally, and my great-grandfather, Papa Pete, who spoke only German, had a full head of white hair and a white mustache, and took tremendous pride in never having been to a doctor in his life. His generation believed that if and when you went into a hospital, you never came out again.

The grandparents all lived downstairs, and we lived upstairs. I was in kindergarten then, and in my memory, it was blissful. If my mother was busy, I would just wander downstairs and find a playmate. I thought Grampa Carl was the only one who knew the right way to tie the bows on the back of my dresses. And I played with Papa Pete every day. I don't remember ever having any difficulty talking with him, joking with him—but I didn't speak German, and he didn't speak English, so how could that memory be right?

One day, when Andrea was two and taking a nap, my mother and Gramma went next door to a neighbor's for coffee. I was playing with Papa Pete in the living room, jumping around, hiding behind the sofa, and he was finding me, coming around the other side and saying "Boo!" and then laughing. Suddenly he put his hand to his chest, said, *"Ach, liebling,"* and sat down on the sofa. And then he died. He was ninety-one.

I waited a second and then sat down on the sofa next to him, half expecting him to open his eyes and say "Boo!" again. Minutes passed, maybe five, maybe ten. I took his hand. And gradually I had a feeling that something was wrong. "Papa?" I said softly. I knew I'd better go next door and get my mother. So I stood up and kind of patted his arm a little, and then I went to the neighbor's.

When my grandmother came to the door, she was slightly impatient. "What is it?"

"Something's wrong with Papa . . . ," I started, and in seconds both she and my mother came crashing through the screen door, practically flattening me. They were hysterical, first for Papa, then for me. I had been in the room with him, and he was dead.

They wouldn't let me back in the house. They made me go down the street to my friend Lana's house. From there I watched the first aid squad come, the ambulance lights flashing, the bell clanging. I wasn't scared. I just couldn't understand why I couldn't go back over there, where the excitement was. Where Papa Pete was.

When I saw him in the casket, everybody carefully explained to me that he couldn't play with me anymore, that he had gone to heaven. Gone. But he's right there in front of me, I thought. And I clearly remember now the feeling of being sad and, finally, a little frightened. That first-time feeling of "getting it." Gone, and not coming back.

Grampa Carl died of a heart attack later that same year. And then, when I was twelve, my mother's sister, Jackie, died of a cerebral hemorrhage, leaving three daughters behind. She was only thirty-six, and it was awful around our house for weeks, everyone was so sad.

But the grandmothers, Gramma Sally and Gramma Hazel, my mother's mother, both lived for a long, long time. They even outlived their children, my parents. They were a constant part of our lives, and not just at holidays and birthdays and funerals. They were part of my own daughter's childhood, part of the extended family that welcomed her and raised her. From them I learned about the wisdom of old age, about the importance of family— and about the power of matriarchs.

Each night, my dad would read fairy tales to Andrea and me at bedtime, and in every single story, the princess was fair-haired. "Hair of gold, hair of sunlight." Like Andrea had, and all my cousins. The only ones with dark hair were the stepsisters or the sorceresses or the wicked stepmothers. One night, halfway through a story session, I started to cry.

That's when Dad found Snow White for me. "With her hair as black as night," he would read, "and skin as white as snow, and lips as red as roses." He began to bring me Snow White books and toys and knickknacks. I could probably open a Snow White museum with what I've collected since. I grew absolutely certain that Snow White had been created just for me. She wasn't wishy-washy—she marched those seven dwarfs around like a drill sergeant—and yet she still got her Prince Charming.

When I was ten, I got my first part in a school play, a musical, as an Indian princess. This was years before politically correct casting (especially in grade school), and with my cheekbones and coloring, I would be a prime candidate for the Indian Princess for years. This first time, the cast was supposed to be all sixth graders. Although I was only in the fifth grade, they bent the rules and took me because I had long black hair and could sing.

The way this happened is important only because it's the way my luck continued to break at each turn of the road in my career: There would be an obstacle, a roadblock, a perfectly good reason someone would tell me, "No, you can't even audition for this part." And then something would happen, and the obstacle would disappear. Or the roadblock would push me, gently, in a direction I hadn't even considered, and option number two would end up being far more desirable than option number one had been. Loni's Luck, Dad called it.

Back then, being the queen of the first grade, the queen of the second grade, the queen of the third grade . . . well, it was pretty much fun. The Disney cartoons and the fairy tales I was reading made royalty a suitable vocation. It gave you access to the Handsome Prince, after all. And for someone with my self-righteous devotion to perfection, being crowned queen on a regular basis just seemed like a natural state of affairs.

When I was fourteen, my mom saw an advertisement in the paper that a downtown department store, the Emporium, was having a contest for "Miss Thermo-Jac." Thermal clothing—Minnesota, you know. The deal was, you had your picture taken in an item of Thermo-Jac clothing that you selected, and then, the following weekend, the winner's picture would appear in the newspaper. That's how you'd find out if you had won. And if you did win, you got to keep the article of clothing you had worn for the picture. I was a little reluctant at first, but when I saw that white jacket with fur around the hood, I was convinced. So I posed, we went home, and I didn't think much about it. Except, of course, a passing thought now and again about that coat. And I was also quite aware that, at least this once, I had pleased Mom.

The next Saturday morning, about ten minutes after the sun came up, my mother rushed out the door to scoop up the newspaper. And there I was, the winner. Mother was so proud—she showed my picture to everybody—and I got to keep the beautiful white jacket with the fur hood. *Hmm,* I thought. This all seems pretty painless.

After that, she entered me in everything, and I cheerfully went along for the ride. Over the years I was Miss Thom McAn (with shoes for prizes!), Miss Good Grooming, Miss Country Style Ford, Miss St. Paul Open—Miss whatever you have, Loni was in it. Each had a prize attached, and a newspaper photo. Soon I was being paid to model in local department store fashion shows. By the time I was in high school, I was working regularly. At a time when other girls were begging to wear makeup—or deciding in protest not to wear any at all—I wore it quite happily almost every day, along with upswept hair, high heels, and white gloves.

St. Paul and Minneapolis—the Twin Cities—have always been very culture-centered, with small community theater companies and dinner theaters growing up around a nexus that included the St. Paul Chamber Orchestra, the Minnesota Opera, the Minneapolis Orchestra, the Children's Theatre Company, the Walker Art Center, and the prestigious Guthrie Theater, which opened in 1963. Performing artists of every kind came through town, and I went to everything I could, imagining myself in their shoes. In 1960, when I wasn't cast in our high school's production of *The Diary of Anne Frank,* I auditioned with the Roseville Players and the Roseville Little Theater, a community theater quite near my home. No money, of course, but parts—little ones at first, then bigger ones. All that mattered to me was that I was doing it. I was onstage, singing, dancing, being funny, or being elegant. Being somebody else.

During this time, my mom sent me on weekends to Patricia Stevens School, a finishing and modeling school in St. Paul. Here, she hoped, I would learn to walk, learn deportment, learn which fork was which, learn how to apply makeup, how to fix my hair—I would be "finished." It was good training for me, and often fun—kind of like playing another part—but the people there weren't terribly encouraging about the way I looked. Lips too big, nose too pug, face too wide, hair just too-too. *Tsk, tsk,* they shook their heads. Probably not much hope for you.

I was in junior high school—and had just started to go out with boys—the first time somebody said to Mom, "Your daughter's sexy." She was amused, I think, and grinned when she told me,

"So-and-so thinks you're sexy." And I remember thinking, well, that's just so *weird*. I mean, what does that mean, really?

I don't think that I really knew then what sex appeal was—but whatever it was, I seemed to have it. I was fully developed quite early, and that, along with my dark hair and coloring, must have made me seem exotic indeed. But it was almost as though the way I looked didn't have anything to do with me. There I was, running around in short shorts, fairly clueless about the havoc I was wreaking. By the time I was in my early teens, there were boys out in front of the house all the time, with their bikes and motorcycles and cars. My poor dad would just clutch his head with his hands, shaking it back and forth, muttering, "Oh, my God."

Sometimes there would be a fight, and Dad would have to go out and be the peacemaker. I stopped dating a guy once, and he made a scene in the front yard. I can remember looking out the window, and there was Dad, comforting him.

"Loni, why did you treat him like that?" Dad asked when he came back in the house.

"Well," I said, "there's this other guy who wants to take me out, and I think he's kind of cute, so . . ."

But what a disappointment I must have been to those boys—because whatever they expected, they sure didn't get it from me. I mean, I looked like I looked, but underneath was this prissy Lutheran Sunday school teacher, prone to giving lectures on swearing and the dangers of "going too far." Imagine *Saturday Night Live*'s Church Lady locked up in Sophia Loren's body. My looks belied who I really was. Which, I believe, is true to this day.

I went steady with Tony in high school, and when he went off to California to college—he was two years older than I—we were still going steady, but . . . well, he was in California and I was in Minnesota. Then I met Ken, who was going to West Point—he was the goalie for their hockey team—and somehow I ended up pinned to him. So there I was, going steady with a guy in California, pinned to a guy at West Point. But they were in different time zones, right? And it's not like I was having sex with anybody—because that wasn't what I did, remember—so it wasn't as dangerous as it sounds.

During the high school phase of my Miss This, Miss That period, I got to know the local news photographers. And whenever celebrities would come to town, the photographers would call and say, so-and-so's going to be here, or there's going to be a big concert, so Loni, just come down and we'll take your picture. They would plant me in a strategic location, and I'd get picked out of a line for tickets, or out of a concert crowd, and get to meet the celebrity of the moment. The next day, there would be my picture in the paper with a caption reading something like, "This lucky fan, Loni Kaye Anderson of Roseville, was just thrilled to meet so-and-so." And they were right, I usually *was* thrilled.

One afternoon in 1963, the popular singing group The Brothers Four, who had hit the charts a couple of years before with "Greenfields," was going to appear at the Orpheum Theater in St. Paul as part of the movie premiere of *55 Days at Peking*, starring Charlton Heston and Ava Gardner. They had recorded the film's theme song, "So Little Time," and were coming to sign albums. The Brothers Four were a very big deal indeed: Within two or three years, they performed on more than two hundred college campuses, as well as on *The Ed Sullivan Show*, *The Pat Boone-Chevy Showroom*, and *Sing Along with Mitch*.

So when my photographer pals called me, I dressed right up, went to the theater, and had my picture taken meeting the members of the group. And when a case of mistaken identity led someone to ask me, "Oh, Miss Gardner, will you sign my album?" I just giggled and went along with it, signing "Ava Gardner" with a flourish.

The Brothers had all been University of Washington students just a couple of years before, and as I chatted with them, they seemed not a lot different from the guys in my own hometown—although, as one friend of mine said, they did record great make-out music. One of them in particular—Bob Flick, the bass player—made my heart beat just a little faster. Remember the time in your life when "boys" were "cute"? Well, Bob was cute—although he wasn't a boy, he was twenty-four. When I told him I was in school, he assumed I meant college, which was fine with me. I wasn't about to admit I was seventeen.

We started to keep in touch, and I would see him whenever the group came through town. I also traveled to see him when the Brothers were in concert in other cities.

For someone who fantasized being in a Carole Lombard movie (as Carole Lombard), I was in heaven. Boyfriends on both coasts and one on the road—what a setup! I got lots of fun mail—and had my weekends free for modeling work at the Emporium department store, where I was on the elevated runway on Saturdays, as well as on Monday and Thursday nights, when the store was open late.

The commercial buildings in St. Paul are all connected to one another with skywalks and tunnels, because the weather is so severe in the winter. The stores are connected to banks, which are connected to office buildings. People often walk through one place on their way to another. One Saturday, I noticed this good-looking man, nicely dressed—suit, tie, trench coat—walking through the store, heading toward the back of the building. Just as he passed the runway, he did a triple take at me. Then he just stopped and watched me for a few minutes. And then he left.

He came back several times during the day. And then on Monday night, there he was, and on Thursday night, there he was again. We kind of half smiled at each other, one of those "Do I know you?" looks. And then he walked right up to me.

"I've seen you before. Do you work around here?" I asked.

"Yes," he said. "I'm a lawyer. I park on the parking garage ramp and then go through here on my way to the office." He asked me when I got off work, and he asked me if he could walk me to my car, which was also in the parking garage. I said yes, thank you, that would be nice.

Can you *imagine* that happening today? Walking into a parking garage with a man you don't know? I look back now at that girl, with her black hair piled up on her head and her high heels clicking along on the parking garage cement, and I just shake my head at the picture.

When we got to the car, he said, "May I take you to dinner or something sometime?"

I smiled up at him, and said, "Oh, thank you, that would be lovely," and in my head a bunch of alarm bells went off: This is a grown-up, a man, a lawyer. I can't tell him I'm in high school. Let alone mention the three other guys. My God, no *wonder* my dad was a wreck all the time.

I told my parents I was having dinner with some friends after I finished my modeling work on Saturday night. And Wendell and I—his name was Wendell—went out on our first dinner date. The next week we went out again. And then again. I still hadn't confessed my age. I would meet him after work, all dressed up; he thought I was a career girl.

And I thought I was quite the worldly sophisticate. I liked it when people thought I was older than I was. It was like playing a game. I wore makeup when hardly any of my friends did, and high heels much of the time. In fact, in the high school yearbook "Best of . . ." supplement, the caption under my "Best Looking Girl in the Senior Class" picture reads, "Will our Valentine Queen ever wear tennis shoes?"

And then, one night, Wendell told me he had fallen in love with me. For a minute I thought, well, OK—I mean, everybody says that. But he was twenty-nine years old, and I was seventeen. The going steady, the being pinned, the boyfriends . . . this wasn't like that, and I knew it.

And then he said, "I want to meet your parents."

Oh, dear. "Wendell," I said slowly, "there's something I need to tell you." I gulped. "I'm in high school."

Well, he completely lost it. His face turned white. He took a breath. And then he got up and went away.

In a few days he came back, through the store. And he said, "I don't care if you're in high school. I love you, and I'll work it out."

I took him home to meet my parents. Wendell dressed real young that night and acted kind of goofy. Kiddish, almost. My dad took one look at him and took him aside and said something along the lines of "Hey, you, just what the hell is going on here?"

It turned out Wendell was in the Minnesota House of Representatives and was soon going to run for state senate. He was into politics, he wanted it to be his life. He told my folks, "I love your daughter. I'll put her through college. I want to have children with her. I'll take care of her." And oh, by the way, he was having this dinner for the governor in a couple of weeks, and would I come and be his hostess?

My mother was so thrilled she could hardly breathe.

I knew I was finally out of my league. I couldn't do this. Here I was worrying about whether I was going to the sock hop, and he was talking about my entertaining the governor! I said, "Uh, excuse me. My turnabout dance is coming up at school, and I think this is going to get in the way of it. And there's this guy in California, and this other guy at West Point, and what about Bob. . . . " It was a scene. And so Wendell went away again. And this time he stayed away.

And was soon married, to the woman he had been seeing when he met me, the woman he truly loved, the one who had been right for him all along. They had four children. He made one more important appearance in my life (more on that later), and in 1971 became the thirty-third governor of Minnesota. And in 1976, when Walter Mondale became Jimmy Carter's vice president, Wendell (in a very controversial move) appointed himself to Mondale's position in the U.S. Senate, where he served until 1978. Just think, I could've been Loni Kaye Anderson-Anderson, the governor's wife. The senator's wife. Yikes.

The first time I ever flew on an airplane was on a trip to Seattle, when Bob Flick invited me there during the summer to meet his parents. I went for four days, for my birthday—which was my eighteenth, but Bob still didn't know that.

He took me out to dinner at the Space Needle, on the Seattle World's Fair grounds. I was thrilled when he told me that Harry Belafonte and his wife, Julie, would be joining us for dinner that night. He was performing someplace in town, and The Brothers Four knew him—I guess they all kept running into each other on the concert circuit. I thought, this is so fabulous, I'm going to faint with happiness! All during dinner, I just babbled on to Harry about what a major fan I was, how thrilled I was to meet him, how special he had made this birthday.

And then, to top it off, we were invited back to one of the other Brothers' houses after dinner and he had also invited the Belafontes. There was Harry Belafonte, sitting right in front of me in an overstuffed chair, just like a normal person, with his gorgeous wife curled up at his feet.

"Since this is your birthday, and I didn't bring a present, how about if my birthday gift to you is a song?" Harry asked. And then he sang, a cappella, "Jamaica Farewell." If I close my eyes this minute, I can still hear that honeyed voice and see all of us sitting there in a hush, hanging on every word and note that came out of his mouth.

Years later, at Christmas in 1992, Burt and Quinton and I were at Lake Tahoe spending the holiday with my daughter, Deidra, and her family. We had tickets to see Harry Belafonte, and after the show, we all went backstage to thank him for the wonderful evening he had given us. As we were introducing ourselves to each other, I told the Belafontes that it wasn't the first time we had met. "You don't remember this," I said to Julie, "but a long time ago, I saw you and Harry in Seattle." And I told her the whole story.

"Harry," she said to him, with this delighted look on her face, "you have to hear this story! You sang for Loni on her eighteenth birthday!" And it was such a joy that night to be able to tell him about the special gift his music had always been to me. Years ago there was a beautiful lullaby that both Harry and The Brothers Four recorded, called "Turn Around." I sang it to my Deidra when she was little, and then I sang it again to Quinton, and today I sing it to my granddaughter, McKenzie.

Bob Flick and The Brothers Four provided one more amazing adventure for me. They were playing in Chicago, and I took the train there for the weekend. Bob had talked to my dad about the arrangements and had assured him that although I would be staying in the same hotel as the group, I would have my own room, which I did.

Now, here is this good-looking twenty-four-year-old guy, in a very popular singing group, touring the country, playing at colleges, and selling records like crazy, with girls, I think it's safe to say, flinging themselves at him. He must've had lovers somewhere along the way. But not me, the ultimate Minnesota virgin. In all the months that we saw each other, I have to admit that yes, there was some pretty important necking going on. Three, four hours of kissing. But no petting—in fact, the most I ever took off was my shoes. The unspoken rule was: no sex. That was everybody's rule, I thought, and I wasn't breaking it, so what was the harm? I had no way of knowing, back then, what it must have been like for him. But I imagine he was often ready to tear his hair out. Or tear something out.

The trip to Chicago had me totally giddy. The day of the concert, I went shopping at Marshall Field's and came back to my hotel room in a frenzy of preparation. I remember exactly what I wore: a turquoise knit sheath, sleeveless, princess style, curve-hugging. Very high pumps. Lots of hair, swept up. Eyeliner that in my memory seems applied with a trowel.

When we got to the auditorium that night, it was already jam-packed with girls who in my place probably would've been a little more generous to Bob than I had been. And after the guys came out onstage, the audience went nuts. When I heard, "This song is for Bob's girl, who's here tonight," I blushed with happy embarrassment as they sang "Seven Daffodils." My gosh, I thought, there will never, ever be another night like this one!

Backstage after the concert, Bob told me, "We've been invited to go to a party at a real neat place. A mansion."

"Oh, great," I said.

"Yeah, it'll be cool," he said. "It's at Hugh Hefner's."

Now, I didn't know Hugh Hefner from a hole in the wall. I had never seen *Playboy* magazine. I had not a clue. But I didn't want to seem dumb, didn't want to be caught asking, "Who's Hugh Hefner?" I was always pretending to know more than I really did, because I was determined that nobody would think I was this twerpy girl from the sticks. I thought, *hmm,* a mansion. In Chicago. Well, maybe he's a politician or something.

"This will be fun," I said to Bob. "We'll have a good time."

When we got to the mansion, we entered, I think, at the top floor. I remember Bob and I walked into what must've been the main social room. Everywhere I looked, I saw beautiful, voluptuous women. It was as though the room were furnished with women instead of furniture— gorgeous women in cocktail dresses, all colors, all styles. I was stunned at their glamour. And their bodies! My goodness, I thought.

As we were being introduced to people, I was trying hard not to gawk. And as the minutes went by, I felt dumber and dumber. I was sure they knew how young I was, what a hick I was. I was certain that any minute, someone was going to march right up to me and say, "Young lady, you have to go now. It's past your bedtime."

And then this man walked over to us, bracketed on either side by a beautiful young woman. And he was in pajamas! Silk pajamas! Bob said, "Loni, this is Mr. Hefner. He's the owner of this house."

As we shook hands, I thought, this is so odd, and quite interesting, too. I can't wait to get home and tell Mom and Dad about all of this.

"I think we need you in our magazine," said Mr. Hefner.

"Why, Mr. Hefner," I said, "that would be lovely." Bob must have told him I was a model, I guessed. First the department store, then newspapers—and now a magazine possibility? Terrific.

"No, really," Mr. Hefner said. "I'm serious."

I looked up at Bob and batted my eyelashes, saying, "Isn't this nice?" and he was looking back at me with an expression I couldn't read. God only knows what was going on in his mind.

In the mansion there was a swimming pool on a middle floor, and as you went down to the lower floors, you could look into the pool through glass walls and see people swimming. You could either take the stairs or slide down a fireman's pole. We took the fire pole, a quick (and funny, for me in my snug dress) trip down to where we could see the swimmers—all in bathing suits, by the way—and then we went into another room, to where the live music was. My head was spinning.

At this point in my life, this was the most amazing thing that had ever happened. I'm about five minutes out of high school, and I'm at this glamorous place with this wonderful guy. A magazine publisher I don't even know is taking me seriously as a magazine model. I'm thinking, well, it just doesn't get better than this. And in the middle of being dazzled, there's a new thought in my head: I want to be married to a celebrity. Now, I'm not thinking that I want to *be* a celebrity, I'm thinking instead of the kind of life I could have if I were married to one. *This* kind of life, the one I see all around me.

Someone introduced me to Shel Silverstein. He's got a beard (I didn't know many men with beards back then), and he's got a guitar, and he's singing songs. "I want to sing a song for you," he said.

"Why, that would be just lovely," I said, trying to be casual.

He proceeded to sing this funny song about "never marry a black-haired woman" and all the reasons why. And then the song went on, never marry a blonde-haired woman, and never marry a redheaded woman, and, ultimately, it's best to marry only a bald-headed woman. When it was over, we were all laughing and applauding, and then he said he wrote the song. I was so impressed. Everyone here certainly is unique, I thought.

"I would like to have your address," said the nice Mr. Silverstein to me.

"That would be just lovely," I said, unable to come up with another adjective.

"Because I'd like to send you the song. And you know, you really should be in our magazine."

My gosh, I thought, this modeling thing is really beginning to take off here. I must just *reek* of model. But of course I never ask anyone to show me the magazine—because I don't want anybody to know that I don't know what magazine they're talking about. I figure I'll just do some detective work on my own when I get back home.

When I got back to Roseville, my mouth was going a mile a minute. I could hardly get the words out fast enough, telling my parents about this amazing trip of a lifetime.

"And Bob sang a song to me," I gasped, "and after the concert we went to this mansion, and this guy came out in his pajamas, just imagine," and I took a breath, "and his name is Mr. Hefner, and all these beautiful women were there, and he wants me to model in his magazine, and this other man, Mr. Silverstein . . ." And then I stopped, noticing the look on my dad's face.

"Wait, wait, wait," he was saying, holding his hand up in the air. "You went to Hugh Hefner's? Mansion? His *magazine? You?*" His eyes were popping out, his voice getting louder. Oh, my God, I thought, what horrible thing have I done?

And then he went to the corner store, and he brought back a *Playboy* and showed it to me. I so clearly remember feeling nauseated—not just from the surprise of the pictures, although they were certainly a revelation to me, but the knowledge that my dad knew about these things. And I had shocked him, upset him so. I started to cry.

He poured me a little shot of something, brandy, I think, and said, "Drink this, it'll make you feel better. I'll get over it, once I've talked to Bob about it." I just sat there while Dad tried to get Bob on the phone, muttering, "What was he thinking, taking you to such a place? I can't imagine what was going on in his head."

I couldn't get over what a major big deal this all was. I never saw one scandalous thing at the mansion: no drugs, no nude people, no couples behaving inappropriately (although I found out later that if I could've gotten a closer look at the grotto in the pool, I might've come away with a different impression!). But as I sat there, listening to my dad, I remembered that Mr. Hefner had asked me if I wanted to take a swim in the pool, and I told him I didn't bring my suit with me, and everybody laughed. That was the thing that embarrassed me for years afterward. How stupid they must've thought I was.

I've never met Hefner since, although I've always wanted to tell him the story. I did get little notes from Shel Silverstein off and on for the next couple of years, and he sent me the song and repeatedly said he thought I belonged in "the magazine."

I've had more than one offer from *Playboy* to pose over the years, starting during the first season of *WKRP in Cincinnati*. Around the same time, I received an inquiry about doing a feature film of the Little Annie Fannie character. I said, oh, no, I don't think so. I had a daughter by then, and the idea of her going off to school and encountering some kid holding a fold-out nude of Mommy, complete with the staple in the navel . . . well, it just wasn't an option for me.

And I've always been glad I never did it. There may be aspects of my past that will continue to haunt me, but at least there are no nude photographs. There is a computerized Loni nude floating around on the Internet, but it's somebody's rendition; I've never posed. Part of me was always flattered to be asked, of course. But another part of me remembers the look on my dad's face, the sound of his voice. Times may have changed; that memory never has.

Chapter 2

When I graduated from high school in 1963, I went off to the University of Minnesota wanting only to do the things I loved and not thinking of a career. I decided to major in art—I was painting, sculpting, and designing and sewing my own clothes—and also to investigate the campus drama department. But as a freshman, of course, there were the basics: English courses, history courses, and figuring out how to get from one side of the campus to the other. And boys. I was still seeing Tony (in California) and Ken (at West Point) and Bob (on tour). And now, at school, Rick, who looked like Robert Redford.

It's important to remember that we hadn't hit the sexual revolution yet, or the women's movement. For me, life was still halfway between a Doris Day movie and a TV comedy/variety show, interrupted only briefly by Bible stories at Sunday school. I liked to dress up in pretty clothes, get good grades, make a little money with my modeling, and find a way to balance a lot of boyfriends while maintaining my status as a "good girl." If there was a conflict inherent in any of that, I didn't see it.

My parents loved to take us on great driving trips, and this year, Dad had announced, we were all going to Florida during Loni's spring break. I told Tony, and I told Bob, and I told Ken, and I told Rick.

We had reservations in Miami, at the Americana—which is now something else, I think. It was all very grand, very fancy, very pink. The first night, I had a date with the lifeguard Andrea and I had met that day on the beach. He was suntanned and muscled and mysterious behind his dark glasses. When he came to our suite that night to pick me up, it turned out that he was quite cross-eyed. That night, I had my first serious drink.

We went to a party being thrown by some people he knew, and I had a brandy Alexander. I was quite delighted with it—my drug of choice has always been chocolate—but decided in about five light-headed minutes that one was my limit. My date, however, had a number of them and became rapidly, totally smashed. I drove us back to Miami, in his car, having no idea from block to block where I was. When I made it back to the hotel, I stepped quickly out of the car, leaving my sodden date in the passenger seat.

"Miss," called the doorman, "what about this gentleman?"

"I dunno," I said as I went into the lobby. "I guess he's your problem." It was an auspicious beginning to a memorable vacation.

There was a floor show at the hotel—this was Miami, remember—and the main attraction was a topless ice skater. Once my parents found out about that, they were not happy. Each day on the beach, people would say to me, "Oh, you were wonderful last night, you just looked lovely." I would stop and think, *hmmm,* what was I wearing last night? Within a couple of days, the Anderson family found out that their elder daughter was a dead ringer for the topless skater. My dad, already irritated at handing out dollar bills each time he wanted a towel or his own car, needed only the ice skater connection to move us immediately to another hotel. We went to the Holiday Inn, right on the beach, and Andrea and I quickly set about the business of serious beaching.

Rick, the boyfriend from college, had shown up, along with a number of our mutual friends from school. Then Ken flew down from West Point. I just barely managed to keep them from running into each other. Then Tony, the boyfriend in college in

Santa Barbara, called from school. My dad finally had a fit and blew the whistle on me. "She's out with I don't know who!" he said, out of patience with running an answering service. Results: Ken takes back his pin, Tony tells me, "I never want to see you again, good-bye." Bob is on the road with the Brothers, and although he's calling, he can't quite get to Florida that week. Phew. I manage to keep Rick safely in the dark.

All our friends from school rented motor scooters, which led to a big collision that put Rick in the hospital with contusions, cuts that needed stitching, blood everywhere, and a lot of pain. When we visited him, he was wrapped like a mummy and depressed at what had happened to his vacation. We tried to cheer him up by having a four-team wheelchair race in the hallways, but when that didn't work, we decided that he didn't belong there.

We snuck back into the hospital after hours, put him on a gurney, covered him like he was a body, took him out a side exit, slid him into a wheelchair (no easy feat, since his legs were so bandaged he couldn't bend them), then into a car, and we took off. The plan was to stash him with some other friends of ours, who were staying at somebody's house, with somebody's mother. The trip, I think, came closer to killing him than the scooter accident did.

Within an hour the painkillers were wearing off, and it was clear that Rick really did belong in a hospital. Chastened, we called an ambulance to come and get him.

While we were all waiting at the house for Rick's ambulance, someone's ex-boyfriend showed up, wanting to pick a fight with the current boyfriend. A nasty scene ensued. The girl's mother was there (I think it was her house), and she had been drinking a great deal. As we got Rick onto the gurney to go back to the hospital, the woman suddenly turned on me and snapped, "Get out of my house, you dirty spic."

When this woman used those words—in a tone of voice that was frightening—I knew it was about the way I looked, that the way I looked made her hate me without even knowing me. My hair was black and naturally curly, and I always got very tan very quickly. There had always been mumbling about what my ethnic mix was; Mom once told me she used to keep me in the house in the summers when I was little, because people made fun of me. I even heard my blonde, blue-eyed cousins talking one time about how "there must be Negro blood in there somewhere."

But my parents had always been adamant about the wrong-headedness of prejudice, about calling people names because of their color or their country. It wasn't Christian, for one thing; for another, I went to the University of Minnesota, which even in the early sixties looked like the United Nations. But when this woman snapped at me, it felt as though she'd spit on me instead. All hell broke loose out in front of her house. Yelling, shouting, tears. "How can people talk like that, how can they be so mean?" I wept. Managing to get Rick back into the hospital seemed like the least of our worries.

When that vacation ended, my dad said he would never take another one with me again, not ever.

While we were in Florida, a couple of friends from school entered me in the Miss Roseville pageant, as a sort of joke. They sent in one of my modeling pictures and a résumé, thinking I would get a laugh out of it. By the time we got home, my picture was in the paper, and the pageant was a week away.

"Well, Loni," said my mother, "you'll just have to do it. I mean, it's in the paper."

"Mother," I said in my most exasperated tone, "this is not like Miss Thom McAn. This leads to Miss Minnesota, then to Miss America. You need a *talent* for this. I have to tell the pageant people this was all a joke!"

But my mother was determined. Backing out now would embarrass the family. Prepared or not, I was in the pageant.

There was no time to come up with a musical number, find an accompanist, rehearse. So I decided to go for the judges' funny bones and recite Dorothy Parker's "The Waltz."

In Parker's piece, the narrator is hysterically ambivalent about dancing but can't seem to say no. It seemed appropriate for the way I was feeling. At any rate, I had a good time with it and won the talent part of the competition. And the evening gown part, and the swimsuit part, and the Miss Roseville part. I was pretty astonished. That astonishment carried me into the regionals, which I also won, and then I went on to the Miss Minnesota pageant.

This had all snowballed in the weeks after the Florida trip, when I still had a very dark tan. It was a dark tan even for Florida—in fact, we had been asked to leave a restaurant in Georgia on the drive back home, because they were so sure I was black—so I stood out like a signpost in Minnesota. I started getting little notes (anonymous, of course) that said things like "We don't want a nigger for queen." And "Black women have their own pageant." There it was again, that irrational cruelty about skin, about race. I became incensed, and not just for me. I was getting more than an inkling of what it was like for people who experienced this treatment in other, more serious ways. I got tense and angry. I began to feel like picking a fight; it didn't matter with whom.

For my talent performance, I had been preparing the scene from *West Side Story* when Maria learns of Tony's death. I think my mother and I must've seen that movie six times. (In fact, I went to the Minneapolis premiere at the Orpheum Theater, and somewhere in my memorabilia there's a picture of Richard Beymer, the movie's Tony, signing an autograph for me. Hard to believe what a credible creepy, villain he was in *Twin Peaks!*) We had the cast album, and I knew every song by heart. For the pageant, I sewed my own costume and constructed a small set. I decided that since I didn't have much of a chance for the beauty part, I wanted somebody to take the performance seriously.

A friend of mine, Barbara Hasselberg, had been in the pageant a couple of years before and had come in runner-up. I had modeled with her a few times and was glad to see that she was back this year as Miss Bloomington. At least, I thought, I have a friend to have some fun with. But it was apparent that Barbara viewed this contest in a different light than I did. To her it was very important. And she wasn't the only one. There were serious mothers backstage, and some of the girls were crying, and there was a tremendous tension running through the room, like an electric wire that you can't see but can hear humming.

When I went in to the judges for my interview, one of them said to me right off, "You don't look like an all-American girl to me. You're much too exotic and probably won't be placing anywhere in this pageant. But hey, you know, we could go a long way with you in the Miss Universe pageant. That's strictly a beauty pageant, no talent or anything, and they really like exotic women."

I bit my lip to keep from saying something I'd regret. Up until this contest, I had been having a good time, playing dress-up, playing Miss This, Queen of That. And then the notes started coming, with the racial slurs. And now I was being told they couldn't market me, that no matter what I did, I was not what they wanted. And I resented it. Anger makes me quiet; combined with rejection, it makes me competitive. When I performed my talent segment, I poured all my feelings into it. I guess it was scenery chewing, but the sweat was running down my back when I was done, and I was crying.

Barbara Hasselberg's discipline and focus paid off for her—she was crowned Miss Minnesota that night. And I was named her first runner-up.

At the party after the pageant, Barbara said, "I really want you to meet my brother. His name is Bruce." I had known her casually for a couple of years, but I didn't know she had a brother. "And I want you to meet my folks, too," she said. Her parents had been in the audience, as were mine, and as the introductions were being made all around, up walked this six-foot two-inch, blond, blue-eyed hunk of a gorgeous man. Barbara's brother, Bruce.

Everything about Bruce that night was just too much of a good thing—terrific personality, good looks, lots of smarts. He was twenty-five, did something or other in sales, I thought I heard him say. We were all giddy with excitement about Barbara's victory, and in spite of my tight jaw earlier in the evening, I had decided that not only was I going to have a good time, but Mr. Bruce Hasselberg would be my consolation prize.

Until now, with dating and boyfriends and a jam-packed calendar, I had been the one in the driver's seat. But Bruce was a
different story. He left no doubt that he was the one in charge,
both on and off the dance floor. We laughed and flirted and
carried on like crazy. We went out by ourselves after the pageant
party, and three weeks later we eloped. I was still just eighteen.

I didn't even have time to call all the boyfriends, it happened so
fast. For some reason—infatuation-addled hormones, probably—
the decision to run off and marry Bruce didn't seem odd to me.
He was Miss Minnesota's brother, after all. It didn't seem like a
mistake; it felt like the natural next thing I was supposed to be
doing.

We eloped to Sioux Falls, South Dakota, because you could
have a blood test in the morning and get married that same afternoon. Ever the sophisticate, I had worn a black sheath and
heels and pearls, and when we got to Sioux Falls, I thought, gee,
maybe I should go find something a little more bridal. But when
we went into the Sioux Falls Penney's, I saw a sign on the first
floor that read THIS WAY TO THE MOVING STAIRS, and I said
huffily, "Oh, no, I'm not going to find anything I want in here."

Our wedding night was one of the great disasters in the history
of sex on this planet. I had always been this teeny girl who
couldn't even wear a tampon. I looked at Bruce and thought,
there is *no way* there is ever going to be sexual intercourse in our
life. But at a moment like that, "Get away from me!" isn't particularly effective. We made a clumsy attempt at lovemaking, and
afterward I pushed him away from me. It was painful and embarrassing, and not at all like the tender and romantic wedding
night I had dreamed of.

For someone who had been passing herself off as a woman of
the world, I knew hardly anything at all about the physical act of
sex, and what little I did know was useless. And Bruce, for all
the impression he gave of a worldly young man, didn't know
much either. He had no idea how to be gentle or understanding,
or how to slow down, or how to help me not be afraid. Obviously he'd had a few girls, and the guy climbed on, and then the

guy climbed off. "God *damn* it, Loni," he sputtered in under-standable frustration when I put him off night after night. "Just what the hell is your problem?"

My problem, I think, was that I was a good kisser, with a body that advertised something its owner had no idea how to use, and my idea of wedded bliss came from an amalgam of my parents' marriage and the romantic movies I'd seen. For a smart girl, I was pretty dumb. And naive. A dangerous combination for a new husband, one who was in many ways as naive as I was.

We went home to face the music. Everybody was so angry with me, everybody was saying, "You've made the biggest mis-take of your life." I would have to abdicate as Miss Roseville, of course, and as Barbara's Miss Minnesota runner-up, and the whole town was chattering like mad. But I was still Miss Perfect. "*Excuse* me? I don't make mistakes." At least none that I would admit.

We stayed at my parents' for about a month, just long enough for them to put together what my mother called "a real wed-ding," at the church, with a reception at the country club after-ward for more than one hundred fifty people. By then, of course, the tension between Bruce and me was so thick that we could've sliced it instead of the wedding cake.

Andrea wore a stricken look on her face much of the time, and the night before the church ceremony, she said sadly, "I'm really going to miss you—it won't be much fun around here anymore." She had no way of knowing that for the bride and groom, it already wasn't much fun. As the family preparations swirled around us, we were like robots in the middle of a bad dream. In fact, the marriage could probably have been annulled at that point, if I hadn't been pregnant—which I didn't yet know I was.

My parents suspected that something was wrong with the newlyweds, but they thought it had to do with the close quarters, with all of us living under one roof. Actually, Bruce and I were under two roofs, since Dad had fashioned an apartment for us in the basement. Mom and Dad gently advised us that we needed a place of our own, to make a new beginning, and they helped us find an apartment in Richfield. We moved in with all our wedding presents, but location was the only thing that had changed.

From the first day, we argued almost constantly— about money, about responsibilities, and, of course, about sex. The poor guy had married someone who didn't want to have anything to do with him. He started staying out all night, coming home at four or five o'clock in the morning. There was no food, because there was very little money—he sold pots and pans door-to-door, I discovered, and the only one who was bringing in anything like a paycheck was me. In a plot twist that was ironic-bordering-on-tragic, I was Miss No-Frost Eskimo for the Minnesota Gas Company, a TV ad campaign in which I wore a parka, boots, and a bikini and drew entries and announced the name of whoever had won that week's frost-free appliance. When I brought my paycheck home, Bruce forged my signature and disappeared again.

One night he came into the apartment with a brand-new hunting rifle he'd bought. When I saw it, I started right up on him about "Where are the groceries?"and "How come you're spending my money?" And he came right back at me with "What kind of a wife are you?" which led, of course, to a heated discussion about our nonexistent sex life. He picked the rifle up from the couch and shouted, "If you don't have sex with me, I'll shoot!" I didn't have sex with him, he didn't shoot me, and neither of us got any sleep that night.

It had been only a couple of months since the night we'd met, but we were already an eternity away from the excitement of our whirlwind courtship and elopement. We were in so far, with absolutely no idea how to backtrack. We couldn't go to our parents, we couldn't go to a minister, and for people who had been brought up the way we had been, marriage counseling or therapy was part of life on some other planet. The fights escalated to such a fever pitch that once, when we had argued our way out into the hallway of the apartment building, he tried to push past me and accidentally shoved me down a flight of stairs. I don't know which of us was more frightened.

I stopped going to classes; except for my forays as Miss No-Frost, I didn't leave the apartment. When I missed a period, which had never happened to me before, I was puzzled.

"Maybe I'm pregnant," I said to Bruce.

"Maybe it's an immaculate conception," he cracked.

One day when he was out, I started cramping and called my mother in tears, telling her I needed to go to the doctor's. And that poor man had to break the hymen to examine me—and to discover that yes, I was indeed pregnant. "But we haven't *done* anything," I cried. How could I be pregnant if we hadn't actually ever had sexual intercourse?

"The hymen isn't a full closure," said the doctor. "If it were, you wouldn't be able to have a period." Young sperm, he went on to explain, to my complete mortification, can swim around in there for forty-eight hours. "And besides," he said, "whether you believe it or not, young lady, you're pregnant."

My mother was completely shocked, and so was Bruce. "This can't be my baby," he yelled that night. "We never did it!"

Under protest, he went with me to the doctor and heard the same explanation I had heard. By the time we got home, he was completely panic-stricken. "I can't be a father," he shouted. "I'm not ready to take care of a family! We can't have this baby, we just can't!"

"Surely you're not suggesting . . . ," I asked, my voice shaking. What was he suggesting? It was 1964. Abortion was illegal in the United States—you went to back alleys or you went out of the country. And besides, I said, trying to be the voice of reason in the middle of my own terror, "Even if that's what you mean, we can't, we just can't."

Bruce got completely hysterical at this and started hollering. "That's not what I meant! But I just, I just won't . . . !" He grabbed me by the shoulders as if to shake me, then changed his mind, shoving me away. I lost my footing and stumbled, falling to the floor. I was sobbing and so was he, but he turned and left the apartment. He didn't come back for three days.

There was nothing to eat except a can of tomato soup and some crackers. I had no car, so I went over and borrowed some milk from the couple across the hall. I came back, put my nightgown on, heated up the soup, and then sat on the couch and drank it from a cup, finishing off the crackers, too. And then, I think, I just sat there. I couldn't imagine what I was supposed to do next.

Now, I must've gotten up to go to the bathroom at some point. Maybe I stumbled around or crawled into bed. I know I didn't answer the phone (did I even hear it ringing?) because when my parents finally came and the apartment manager let them in, they had been calling for three days and were completely frantic. I remember my dad coming over and putting his arms around me, and my mother behind him, crying. "We're going to take you home," Dad said quietly. "You're coming home with us now."

He went off and rented a little U-Haul trailer, while Mom rushed around and packed. When he got back, they started carrying my clothes and some wedding presents out to the car, all the time talking to me like I was totally crazy—that gentle, soothing monotone you use with someone who's out of it.

All of a sudden Bruce appeared in the hall, shouting at the top of his lungs. "Andy," said my mother quickly, "let's just get her out of here."

My dad lunged at Bruce, but Bruce sidestepped him and reached for my hand. He had given me a ring—and quite a ring it was, too, one and a half carats, I think. He snapped, "You're not leaving with this!" and before my dad could stop him, he had yanked it off my finger. Then he stepped away.

Somehow we managed to pile into the car, and Dad drove us home.

The next day, we all sat around the table and said, "What are we going to do?" Both of my grandmothers were there, too. Andrea, a junior that year, was repelled by the mess and determined to keep her distance. She was frightened for me and couldn't understand how all this could have happened. And didn't want any part of it. But the rest of us talked and talked, and I cried, and Mother cried, and then we talked some more.

We were a very traditional family, with a long history in a church and community that were both very conservative. I had been, up until that moment, a very public teenager in that community. Both my grandmothers suggested that I give up the baby for adoption and start my life all over again. Because, they said, no one would ever want me.

"This is the end of your life if you keep this baby," they said, quietly and seriously. "No man wants a woman with another man's child. Your life is ruined. You must give up this baby."

At their words, something inside of me finally came to the surface. "Wait a minute. This is my baby," I said, looking at the people around the table, the people who loved me, whom I loved. "I *only* want this baby. I don't want anything else."

Well, the grandmothers gasped, and their eyes rolled back in their heads, and everybody started talking at once. "No, you don't understand," I said. "This is *my baby*. This is the most important thing in my life, and nobody's talking me out of it."

So they backed off a bit. "Let's not upset her anymore," they said. Poor Loni, she's gone a little crazy.

And then I said, "I want to get a divorce."

A divorce? With a baby on the way? Heaven help us all. Nobody will ever want her now.

We didn't have such a thing as a family lawyer. No one in our family had ever needed a lawyer for anything. As for me, I knew only one lawyer—Wendell Anderson.

So I called Wendell and told him what had happened. Rick was still in touch with me, calling to make sure I was OK. Tony, of course, wasn't speaking to me at all; I'd pretty much broken his heart. Bob was still sending flowers; he didn't even know I'd gotten married. Telling him was no fun at all.

For the first three months of the pregnancy, I didn't look pregnant, I just had huge breasts. (Well, I'd always had huge breasts, but they were even bigger now.) When I went to Wendell's office, I got all dressed up. I was very Jackie Kennedy–looking, I thought, in my fake leopard coat, and my fake leopard pillbox hat, and my black dress and long gloves. I was so conscious of this very serious, adult thing I was about to do, going to a lawyer's office to talk about getting a divorce. I felt like I was going to a funeral.

By this time Wendell was married—as I said, to the girl he had truly loved all along. But I was so needy that day, weepy and nervous. He put his arms around me, saying how he should've been there, he could have . . . I don't know what, protected me or something, "If you had only married me," he was saying. I had been wronged, and this kind, chivalrous gentleman was outraged, but his reaction scared me.

Now, I'm totally off men at this point, right? Because all men want the same thing. All I want is a divorce. I am *off* men—and here's this man putting his arms around me. At first I just stood there, as cold to him as I've ever been to anyone. And then I walked out the door and went home and told my dad. Who then went to see Wendell in his office.

When he came back, Dad said, "What a nice man. He'll handle your divorce. But he doesn't need to ever see you or speak to you again, except for court. He says he feels too protective but doesn't want to upset you. So he doesn't need to see you, unless I'm there, too." Fair enough, I thought.

The divorce itself became very complicated. When we first went into court, the judge said he wouldn't hear my petition. In fact, he refused to hear it. "Because pregnant women aren't in their right minds," he said.

"And you know this firsthand," I snapped, "because the last time you were pregnant, you were not in *your* right mind?" I thought, did that come out of my mouth?

The judge said firmly, "Young lady, if I hear one more word out of you, I'm going to find you in contempt of court and fine you."

What's happening to me? I wondered. I want to fight, I want to yell at him, and I have absolutely no desire to be ladylike. But he stuck to his guns, and Wendell strongly advised me to keep my mouth shut. And so there was no divorce until after the baby was born.

In the meantime Bruce went completely haywire. He came to

my parents' house, he called every day, he cried on the phone. He was wrong, he said. He loved me. He wanted us to be a family. He would throw himself at the front door, pound on it, yell through it. And I would think, he doesn't even know me—how can he believe he loves me after all of this? I thought he was completely crazy.

What he was, of course, was distraught and heartbroken and very young, as was I. He may have been out of control, but he was neither malicious nor dangerous.

Over the years we've gradually mended all our fences. Once the heartache and confusion of the first years were over, Bruce and I realized that we had created a child together—our daughter—and that we had to put her interests and welfare ahead of our mistakes. I stayed close with his parents, who although supportive of the divorce said that I would always be their daughter-in-law, and I stayed close to Barbara, his sister. I even stayed with her when I went to New York for work. But this stage of our relationship didn't come easily, and it didn't come anytime soon. We still had a few scenes and confrontations ahead of us.

So now I am a pregnant former beauty queen, living at home, trying to figure out how I got myself into this fix. No college, no job. All the boyfriends are pretty much gone, although I did get flowers from Bob Flick. And then dear Rick-who-looked-like-Robert-Redford came back into the picture and asked, could he be my friend? Could he stand by me and be supportive, and would I let him be my friend?

Imagine how embarrassing it must have been for this nineteen-year-old boy to be so loyal and generous to a girl who had not only hurt him, but made a big public mess besides. His friendship was the most generous gift anyone could have given me.

During this time, Rick's dad was killed in a plane crash, and he asked me if I would please be with him at the funeral. "This is the girl I love," he said when he introduced me to his family and friends. "And if she ever changes her mind . . ." They were all looking at him, then looking at me, hugely pregnant in my midnight-blue maternity dress. Being a mother now, I can't imagine what was going through Rick's mother's head on that difficult day.

During the months of my pregnancy, although Bruce made unpredictable and emotional appearances every so often, everybody else spoiled me rotten. My Gramma Sally took it as her personal duty to teach me how to cook. We would plan menus, and go to the market, and rattle the pots and pans around. Thanks to her, I became an excellent cook—and a spectacular baker. Cooking and eating, cooking and eating. At eight months, I had gained sixty pounds. I could barely move.

One Friday night, I baked a fabulous chocolate cake with white frosting, while my dad was watching *The Tonight Show*. I had been to the doctor the day before, and he had said I wasn't due for another three, possibly even four weeks. I decided that since I had made this cake and Dad and I were both up, what the heck, I would just sit down and eat a piece of cake with him. Just a sliver. And then I had another sliver, and then another, and pretty soon I had eaten the entire cake. A chocolate sheet cake, with vanilla icing, and I had eaten it all.

"Boy," I said to Dad, "I'm *really* uncomfortable."

He laughed. "Well, after all, you did just eat an entire cake." And then I started laughing, too. Which made me feel even worse.

"No, really," I said, trying to catch my breath. "I feel like I'm going to explode or something."

This made him nervous. "Let's call the doctor," he said. I didn't want to, I felt foolish. But he insisted.

When I called the doctor, he said, "It's the cake, not the baby, Loni. You're not due for weeks yet." He advised me to take antacids—which would never happen today—and said if that didn't settle things down, I could take a sleeping pill. Which would *absolutely* not happen today.

"I would feel better if I could just lie down," I said to Dad. But once on the couch, I had to sit back up again.

Weeks before, I had asked the doctor what labor would be like, and he had said, "Well, you know, you'll have a pain, and it'll be different from any other pain you've ever had in your life. And when you get another one, start timing them. When they get about twenty minutes apart, call me. When they get five minutes apart, come to the hospital." It sounded simple. But I wasn't having pain, exactly. I was just . . . uncomfortable. So there was nothing to time. There was just this constant, pressing feeling of . . . well, that I'd eaten an entire chocolate cake.

Dad said, "I'm going to have your mother drive you to the hospital, just to have them take a look at you."

"But, Dad," I whined, "what will they think there? They'll just send me home because I'm so stupid, because I ate a whole cake. It will be so embarrassing."

"I don't care if you're embarrassed, you're going to the hospital," he said firmly. He had Mom on his side; better safe than sorry, they both agreed. He would stay at the house with Andrea and wait for news, since hanging around a maternity ward wasn't part of his plan. Besides, back in those days, that's what the menfolk did—wait for the baby news.

It was now close to midnight, and as they bundled me into the car, I continued whining. "This is so embarrassing."

"Will you quit this," said my mother. "You're driving me totally nuts. We're doing this for your dad, and we'll call him from the hospital and tell him that everything's fine."

We headed for Bethesda Hospital, where I had been born, and on the way we had to cross the railroad tracks. When we hit the tracks, I said, "Whoa! Mom? I think that was a pain! I think that was really something!"

"Oh, great," she said. "Now you're having some kind of psychosomatic thing."

When we got to the hospital and the nurse came to greet us, I just started blathering to her, motormouthing like crazy. "I think this is just gas, I made this cake, and then I ate it, but I can't get comfortable, and then we hit the railroad tracks, and, and, and . . ."

The whole time she was nodding, saying, "Yes, dear, yes, dear," as she took me into an examining room and put me into a gown.

"Just get right up there on that table," she said, "and we'll take a look."

There was a little step stool, and as I stepped up on it and started to slide onto the table, my water broke.

"*What was that?*" I asked the nurse in a panic.

"Well," she said, "I don't think you're having gas pains."

And all of a sudden it hit me: I'm having a baby. And I have only one question: *Where are the drugs?*

I had been telling my doctor since day one: I don't want to have any pain. I want drugs. You don't understand, doctor. I want this baby, you know (but if somebody else could actually have it *for* me, that would be good), but because I don't want to have pain, you *will* be giving me drugs, right?

"Yes, Loni," he had promised. "We will be giving you drugs."

But no, says the nurse. "I'm afraid it's too late for drugs. You're already dilated eight centimeters."

She might as well have been speaking Greek to me. Twenty-seven years later, when my daughter had her baby, she knew from the first detail to the last what was going on inside her and what was going to happen to her. But nobody had ever explained anything to me. My mother had told me the process was like bad menstrual cramps, and that's all I knew. And I had never read any books about having babies—I only read cookbooks during my pregnancy. And I was getting pretty mad.

"You people are making my life miserable," I wailed. "I don't know what 'dilated' means, and I don't care, I just *want my drugs!*"

At this point my mom has come into the room, and as she's saying something like, "Now, honey, calm down," I get this one, huge, really terrific pain, and I shout, "That's *it,* I don't want to do this, stop this now!"

I had never been a person who yelled, and I always got nervous around people who did. But at that moment, it was like I was standing outside myself someplace, watching Loni tell everybody off. "Nobody told me it was going to be like this," I'm wailing. And everybody's got this look of slight disgust, like, this girl is a real pain in the behind.

Luckily, it was a quiet night, and I was the only one in the labor room. Every time I had a pain, I just screeched to my mother, "You didn't tell me it was going to be like this!"

"Honey," she said quietly, "I was in labor eight hours with you. And Bruce's mother was in labor for twenty-six hours." This just made me howl. I was one of those miserable, awful, petulant-in-labor people, and nobody was telling me how to breathe, or how to focus, or anything.

Ultimately I think I had about eight really hard labor pains. There are women who will read this and want to throw the book across the room. But I was just a kid.

When the nurse says, "I think it's time," and wheels me into the delivery room, I'm still hollering for my drugs, and everyone's starting to chuckle just a little—because the baby's almost here. "There's a mirror over your head if you want to watch," says the doctor. *Watch?* No, thank you, I think I'll watch the clock instead.

They had strapped my hands to the bars on the side of the bed—aluminum ones, they must have been, because while I was watching the clock and Deidra was making her appearance, I bent the bars. I know now that for labor, it was a relative walk in the park. I was uncomfortable for about an hour, and from the time my water broke until she was born, it was only about forty-five minutes.

"It's a little girl," said the doctor. And I just thought, wow. My girl. I got my girl.

I had prayed every night for a little girl. I knew how to take care of a girl. No need for a man in my life if I didn't have a little boy, no need for a masculine presence. Or so I thought. Even though I'd never had brothers, I knew that a little boy needed a man around. But I just wanted it to be my little girl and me; I thought I didn't need anybody else. Now that I've got my little girl, I thought, life is good. I started to slide into bliss.

When Dad arrived, he said, "We've got to call Bruce."

"Do not call Bruce," I ordered. We were not divorced yet, of course, because the judge wouldn't do it until the baby came. But I did not want to see him. I didn't love him, I wanted to forget that we had ever been married, and I certainly didn't want him to have anything to do with my baby.

"Loni Kaye," my dad said sternly, "Bruce is the father of this

little girl. He has a right to know, and I am going to go call him."
I wanted to argue, but I was really tired and felt myself going off
to sleep.

Bruce was in the navy reserves then, and he was out of town
with his reserve unit. As a matter of fact, Dad found out, he was
in the brig on this particular night. I don't know why he was in
the slammer, but at the news of his fatherhood they released him,
and when I woke up, there he was, trying to hold my hand. I
shouted for the nurse and turned my head over to the other
side—and when I opened my eyes again, there he was, standing
on that side of the bed. Finally I got so hysterical that the nurse
asked him to leave.

The next day there was a huge blizzard in Minnesota, and
nobody could get in or out. I was in a room for two, and I was
alone. This was before rooming in, and Deidra was in the nursery.
It was the strangest time. I had never been by myself before. I
spiked a temperature—I had some kind of infection—and they
wouldn't let me see Dee. Then, when they gave me a penicillin
shot, I had an allergic reaction and went into shock. I hadn't had
one sick day during my pregnancy, no morning sickness, no nau-
sea, and now I was miserable, delirious, and completely alone,
with raised hives from the top of my head to the bottoms of my
feet. They wouldn't let me out of my bed, and they wouldn't
bring my baby to me.

I was running a fever of about a hundred and three degrees
and in my addled state decided to take matters into my own
hands. I climbed out of bed and started sneaking down the hall,
practically hanging on to the wall, trying to be inconspicuous,
trying to find the nursery. Everything was spinning around—in
my memory, the black and white floor tiles were undulating
under my feet. When I got to the nursery and figured out which
little one was mine, I just leaned on the window and looked at
her for the longest time. It was very quiet. It seemed she was
looking right back at me, her big hazel eyes calm and steady. And
then all of a sudden a nurse spotted me and yelled, "Oh, my
God!" scaring me half to death.

They got a wheelchair and hustled me back to bed. I cried and cried. I was just this kid, practically, and the storm outside was keeping everybody out, and my infection was keeping me from the baby, and I was so lonely. In the week I was there, they never did let me have Deidra in my room. They gave me a shot to dry up my milk and medication to combat both the infection and the allergic reaction.

In a couple of days the storm quieted down, and my parents came, and Andrea, and my friends, and Bruce's mom and dad. And I finally got flowers—from Bruce, and from Tony, and white roses from Rick, and a beautiful baby blanket from Bob Flick, from I. Magnin, which I had never heard of. There was this one unpleasant nurse—you know how you remember these kinds of people, who seem to have a way of showing up in the middle of other people's kindness—and she said to me one day, looking at the presents and the flowers, "Well, just who *is* the father of this baby, anyway?" And I just snapped. I cried and cried and cried, that somebody would think that of me and say something like that to me. Because I was such a good girl, you know? And of course, my hormones weren't really stable at that point, either.

It was an interesting time for me, emotionally and physically. I crashed to a hundred and two pounds during those first six weeks and wasn't allowed to take care of Deidra when we first got her home, wasn't allowed to get up at night with her at all. Mom did everything in the beginning. Gradually I got up with her during the day, fed her, played with her, got to know her. This beautiful little hazel-eyed girl, with hair of gold, who was mine. And only mine.

Deidra was a serene baby, and it was calming and reassuring to hold her, to feed her, to gently rub the top of her head and feel her against my heart. All the months that had come before, all the silliness and drama and heartache, didn't seem to have much to do with me. I wasn't the girl at the beauty pageant, or the one at the wheelchair races in Florida, or the bratty one in the delivery room. I was this baby's mother.

After I got back on my feet, I registered for school in September. My parents had agreed that yes, I could live with them, and they would be happy to baby-sit occasionally. They certainly weren't going to throw me out; they loved me, and they loved their little granddaughter. But since I had made a choice to live as an adult, they fully expected me to take responsibility for the consequences. I would pay rent and personal expenses for the baby and me. Dad would lend me money as needed, he would take care of us, but he would keep a ledger, and I would be expected to pay it all back. No compromises, no negotiations.

"And," said my dad sternly, "you will have to pay your own tuition and buy your own books. So you'll have to get a job."

Some might say he was too tough on me. I admit I thought so, too, at the time. Now I think that he gave me a great gift.

Chapter 3

My life became a series of things I was late for. I had started off with a full academic course load but soon dropped down to half. For work, I modeled for a local furrier. It was a beautiful store, with thick carpet, crystal chandeliers, gorgeous fitting rooms, and customers who spent more money in half an hour than I made in a month. I worked a forty-hour week, scheduling my courses around my modeling, and I cleared fifty-seven dollars.

And when I came in the door of my parents' home at night, my mother went off duty—she handed Deedee to me, and that was my job for the rest of the evening. Feed her with one hand, turn the pages of a textbook with the other; try to write a paper with her on the bed.

I was certainly not an A student anymore. I got decent grades in the courses I liked, but nothing got enough attention. Deedee didn't get the best mother, the school didn't get the best student, I wasn't the best daughter or big sister. I sleepwalked through my job, spread too thin and just making it. I had pneumonia twice during my college years, and one long battle with mono.

I had started as an art major, wanting to paint and sculpt as I had done in high school, but my parents soon convinced me that it wasn't a practical choice for a single mother. I switched to education. I stayed with the art courses, thinking that if I couldn't be an artist myself, maybe someday I would teach them.

I wasn't teaching Sunday school anymore, though. Resurrection Lutheran had decreed that I couldn't come back there as a divorced mother; I would be a bad influence on the young girls. This "punishment" stung almost more than anything else that had happened. I had always taken my classes to heart; I didn't just walk in on Sundays and lecture the students on good and evil. We explored the culture of the times—the food the people ate, the clothes they wore, the political and social history that created the landscape of both the Old and New Testaments. Besides, if nothing else, I might've been a good object lesson for the kids. But there was no balm in Gilead—I was out.

When I told my mother what had happened, I expected her to say, "Well, you got what was coming to you." But instead she became very angry, and so did my father. At the church, not at me. And in protest, my family left the place that had been at the center of our lives as far back as I could remember. I was astonished. I began looking at them, especially at my mother, with more respect and appreciation. I was just beginning to understand how much I needed her.

In the meantime Bruce was behaving like a madman. Calling and calling, hanging around wherever I was, showing up suddenly outside of work, outside of class. Nowadays I guess we'd probably call it stalking. He took my car apart so I couldn't go anywhere—I came out of class one afternoon, needing to get to work, and it wouldn't start. He followed me home from work and cruised the street after I went into the house. I looked out the window late one night, and there was his car, parked in front. Even my dad was unnerved by it.

I didn't have a boyfriend. Rick had continued to be a close, supportive friend, but by this time he had a girlfriend. Bob had come back into my life after the baby was born but couldn't handle the idea that not only was I no longer the poster child for virginity, I was somebody's mom now, and the child was another man's. Besides, I had no time for a man in my life. I had to work, go to class, study, and be a mother. I couldn't imagine a man fitting into the mix, and I didn't want one anyway.

But after a while, the very absence of wanting began to bother me a little. My parents were a couple, my sister was dating, there were couples nuzzling and holding hands all over my college campus. Was I always going to be alone?

When Deedee was two, I picked up the phone book and went through the yellow pages until I found the name and number of a Lutheran church in downtown St. Paul. "Downtown," to me, must've meant more sophisticated. I made an appointment with a church counselor there. Maybe, by returning to a familiar source of comfort, I would get some help figuring out what I was supposed to do next.

I spoke with a young psychologist (he was about thirty, I think) from Lutheran Family Services, who listened thoughtfully while I told him about the last three years of my life.

"And I think I hate sex," I said, the tears rolling down my face. "Except for this child, I hate everything that happened to my life because of it. I'm like dirt under people's feet, a social outcast, divorced; at school nobody even talks to me. I don't have any friends. And I don't ever want another man in my life. I can't imagine marriage, but I don't want to be alone. What am I going to do about this?"

He leaned forward and quietly said, "But, Loni, you didn't really have sex. You didn't make love to anybody, nobody made love to you. And you didn't have a marriage. In many ways, none of this really happened."

He said that one man was not all men, and that the sexual experience Bruce and I had was in no way typical of sexual behavior between people who cared for each other, who desired each other. He said that it was time I stopped seeing my life as some kind of punishment from God. And then he said (and remember, this was the sixties) that he recommended I have an affair.

"But choose carefully," he cautioned me. "Find someone who is gentle, supportive, understanding. Someone who is experienced, someone you can trust. And start all over again."

"I'm not sure I can do that," I said.

He smiled. "Give it a little time," he said. "I suspect you can."

I had begun spending time in the theater department, working toward a minor. I took stagecraft courses and costume design and acting. When I said I wanted to audition for a play, my parents were appalled. I didn't have enough time; what was I doing being so frivolous? But I rearranged my schedule, bound and determined to find the time.

People in the theater seemed more willing to accept me, more open to a student who was also a mother. I'd go to a party and bring Deidra, and she'd fall asleep in the pile of coats on the bed. I still didn't drink or smoke or swear; I was still that person I had been before, except that now I was a mom. And a little less judgmental, maybe. If someone was smoking a joint in the corner of a room, I'd make a face, but I didn't deliver a lecture.

I became friends with the assistant to the head of the theater department, a man who was ten, maybe twelve years older than I. Don was separated from his wife (it was his wife, in fact, who had told me of the separation) and had a small son. Handsome and fair, with sandy hair and blue eyes, he was the kind of man I had always imagined or hoped I would be with: educated (he was working on his Ph.D.), dignified, complete with a pipe and leather patches on the elbows of his tweed jacket. Gradually we began to see each other outside of department gatherings.

His son was a couple of years older than Deedee, and we would take the kids places together, for ice cream or to a playground. He genuinely liked my daughter, and I liked the way he was with her. And he loved the theater, telling me about playwrights I hadn't heard of, actors I didn't know, plays I hadn't read. In time, he became my first lover.

Don was all of the things that the minister had advised me to find: kind, gentle, patient. He was, I think, the first man I really loved. He was my sexual awakening, he was my mentor, he made me feel alive. He made me feel that life was full of wonderful possibilities and that I could hope for things again. It was the first real joy—emotional, sexual, spiritual—I had ever had.

When my parents found out about the affair, they became enraged. He was, after all, still married, and although I had had nothing to do with the separation, they thought I was being irresponsible. Don even went to them and told my dad that he would get a divorce, that he wanted to marry me. But they were having none of it. And then they leveled the big guns: If I didn't end the relationship, stop spending time around the theater and start acting like the respectable mother I was supposed to be, they would go to court and take Deidra away from me.

This was the first serious battle I had ever had with them, and it was nearly a major break with my dad. I don't think they would ever have followed through on the threat; I think they were just trying to turn me around. I believe it was about their deep love for their granddaughter and their passionate desire to protect her. But their anger scared me, and I told them I would end the affair. It was a lie, though—I continued to see Don.

Once, I even went to his estranged wife. "Whatever is happening between Don and me," I said, "I want it to be open and aboveboard."

Astonishingly, she was very kind to me, but she wasn't ready to hand her husband over. "I'm not sure the marriage is really finished," she said. "I love him."

I nodded. "Me, too."

Soon afterward, she was diagnosed with uterine cancer and went into the hospital for a complete hysterectomy. Don agonized about what to do. I knew he would do the right thing, I knew he would go back to her, so I told him I didn't love him anymore.

I don't think I had ever felt such pain about a romance. And I wasn't prepared for it. Don and Deidra and school and the theater—they were all rolled into one somehow, and I wasn't prepared to lose that dream. I stayed in the theater department, of course, but kept my distance from him. And my parents got what they wanted.

Around the same time, my dear friend Rick, who had stood by me through everything, disappeared while piloting a private plane on a fishing trip in Canada. I couldn't accept that he was gone, or that he had died in the same way his father had. It was twenty-eight years before they even found the crash wreckage.

He looked so much like Robert Redford that every time I've seen Redford in the years since, I've caught sad, gentle hints of the man Rick might've been, with laugh lines in all the right places and eyes reflecting the maturity of a full life. For months after the disappearance, I half expected him to just show up, like he'd been in the wilderness and had decided to walk out that day. But he was gone.

It occurred to me halfway through college that I wasn't a student, I was a theater person pretending to be a student. All I wanted to do was get out. I did my student teaching so that I could get my certificate, but when I walked into that high school class, the wave of adolescent energy and mania that came at me was just too much. I knew I wouldn't be a teacher. I didn't *want* to be a teacher. I wanted to be an actress. Period.

I auditioned for everything. I was cast in Ibsen's *Brand,* directed by Douglas Campbell of the Guthrie Theater. I played a pregnant peasant woman and got high praise from Campbell for knowing how a pregnant woman walks. "I just stopped walking like this myself a few months ago," I told him.

I made it into the University of Minnesota showboat, which was a paid, ninety-dollar-a-week job; Linda Kelsey, who was so terrific in *Lou Grant,* was in the showboat with me. Years later, we were right across the street from each other on the MTM lot, and we used to laugh about how our accommodations had improved since the showboat days.

A famous Indian director, Balwant Gargee, came to the university to direct a play called *The Little Clay Cart,* based on an ancient legend that is in some ways India's version of "Cinderella." The lead is a courtesan, Vasantasena, who is *the* woman in her village—the most beautiful, the most sought after. Men shower her with gifts until she actually chooses someone.

The production was part of an important cultural exchange, a very big deal, and the auditions were open only to graduate students. Although at that point I looked more like an Indian courtesan than almost anyone in the state of Minnesota, I was only a lowly sophomore.

I was in the theater department office one day doing an errand, and the chairman said to me, "Loni, this is Mr. Gargee, the director of *The Little Clay Cart*." I shook his hand and made all the proper admiring noises, then turned and went on my way.

A few minutes later I heard someone running down the sidewalk behind me. "Miss, miss, are you an actress?" It was the Indian director.

When I told him I was, he asked, "Why haven't you been at the auditions?" At the news that auditions had been open only to grad students, Gargee took me by the hand back into the theater department, saying, "*This* is my Vasantasena! *This* is the way she's supposed to look!" They had me read right there and then, and I got the part.

It was a glorious experience. I got wonderful reviews, and all the Indian students would come and wait backstage afterward to speak to me—and when I came out in my sweatshirt and jeans and sneakers, they were visibly disappointed. Onstage, I had a jewel on my forehead, and my black hair was parted in the middle and braided down my back, flowers woven through the braids. I wore incredible jewels and beautiful silk saris embroidered with gold thread. I had my feet painted each night by an artist and wore bells on my fingers and toes. The way I moved and walked was very stylized, because I was, after all, a myth, a legend. Each night, after I got my makeup on, my eyes all done up, I would look at myself in the mirror, my midriff exposed, the bells jingling, and I'd think, oh, wow. This is acting. Even my reluctant parents were astonished at the transformation, and at the reception the play got. It was here, I think, that they began to rethink "Loni's hobby."

That whole experience was so intense for me, so all-consuming of my emotions and my attention, that when the play ended, I was bereft. Because one of the hardest things I had to learn about being an actress was that the play, or the movie, ends. And then you go back to real life. You make a home with people when you're on a project with them; it's a little like being away at camp or being on a ship. You have a common mission, a common goal. And then the next day it's gone. It's the place where reality and fantasy slam up against each other, and it's always made me a little bit sad.

When I completed my degree and got out of school, I told my parents how much I really loved acting, how much I wanted to do it. And they basically said, "Well, that's all very well, but you have to get real now—you have to find a job."

Patricia Stevens School in Minneapolis—the very one Mom had sent me to, only I'd gone to the branch in St. Paul—was not just a modeling school but a trade school as well, and it required accredited teachers. They had a nine-month course for fashion designing and a math-heavy program for students who wished to be fashion buyers. On Saturdays and two nights a week, there were modeling courses and what they called "self-fulfillment" courses for women who wanted to learn more about makeup, hair, and fashion. I was hired to teach the accredited course for girls during the day, and because I needed the extra money, I also taught the two-nights-a-week and Saturday classes.

I quickly fell in love with my job at Stevens. It was a coming-together of all the things I had learned to do and that I enjoyed. Art, modeling, performance, clothing design. I was sewing all my own clothes then, and Deidra's as well. I taught movement and dance, and fencing, which they'd never had at Stevens. We had a television class, where students could learn how to perform for the camera. I was encouraged to be innovative at Stevens, and they treated me like a professional. At twenty-three, I was making a nice living. And little by little I was slowly paying back Dad's ledger account: twenty-five dollars for the dentist, seventy-five dollars for car repairs, twenty dollars for Deedee's shoes.

I went back to community theater, winning roles in *The Three-penny Opera, Can-Can,* and *Any Wednesday.* With performances on Friday and Saturday nights and Sunday matinees, I could still teach my day class on Saturday, as well as the regular classes during the week. I'd get up with Deedee first thing in the morning, have breakfast with her, and send her off to school. Most nights I would be home with her for dinner, read her stories, tuck her into bed. Something had to go, of course, so I didn't date much.

Besides, Bruce was prepared to make life miserable for anyone I dated. If I went out with friends after work, he would show up and make a scene; one night I actually did have a date, doubling with another couple, and Bruce came into the restaurant and promptly punched out the wrong guy. Another night, a nice young man was walking me to my car out on the parking ramp, and Bruce tried to run us over—and when we jumped behind a barricade, he ran his own car into a wall! This was all because he wanted me back, he said. Somehow, I wasn't convinced.

There was a court order for child support—fifty dollars a month—which he rarely paid. I'd go to the judge, who'd shrug and say, "You can't get blood from a stone," and that would be it. "You want to put him in jail?" he'd ask. "You do that, it won't get you paid, because he won't be working."

On the other hand, I discovered, you can sue anybody anytime you want, so Bruce would occasionally sue me for custody. The first time, the judge spent about two minutes on the case and threw it out. Another time, some years later, I had gone to New York to do a commercial—Arm & Hammer laundry detergent, I think—and Bruce filed papers saying that I was actually there working as a topless dancer. The last time he filed suit, the judge said to him, "If I ever see you in my courtroom again, I'll throw you in jail just on general principles!"

I think Bruce's strategy was: Come back to me or I'll bug you the rest of your life. Sometimes the bugging was a nuisance; sometimes it was frightening. When he started calling my dates and threatening them—heck, he even called their mothers!—I began to get scared. If there had ever been an idea in my mind that Deedee and I would leave my parents' house and get a place of our own, that ended it. "Don't worry, Loni," my dad said. "He's all talk."

My best friend was a woman named Nancy Jackson, married to a policeman, with two little girls. She worked at Patricia Stevens, too, and we often rode to work or had lunch together and got our little girls together for play dates. Nancy was very unhappy with her husband, whose name was David. They had been married very young, and although the love had gone out of their relationship, David had a temper and had threatened to kill Nancy if she left him. He followed her; he monitored her phone calls. Everything that she told me David had said to her, Bruce had said to me.

"But you did it, Loni," Nancy said. "You did it, and everything's working out for you. You're my inspiration. And I'm going to do it, too. I'm going to leave David."

I thought about it and said to her, "Nancy, you have to do whatever makes you happy, whatever will give you and your girls a good life."

After I began making my living doing theater work and quit the job at Stevens, Nancy and I continued to stay in touch. Eventually she left David, and they were divorced. Soon after, David had a new girlfriend, and Nancy had met someone else, too. "See?" she said happily. "Everything's going to be fine."

Nancy's new sweetheart had been married before, too. His former wife had been found to be mentally unstable, and he had custody of his children— all eight of them. When he and Nancy became engaged, it was with the sense of a great adventure, as they made plans to raise their children together. When the engagement became public, David flipped out.

He went to his superiors and said, "I want to kill my wife. You better take my gun away from me." So they took his gun away and arranged for him to see the police department psychologist, who said after I don't know how many visits that he was just fine. And then they gave him his gun back.

One morning, Nancy's father called me. "He's killed Nancy," he said.

What David had done, after the department had given him his gun back, was pick it up, drive straight over to the apartment, and, in front of their two-year-old daughter (the older girl was at school), shot Nancy dead. The fiancé jumped in front of him, trying to protect the little girl, and when David shot him, he fell on top of her and died. David then called the police and shot himself—leaving a little girl in a room with three bodies and leaving all ten children without parents.

The news rocked me, and the loss of my friend broke my heart.

I couldn't believe that she was there one minute, full of plans and hope, and the next minute she was just gone. I wondered what made Bruce, in his anger at me, say all those things, threaten all those things, and then not do them? Whereas David said and threatened, and then made good on his threats. What makes one man step over that line and another man not?

I tried to keep in touch with Nancy's daughters after that, but I reminded them too much of her, I upset them. Now they're the age Nancy was then, the age I was.

Years later, on his deathbed, my dad told me—and I can say this now, because he's safely gone—that he had talked to a man, a man who killed people for a living. He said that he had paid this man, and if Bruce ever had done anything to hurt me or Deidra, this man would've killed him. "It was understood," Dad said, nodding slightly as he remembered. "If anything had ever happened to you, that's it, he would've been dead."

At that moment I finally understood that my dad's passion, for my mother, for the things that he loved or believed in, carried through to Deidra and me. That this responsible businessman, pillar of the community, prince of the ordered universe, could make such a plan boggled my mind. Yet in a way, it was typical of how he did things. Shortest distance between two points is a straight line. Cross it and here's what I'm going to do. Period.

Bruce, praise God, came to his senses on his own, gradually getting on with his life as I got on with mine. He married again— Deidra has two stepsisters and a half brother. And we became friends. But it took years, and it took effort. And it could just as easily have gone another, more tragic way.

Chapter 4

The Friars dinner theater in Minneapolis was running auditions for *Born Yesterday*. Equity actors only need apply. I didn't have an Equity card—but they didn't have their Billie Dawn yet, either. So they opened the auditions to anybody, promising to get a card for whoever was cast.

I still had dark hair, but I had played a blonde ditz (courtesy of a wig) in one of the university showboat productions, and everybody started saying, "This is you." So on my lunch hour at Stevens, I went out and bought my own blonde wig, for about $19.95, I think. I took it home, put it on, styled it, put on a snug sweater, snug jeans, and a pair of heels, and sashayed my way to this audition.

Up until this time, my looking older had had everything to do with the way I dressed, not with the way my face was arranged by nature. It's kind of a baby face, with a pug nose and dimples, and before maturity brought the gift of cheekbones, it was a round, childish face. Topped off with silly blonde curls, I looked like a kid just off the school bus.

I sat in the lobby waiting to be called, thinking, I'm just too cool for words. This is my part. Later I found out from the stage manager that when he saw me, he went in to the casting guy and said, "There's a girl sitting in the lobby waiting for her audition.

I think she's your Billie Dawn, but she's only about seventeen."
I was twenty-four.

There are times in this business when the part is just yours.
You know it in your bones. And Billie Dawn was mine. I wanted
it. I *was* it. And I got it. And then the terror set in: If they ever
find out I'm not blonde . . . I kept the wig securely on my head
during the entire rehearsal period. I was certain that if it ever
came off, I'd lose the part with my name all over it, and the
Equity card as well. Equity minimum, at that time, was more
than I made at Stevens.

Opening night I received a standing ovation at the beginning
of the second act. For just *appearing* on the stage. Well, there
now, I've made it, I thought. I'm a star. I'll never have to worry
again. When I remember that moment now, I just want to fall
down laughing at that girl and her mind-bending naïveté. I was
more just-off-the-bus than I knew.

After the curtain dropped, I floated offstage on a cloud. The
audience was still hollering and clapping, and everybody backstage was so happy, and I was so excited that I tore my wig off!
The director—who had also played Harry, my leading man—
looked stunned. "Would you have cast me?" I asked him.

"I'd like to say yes," he said slowly, "but I think I have to say
no. No. Where the hell *are* you in there?"

I got one review that said something like, "Not even topped
by Judy Holliday." I couldn't believe it. I really thought I'd never
have to worry again, that they'd be beating down my door forever afterward. I quit my job at Patricia Stevens. I was a big star
for the whole run—and when it was over, I didn't have a job.
And nobody was beating down my door.

Being Grampa to Deidra had mellowed my dad somewhat—
Andrea and I had been struck dumb one afternoon when we
walked into the living room to find him watching the news as
Deedee set his hair with her doll curlers—but his original rule
held. "What are you going to do now?" he asked insistently.
"What are you going to do for work?"

I called the booking agent I'd worked with all through school
and went back to modeling, one fashion show at a time, one

print ad at a time. Penney's, snowmobiles, desk organizers, Radio WLOL. But there had to be more than this.

Ralph Foody, the actor who had played the attorney in *Born Yesterday* (and who was in the first *Home Alone* movie), was from Chicago. He and his wife, Jan, had been wonderful to me, encouraging me to think past Minnesota. When I called and asked them if I could sponge off them for a week and try my luck in Chicago, they said yes. I packed the requisite 1972 wardrobe—leather hot pants and go-go boots—and took off in my 1967 burnt-orange Mustang Grande with bucket seats, with a gasoline credit card on loan from Dad. I arrived in Chicago with exactly seven dollars.

Shirley Hamilton was the biggest commercial agent in the city at that time, and I went to her office with Judy Fields, who had also been in the play with me at the Friars. Judy looked like the ideal all-American girl—an open, pretty face, great smile, blue eyes, blonde hair. There was always commercial and acting work for girls who looked like Judy, and Shirley had an audition she wanted to send her to. But when Judy introduced me to Shirley, she said, "My God, you look like an American Indian! I have no place for you whatever, I can't even send you out. With that hair halfway down your back and that exotic look, nobody will cast you." Well, I thought, crestfallen, so much for Chicago.

Judy talked me into coming to the audition with her, saying we could go get lunch afterward. There were dozens of women in their twenties in the lobby, signing the check-in sheet. No one knew what the audition was for. I just sat there thinking about how much money I now owed my dad. "Go sign up," Judy whispered to me.

"I can't do that," I said. "Shirley said nobody will cast me."

"Oh, go ahead," she said. "What can it hurt?" I figured, well, OK, as long as they don't take any of my seven dollars.

One by one they called the names out on the list, and when they called mine and I got to the room on the other side of the door, the woman there said to me, "I can't find your name on this pre-approved list."

I'm dead, I thought. "Oh, uh, I just got back into town today, and Shirley Hamilton told me just to come on in." That seemed to satisfy her.

They said they wanted to ask a few questions. Was I allergic to creams and soaps? What kind of cosmetics and cleansers did I use on my face, on my skin? What kind of deodorant did I use, what kind of soap? After they asked and I answered, they said, "Thank you. Here's your thirty-five dollars." Wow, I thought—I sneak in here like a thief, and they're going to pay me for it!

Judy and I went out the door hooting and hollering. We were rich! On the way to lunch, I bought a scarf (with the original seven dollars) for Jan Foody for being so nice to me. After we'd ordered, Judy said, "I'm going to call Shirley to see if I got a callback." When she returned to the table, she said, "Shirley wants to know what happened to my friend who snuck into the audition. Because there is a callback—for you! And if you go, they'll pay you seventy-five dollars an hour."

I went right to the audition callback, which would be filmed, they told me. If I was cast, they said, they'd provide my Screen Actors Guild card. A SAG card? Wow, that was better than a good review.

The commercial was for deodorant; all they wanted me to do was shave under my arms, use two different deodorants, and then tell them what it felt like. Sure enough, one really stung, but the other one, I told them, didn't sting, felt kind of refreshing, smelled wonderful. I just babbled. And then they gave me the cash and I left. And I got the job, which was a national commercial for Secret. And to this day, as God is my witness, I still use unscented Secret Deodorant. Why tempt fate?

When I got back to St. Paul, I started getting little bills, little statements, from Shirley Hamilton. I owed her twenty dollars, I owed her thirty dollars. Finally I called her. "Why are you sending me these bills?" I asked indignantly.

"This is the way it works, honey," she said patiently. "You pay me my ten percent, I'll send you your checks." That's the day I learned about residuals. Within weeks, she had sent me seven thousand dollars. That was August—I had gone to Chicago in July. In a month's time, I had gone from seven dollars to seven thousand!

I asked Dad to get out the ledger, which showed that I owed him two thousand dollars. I handed him the whole amount. And then we went and opened my first bank account. The only thing I bought for myself was a television for my bedroom. I thought I had the most incredibly wonderful life. My little girl was going to be in the first grade soon. I had paid back my dad, I had my own television in my bedroom, I had money in the bank. What riches!

In September I auditioned for *Fiddler on the Roof* at the Chanhassen Dinner Theatre, a wonderful (and huge) place in Minneapolis, and was cast as Tzeitel, the oldest sister. Mom and Dad came to opening night and saw me sing and dance and do all the stuff I'd been doing for years for no money, but now I was earning the grand Equity minimum of a hundred sixty dollars a week. That night, by the time I'd gotten my makeup off and celebrated the opening at the cast party, they were long in bed. But on my pillow was an envelope, with a letter inside. "You were so wonderful," they wrote. "And we are so proud." They get it, I thought. They finally get it.

I did *Fiddler* for fifty-three weeks, eight or nine shows a week, and I never missed one performance. Other actors came and went, people got sick or dropped out to do other shows, but I stayed with it. Sometimes I did commercials during the day—one was an industrial commercial for Maytag, with a pre-*M*A*S*H* Mike Farrell, and Jesse White playing that first lonely Maytag repairman.

Don, my precious friend from the theater department, came to see me in *Fiddler,* and we had a lovely, gentle dinner afterward. His wife had made it through her illness, and they had made it through their difficulties. I was proud that he had come to see me, since he had been so much a part of my dream.

Andrea had graduated from college with a degree in home economics, so that she could teach, and the day after graduation she was married to Steve Sams, her first love. He was (and is) a forest ranger, and after they were married, they began their life of moving from one beautiful part of the country to another. It was bittersweet to see her go; she was everything that my mother had wanted me to be.

Deidra was six and came to *Fiddler,* excited that Mommy was doing something she could understand and enjoy. But what she remembers now is that I missed all her school events. I rarely had dinner with her anymore, or read her a story, or put her to bed, because I was already on my way to the theater. On weekends, when she was home from school, I had matinees. I got home well after midnight every night and rarely got to sleep before one. But I still got up with her every morning at six, had breakfast with her, put her on the school bus—and then collapsed back into bed. Each afternoon I picked her up from school, and we'd have a snack and talk. And then I'd have to head for the theater at five-thirty or six. When anyone asked Deidra what her mother did for work, she didn't say, "She's an actress." She said, "My mommy pretends."

During the *Fiddler* run, I became friends with Art Vestry, the man who played Papa. One night we were having one of those silly backstage conversations, and he asked, "OK, who in Hollywood do you think is sexy?"

I had to think only a minute. "John Gavin. If John Gavin walked in right now, well, you could just cart me away. *Imitation of Life* and *Back Street, Midnight Lace* and *Spartacus, Tammy Tell Me True.* Oh, my."

Art started laughing. He was from Los Angeles, and one of his best friends there, he said, was John Gavin. "I'll get you an autographed picture," he promised. And sure enough, in a week or so, there was a black-and-white glamour shot of John Gavin, signed "To Loni, with love." An immediately prized possession, it went right up on my wall.

The Friars theater had a nightclub downstairs, with live music. One Monday night, when the Chanhassen Theatre was dark, three of us—my still dear friends Jeanne Jensen and John Command, who was in the *Fiddler* cast with me, and I—headed over to hear this wonderful fifties rock group The Diamonds. When we got there, the theater was all lit up, although we knew there was no performance scheduled. It turned out they were springing a surprise *This Is Your Life!* on Dana Andrews, who was appearing at the Friars in *The Marriage-Go-Round*. As we walked through the doors, we looked up to see the glamorous folks in their tuxedos, and there, at the top of the steps, stood John Gavin. In the flesh.

"Oh, my gosh," I breathed. "Wait until I tell Art I actually saw John Gavin."

Jeanne said, "Oh, go up there, Loni. Go up and talk to him." She saw the look on my face. "Look, just go up and tell him you're a friend of Art's, and you've got his picture, and you've always been a fan, blah, blah, blah. What are the chances you'll ever see him again in your life?"

She was right, I decided. I walked up the stairs and said, "Excuse me, Mr. Gavin, but Art Vestry . . . ," and he brightened right up, a five-hundred-watt smile.

"Is Art here?" he asked.

I explained that no, Art wasn't exactly here, not in the room, exactly, but he was in town, and we were doing *Fiddler* together, and probably he didn't remember, but he'd sent me an autographed picture, and, as Jeanne had suggested, blah, blah, blah.

"Well, let's go find a pay phone; we can call Art and say hi," Mr. Gavin suggested. Which we did. First Art and I talked, and then Art and John talked, and there was much laughing, and the whole time my heart was thumping.

When he'd hung up, I said, "This has been such a thrill, and I'll leave you to your evening now. I'm meeting my friends downstairs in the bar."

He flashed the high-wattage smile and shook my hand. "You're a very lovely girl, and I wish you great success in your career."

Well, I'm sure my feet touched the ground on the way back downstairs, but I wouldn't swear to it. I sat down with Jeanne and John, muttering, "I can't believe it, I can't believe it."

It wasn't ten minutes before the waiter came up to the table and said, "Excuse me, miss, but Mr. Gavin has requested that you and your party come up to the theater and join him for dinner, to watch the taping of the program."

I didn't know what to say. "Yes, yes," hissed Jeanne and John. So up we went. I remember what I was wearing that night more clearly than any prom dress: a purple, puffy-sleeved, form-fitting velvet dress (I think the style that year was characterized as "rich hippie") that was long enough to cover my lace-up boots, with Gibson-girl hair piled on my head. Oh, I thought I was hot stuff.

We sat around the table and watched while John gave his part of the presentation, and when he came back and sat down, he told us wonderful Hollywood stories. He was completely charming—he'd insisted we call him Jack—and I began to feel like Cinderella, aware every minute that the clock was going to chime and I'd turn into a pumpkin.

At the end of the taping, there were a lot of people hanging around the table—the local network executives, some reporters, and more than a few quite interested women. When one of them suggested that she would be happy to give Mr. Gavin a ride back to his hotel, he quite nicely said, "Oh, no thank you, I've already made arrangements. This young lady is giving me a lift." I hadn't made the offer, hadn't said a word, but I'm thinking, *whooaa,* I'll take you anywhere you want to go. I'll drive you to Nome. And Jeanne and John said their farewells, grinning and rolling their eyes as they left.

When we got to his hotel, he said, "Won't you come up for a drink?"

Now, I'm not dating anyone, and he's in between marriages (there were movie magazines in those days, and I *knew* these things), so I took a deep breath and said, "Yes."

I had never, ever had a one-night stand in my life, and here I was, walking into a hotel room alone with John Gavin. How far can I let this go, I wondered? When he asked what I wanted to drink, I said the first thing that came to my mind. "Black Russian, please." After two of them, I hurled caution to the wind.

It was straight out of a movie. He unlaced my boots, he took down my hair, he slowly undressed me, and he made glorious love to me. Talk about being swept off your feet. And out of your boots. Don't you remember seeing *Back Street* when you were about twelve? A four-hankie sobfest if ever there was one, and here he is, the most handsome man, even more startlingly gorgeous in person, dark and romantic—and creative—and I'm being transported into a state of bliss I'd never even imagined. With every whisper, every word, I wanted to jump up and say just a minute, let me write this down! I want to keep track of everything. What was that line? Was it from a movie, a play, what? Other women my age might've been looking around for Mick Jagger. Not me.

So hours later . . . I floated downstairs and drove straight home, went right inside, and woke up my mother.

"My Lord, what time is it?" she whispered, her eyes big in the dark.

"It's four o'clock or something," I whispered back. "Never mind, you have to come out in the hall, I have to tell you something. *Ssshh*, don't wake Dad."

She grabbed her robe and followed me into the hall. "What is it, Loni?" she asked with some irritation.

"I just made love with John Gavin." *That* woke her up.

"Oh, my God," she gasped, "that's the most exciting thing I've ever heard!"

I was immediately grateful to her—it was exactly, exactly what I had wanted her to say. I wanted her to be just as goofily thrilled as I was. We sat in my room and talked about it all night long, giggling like fools.

I think the 1995 Loni has to step in here and point out that this was in the early seventies—the part of the seventies that was still in the sixties—and it was a free and different time. For a lot of people, sex was fun and friendly; it was what you did at the end of a date. We couldn't imagine AIDS then, or even sexually transmitted diseases. The worst that could happen was pregnancy, and taking responsibility meant preventing pregnancy. There simply was no fear factor, there was just a celebration, the wonderful humanness of what could transpire between two people. And for this former Sunday school teacher, this particular celebration had been a revelation!

Although Jack had taken my telephone number, I never expected him to call. But he did, and he asked me to come and meet him in Chicago for the weekend. He was president of the Screen Actors Guild then (he'd succeeded Charlton Heston in 1971), and they were having a board meeting. Since the *Fiddler* run had ended, I giddily accepted. It would be a chance to see my friends Ralph and Jan Foody and to take another look at this Jack Gavin person, who seemed to have taken up residence in my imagination.

We had a wonderful time. He wined and dined me, we made love, we laughed a lot. We were like a matched set, me with my head of black hair and him with his. People would just look at us and gasp. I was very conscious of it as a scene—out of a movie. I said to him once, "You know, Jack, the problem with you is, when we get up in the morning, you're prettier than I am."

I knew quite soon that I wasn't in love with him, nor he with me—we were enamored of each other, and we sure had fun together. But life isn't a movie, and mine was still firmly rooted in Minnesota. And he was a big man on the Hollywood movie campus. Gradually we fizzled. But not without my grateful understanding of what Jack and the relationship had meant. My introduction to sex had been so horrific; everything that came afterward came as a balm somehow. Being a woman, a sexual woman, was beginning to be a great adventure. And sharing it with my mother—well, it gave me a window to the part of her that had been inexplicable before. I was learning the mystery of what she and my father shared—that indeed another person could make the earth move for you!

Chapter 5

After the *Fiddler* run at Chanhassen was over, I went back to the Friars again to do *Never Too Late* with Richard Deacon and *Send Me No Flowers* with *Laugh-In*'s Alan Sues. I was now a paid, self-supporting, working actress. I even went to Chicago to audition for shows there, and stayed with Ralph and Jan.

We did a funny brunette vs. blonde experiment in Chicago. There was a theater bar—I can't remember the name of it now, but it's not there anymore. One Monday night we all trooped in, and I was being my own brunette self. Everybody was very nice to me, and it was a very pleasant evening.

The following Monday night we went back. I was wearing exactly the same clothes I had worn the week before—and a blonde wig. In ten minutes I had eight drinks lined up in front of me, sent by guys in the bar. The bartender would put one in front of me and mutter, "Tall man in tweed coat at end of bar," or "Guy with scar sitting on third stool."

At the end of the evening, the bar manager came over and said that the board of directors of Hiram Walker, the liquor company, was having its annual dinner in the banquet room, and would I like to join them? All men, all gray-haired, distinguished. And I said, "For dinner?" He nodded.

It was like playing a part. And I played cute, and blonde, and silly. I had a lovely dinner, and at the end of the evening, they each gave me money for a cab and they each gave me a business card. And I thought, this is what happens to a blonde. I wasn't offended, I was just amazed. And I decided, after that, not to be a blonde. When I was a brunette, nobody treated me like I didn't know what I was doing, as an actress or a person, and I liked that. I changed my mind a few years later, but that's another story.

I had saved a thousand dollars for a vacation, and during Deidra's spring break from school, the two of us flew—first class!—to Disney World for a whole week. I had made us matching seersucker pantsuits for the trip, and bought a movie camera. It was the first vacation we had ever taken together, and we were beside ourselves with excitement.

We stayed at the Hotel Royal Plaza, where almost twenty years later Burt, Quinton, and I would often stay again. There would be a Reynolds Suite, and our family pictures would all be up on the wall. But for this first visit, it was mother-and-daughter only. We ordered up room service breakfast every day. After a swim in the pool, we would take the shuttle bus to the park and stay through lunch, dinner, and the last-call fireworks every night. We rode every ride, went into every gift shop, and walked for miles in the sun. At eight years of age, Deedee became an expert with the camera—although she did have to say "Mo-*ther*!" when I started jumping up and down in front of it every time she aimed it at me.

I couldn't believe how happy I was. Deedee was thriving, so was I, and here we were on vacation in Snow White's neighborhood. Back home, I was being paid to be an actress, and in between plays I was doing commercials—for Montgomery Ward, for Pillsbury, for Swanson frozen foods, for General Mills. In fact, before I ever did *WKRP in Cincinnati*, I was making more money than my dad; he was helping me manage my finances at that point, and he was astonished. That's the thing, I think, that surprises people—that you don't have to be a star to make it in this business, and you don't have to live in Hollywood or New York. There's an entire industry in the middle of this country, with trained and talented professionals making a good living.

Deidra and I were still living at home with Mom and Dad; with my schedule, we all agreed, it was best for both of us. My parents had mellowed, I had grown up, and Deedee had the kind of security and consistency that I couldn't have provided alone.

Reading filled a social void for me—I usually had three or four books going at once; it's what I did during the day when Deidra was in school. I wasn't dating, Andrea was gone, and once Nancy Jackson died, it was hard to open my heart to new friends.

That summer I was scheduled to do *Play It Again, Sam* at the Old Log Theater, on a lake just outside Minneapolis. I had been cast as Sharon, the fantasy woman. An actor named Ross Bickell was going to play Dick.

I noticed at the first rehearsal that Ross was reading *The Murder of Roger Ackroyd,* an Agatha Christie mystery that I'd recently finished. "Oh, I read that one, it's really good," I chirped. Then, with more enthusiasm than was warranted (especially for a fellow mystery fan), I proceeded to tell him Who Did It. It was an auspicious beginning.

At around this point in the seventies, men started—from the weird fashions, maybe—looking kind of unattractive to me. Humans weren't meant to wear those combinations of colors, those plaids and prints, those strange fabrics right out of a chemical vat. Disco fever didn't do anybody any fashion favors, and I think the men suffered more than the women did. Ross, however, came through the decade unscathed.

A classically trained actor with a beautiful speaking voice—and could he sing!—Ross was just terrific looking: sandy hair, clear blue eyes, a constant twinkle. He was from Virginia and had studied drama at Boston University. I was immediately in awe of him. He'd performed at the Guthrie, in *Julius Caesar* and *Uncle Vanya.* He was the real deal.

Rehearsals were great fun, and we had a fast friendship in days. We found ourselves talking at every break, having lunch together every day, going on endlessly about books and music and theater. Ross was living with someone, he had told me. A woman named Pamela. So I decided that what I was beginning to feel toward him had to be about learning from a talented actor, working in collaboration with a respected colleague. And he was a good actor, a really good actor, and I watched him constantly, listening to the way he delivered a line, watching the way he walked across the stage, picked up a prop.

Just before our opening night, we were at a rehearsal, and during a break he said, "Let's take a walk." The theater was right by the lake (everything's "right by the lake" in Minnesota), and it was dusk. We stood and watched as the stars came out, and then he leaned in and kissed me. And I thought . . . well, now the bottom has dropped out of everything.

When the kiss was over, I just looked up at him and said, "What?"

"I don't know," he said, and he sounded pretty miserable. "I'm crazy about you."

I nodded. "I'm crazy about you, too. But you're committed to someone. Aren't you?"

So we quietly walked back to the theater, very introspective, very somber. Opening night came, and Pamela was there. And I thought, well, that's the way it is, we have to work together every day, just get over it.

Every day we saw each other. Every night after the show, we stood around talking about nothing, putting off going to our cars. After about ten days, he kissed me again. And all of a sudden we're necking in his car, and I'm saying, "Wait, wait," just like in high school, because right on top of the thrill, like wet cement, is this overwhelming guilt.

He's heartbroken and guilty, because he really cares for this woman, she matters to him. And so do I. And he won't get further involved with me without telling her. So not only is everything about him right, that is, too. He won't even lie about me! The next day he moved out of their apartment.

Ross moved into a hotel, and every night after the play I went back there with him. Our lovemaking was tempestuous, passionate, enthusiastic, and often interrupted by phone calls from Pamela, sleepless and weeping, having a rough time with the breakup. He's done this to her, and so have I. We've done this horrible thing to another person, and we're happy, and we're miserable.

I started getting home just before Deedee got up for school, and my parents threw up their hands in anger and frustration. I heard the familiar "As long as you live under my roof" speech that we've all heard from our parents, only the primary reason for their anger was their granddaughter. "All right, so *you're* an adult," said my father. "But Deidra is not, she's a little girl, and you're her mother. She's not to know about this, never to know you're not here. You still get up with her in the morning, help her get ready for school. Your obligations in this house haven't changed."

I was exhausted, and exhilarated, and completely, totally in love. I finally brought Ross home to meet my parents and, more important, to meet Deidra. Whatever dating I had done, whatever men I had seen, it had always been outside that house. I'd kept her and my life with her separate. But this man was significant to me and would continue to be, and I had known it from the beginning.

When we had started, it was June. In August the other woman was still a factor; his emotional connection to her, the entanglement, wasn't going away. He couldn't seem to handle it, and we couldn't get beyond it. We couldn't keep our hands off each other, but it was like she was there all the time, in pain, and it was our fault. It was a big, nasty mess.

"I'm going to go to New York," I finally decided. "I'm going to give it a try. While I'm gone, you're going to have to decide how to work this out."

Barbara Hasselberg, former Miss Minnesota and my former sister-in-law, was living in New York City, in an apartment on 65th Street between Fifth and Madison avenues. We had stayed in close touch, and she was willing to let me come and sleep on her couch. Our friendship had been eased along by Bruce's remarriage—to Pamela. (Yes, another Pamela! Little did I know that there would be a third Pam a few years down the road. . . .) I was so happy for him, and so grateful to his wife. She was warm and generous, the best stepmother (and friend) I could have wished for Deidra, and she was key to the kind of healing Bruce needed in his life. After they were married, I never worried another day about Deedee spending time with her dad.

Barbara, however, was living a bit over her head in the Big Apple. Talk about champagne taste—this apartment was eight hundred dollars a month, which was outrageous for 1973, and not just by Minnesota standards. She was working for a cosmetics company, primarily because she was just so beautiful, and when she wasn't working, she was painting the town. Neither one of us had much money, but we *were* centrally located—so we went to the Oak Bar at the Plaza every night for happy hour. Someone would inevitably buy us a glass of wine, which we'd nurse for an hour while we ate the complimentary hors d'oeuvres. The bartender got to know us after a while—I think we were good for his business—and he made a safe space for us at the bar as we wangled our one "meal" of the day.

Between us, Barbara and I found a commercial agent, and that's when I got my Arm & Hammer laundry detergent commercial. And a Mop & Glo floor wax commercial, which was touted as breakthrough "women's lib" advertising. Stephen Collins played my husband (he was the blond, I was the brunette) and we were the new, upscale working couple who shared the housework—I did the laundry, hubby did the floors. It not only got a lot of airplay, it was also written about in the media and advertising columns.

September in New York can be an evocative, magical time. Jack Gavin was in the city to do the musical version of *Two for the Seesaw,* with Michele Lee. I called him and went to see the play, and afterward we went back to his apartment. He was just as handsome as I remembered, and there was a lovely spark between us. But there was no possibility of anything happening— by then, Jack was involved with actress Constance Towers and in fact would marry her a year later. The beautiful, statuesque Connie, who has since become a friend, is someone whose talent and elegance I always admired. She was the perfect partner for Jack, especially when he became United States Ambassador to Mexico during the Reagan administration.

Hearing Jack talk about Connie just made me miss Ross, in spite of being so mad at him. And then, suddenly, Ross blew into New York City. He had loaded up the car one day and driven straight through, and now there he was, camped on my doorstep. "I love you," he said.

"Are we going to be able to be happy?" I asked. "Honestly? Can you get past this damn guilt?"

Yes, he assured me, yes. We decided to stay in New York and continue trying our luck; we went across the Hudson to Montclair, New Jersey, to stay with his sister and brother-in-law and came into Manhattan every day for open calls and auditions. Deidra said later that it seemed to her I was gone for a year; I was actually in New York for two and a half months and got back home twice for week-long visits with her.

The national commercials had begun being aired. Over the next three or four years, I probably earned thirty thousand dollars a year from each of them. We started to think about staying in New York for good. But in October, Pamela began calling Ross again, and very quickly it seemed like we were back to stage one. Ross was and is a nice man, with a conscience; Pam's sadness was torturing him.

Then Art Vestry called me out of the blue and said, "We're taking a New York cast to Jacksonville, Florida, to do *Fiddler* over the Christmas and New Year's holiday. Will you come?" It was my ticket out. I decided to go home and spend a little more time with Deedee, and then go to Florida with *Fiddler.*

When I got home, I told my mother, "If he calls, I'm not here." And of course, the minute he did, she said, "She's right here."

To me she said, "Loni, this is your problem. You're an adult; straighten it out."

I told him I didn't want to talk to him, didn't want to see him. He couldn't put the three of us through this any longer; he had to make a decision. I almost didn't care anymore what it was. But I knew we'd end up hating each other if he didn't decide.

I went to Florida at the end of November, for a six-week run of *Fiddler.* Deidra came down for two weeks over school vacation, and we decorated the motel room with Christmas decorations and went to Disney World together, and had a wonderful time. She danced with all the theater people—the gypsies—until four in the morning on New Year's Eve. She was the belle of the ball, and I was collapsed at the table. Someone at the motel desk came and got me, told me I had a phone call.

It was Ross, in an outdoor phone booth in icy Minnesota, in the snow, with a handful of change. As I heard the dimes and quarters clinking in, I heard him say, "Will you marry me?"

I started crying so hard I could hardly get the words out. "Yes, yes! I'll marry you." Happy New Year, 1974!

I almost couldn't believe that I was going to do it again, ten years after my disaster with Bruce. But on January 28, 1974, we were married in the minister's study at Resurrection Lutheran Church (which had a new pastor by then), with just Mom, Dad, and my daughter as witnesses. My parents were thrilled, and Dad and Ross grew close quite quickly.

Deedee was another story. Oh, she liked Ross well enough, but she had lived all of her life with Gramma and Grampa in a big, beautiful house on the lake. She had always been the center of their world, and now she questioned whether she would receive the same degree of attention from Ross and me. "Why can't he just move in here with us?" she asked. For her, it was more complicated than just moving into a new apartment. She was leaving her family home. "They were my other parents, my security," she says of her grandparents now, remembering the difficulties of those first weeks in the newly reconstituted Bickell family.

We went to Virginia to meet Ross's parents, Nancy and George, and his sister, Robin, who was to become one of my dearest friends, part of the girlfriend gang that includes Jeanne Jensen (who became my secretary) and Jeanne's daughter Linda, who became my manager. In fact, Robin still visits me in California at least twice a year, and since 1980, when I did *The Jayne Mansfield Story,* she has often worked on the set with me as a wardrobe person.

With this marriage, I felt at last that I was an adult, building a family structure that extended beyond the sheltering care of my parents. Ross was strong and loving and fair; Deidra grew to love him dearly and took his last name as her own, keeping it until she married. He was my best friend, and I had to lean on him very soon—because just before we were married, my dad was diagnosed with prostate cancer.

Years before, after Bruce and I were divorced, I told my dad once that I didn't ever want to marry again. He said, "Then I've failed you, as a father and as a man. If you don't want what your mother and I have, if you don't want what a man can give you, then I've failed. That you think you can live without it makes me very sad." No matter how content I was, no matter how self-sufficient I became or how much work I got, Dad always worried that it wouldn't be enough for Deedee and me. Now, with Ross as my partner, Dad began to turn inward, toward the fight he was in and toward the preparations he needed to make.

I wouldn't acknowledge the shift at first, or the significance of the illness he was fighting. He wasn't at risk, I thought, because he wasn't mortal. He was, after all, the one who made everything all right. Soon, I began to know in my heart that everything wasn't going to be all right at all.

Our first year together, Ross and I worked pretty steadily, and we worked together. We did a Hugh Leonard play, *The Patrick Pearse Motel*, at the Old Log Theater, and then went to Denver to do *Star Spangled Girl* with Dwayne Hickman, at the Colorado Music Hall. We were in Denver for six weeks, and Deedee came with us. We enrolled her in the fourth grade, in a public school where a lot of her classmates, for the first time, were black.

"Mom," she said one day after school, "a girl in the bathroom called me a 'honkie' today. What's a 'honkie'?" Oh, boy, we laughed. You can take the girl out of Minnesota, but you can't take the Minnesota out of the girl!

We came back to Minnesota to do a comedy called *Paris Is Out!*, with Pat O'Brien and his wife, Eloise, who were doing a lot of national touring then. Ross and I quickly became very fond of them. One day Pat said to us, "I think you two should move to Los Angeles."

We were making a perfectly good living—the residuals from the commercials were coming in, and one or the other of us was working all the time—and we were settling into our new family. "I don't think we need to go to L.A.," I said. "Besides, the competition there is ridiculous. There's a pretty lady under every rock, and there's a funny lady under every rock."

"Ah," said Pat, "but not so many pretty, funny ladies."

Coincidentally, when *Paris* was over, Ross and I both found ourselves out of work at the same time. And we started thinking. We went to Mom and Dad to talk it over with them. They had sold their big house after Dee and I had gone and had moved into a new, small house. What was going on, of course, was that Dad was winding things up. He was putting things in order for Mom. I didn't want to see it, didn't want to think about it.

"What do you think about L.A.?" we asked. "Should we give it a shot?" We all agreed it was worth a chance. Ross and I had enough money saved to last us six months, we figured. If we didn't make it in Hollywood in six months, then we would come home.

Now, if anybody said this to me today, I think I would laugh for about three hours. There are people in L.A. parking cars after ten years, still waiting to make it. Thank God I didn't know what the deal was then, or maybe I wouldn't have done it. And I couldn't have done it without Ross. I had indeed married my best friend. We did everything together; we shared work and family and books and dreams.

A lot of women say, about remarrying, "Well, there's always the last-minute, second-thought thing." No, not for me. There wasn't a single doubt in my mind about marrying him. He was everything I ever wanted, on any level. He was my soul mate. And when we made the decision to go to Los Angeles together, I knew it would work out right, because we were doing it together.

But I think each turn of my life has had a purpose. There are no decisions I would change. When people ask me, Would you have passed on Bruce?, I say no, because then I wouldn't have had a life with my Deidra. Would you have married Ross? Yes, because if I hadn't, I wouldn't have had the courage to head west, and I wouldn't have had his strong arms and heart during my dad's illness. Would I still marry Burt? Yes, I absolutely would— because with Burt came the joy of Quinton. Oh, I may grieve a lot of things now and then. But I don't regret much.

Chapter 6

We found a town house condominium in the San Fernando Valley, just a short walk from Deidra's school. Two bedrooms and two baths, a pretty living room, and a small garden with a barbecue—and a swimming pool and playground in the condo complex. It felt like a palace. It was all we needed to begin our new life.

The first day, surrounded by packing boxes stacked like building blocks, I just sat down on the floor and had myself a good cry. And then I tackled the kitchen. That's always the first place you have to start in making a new home, I think. You have to figure out the chore paths, which cupboards get used for what, where the food goes. How a kitchen gets put together is an indicator of how the rest of it will go. But you have to get that good cry out of the way first.

Our days were simple. Ross and I would walk Deidra to school, come back, look up recipes and make a shopping list, go out for our auditions and interviews, get lunch and the groceries, come home, walk to school and get Deedee, come back and cook dinner. If there was time, we would all take a swim. It was cold and snowy back home. Under the California skies, all was bright and sunny.

Pat O'Brien helped us find agents within the first two weeks.

One, who had seen me in *Fiddler*, said I could probably work as much as I wanted—as a singer, interestingly enough, maybe in supper clubs. But I didn't want to work at night anymore, especially without Mom and Dad to back me up. I wanted to work during the day, while Deidra was in school, so I could be home with her at night. I wanted to cook her dinner, supervise her homework, go to PTA meetings. The agent said that sounded like television and referred me to Len Kaplan, who then represented me until the mid-eighties.

When a husband and wife do the same kind of work, there's always danger of tension, of competition. Although that's probably true in any career, I think it's especially so in the arts, where egos are fragile. But there seemed to be no competition between Ross and me. We weren't up for the same parts, of course, and besides, our ambitions were different. I wanted work that would let me be available to my husband and daughter as a wife and mother, not just as a roommate. I wanted to work in a job that would allow me also to have a life. Ross wanted to be An Actor.

If we had settled in New York, he would have set his sights on Broadway. In Hollywood, he was aiming for films. His voice was deep and rich (he had great success with voice-overs and commercials), and his idol was Richard Burton. He could sing, he could do comedy, he could do the classics, and from the beginning his reviews had been routinely good. And he had always worked; in the early days in Minnesota, he and Nick Nolte auditioned for the same parts, and Ross was often the one cast. While I had done just fine with my career so far, of the two of us he was the star, I had no doubt about that. I don't think he ever took me as seriously as an actor as I took him. He thought I was cute and funny; I thought he was brilliant.

We were lucky, and we both found work immediately. Ross got important TV guest leads—on *The Tony Randall Show, Logan's Run, Cannon, Police Story, City of Angels*, with Wayne Rogers. I was getting "the girl" parts—on *Police Story, Police Woman, Barnaby Jones, S.W.A.T.* And I began to have luck in comedies as well—*The Bob Newhart Show*, Cloris Leachman's *Phyllis*, and *The Love Boat* (where Donny Osmond and I played a brother and sister in one episode—too many teeth on the nation's TV screens that night, I'd say). If you stay up late enough now, you can find me in reruns all over cable, in boots, minidresses, and various shades of long hair, "the girl" in short-term peril or making one-episode wisecracks.

We began to be part of a neighborhood, a theater community, with cookouts on the weekends, grocery shopping at the same market each week, checking out the same flea markets and antique shops, meeting the same people at auditions. We first met Lynda Carter when Ross was a guest star, along with Bob Hays, on *Wonder Woman*. Lynda soon became a good friend and would be my costar a few years later on *Partners in Crime*. Bob, the crazed pilot of the *Airplane!* movies, has not only stayed close to our family, but eventually married my friend Sondra (or Sam, to those of us who love her) Currie's sister, Cheri. Sam and I kept running into each other at auditions, trying out for the same parts. We decided that the only thing to do was become friends—and that friendship is still an important one to me today.

As well as new friends, we were making a good living—sixty, seventy thousand dollars a year between the two of us, which was terrific by anyone's standards.

Ross had what Deidra now calls a "big presence." Part of it was his actor's training, part of it was his personality, which was powerful no matter what kind of mood he was in. And he, like my parents, liked to take a drink or two. Or three. A little wine with dinner, an after-dinner drink or two, a couple of beers on a sunny Saturday by the pool.

Usually, when he had a slight buzz, he was a pussycat. I used to say to Deedee, "Let's just give Ross a drink and *then* ask him" for whatever it was we wanted, because he would cheerfully say yes to anything. But if a disagreement or an argument came up when he was drinking, it could get scary. He was the kind of guy who, for effect, would slam a door, hit a counter with his fist, or yell really loudly, with that great voice that had been trained to project to the last row of seats in the theater. And he was so intelligent that when he was mad, he could do major-league, below-the-belt put-downs. He knew how to level some-

Gramma Sally and Grampa Carl Anderson (my dad's parents) at their wedding.

My newlywed parents, Andy and Maxine, in November 1943.

Loni Kaye, two years old, after a very successful fishing day with Dad and Grampa Carl.

My first-grade picture. Note the fingernails!

At eleven I didn't look much like my *Scandahoovian* cousins.

Even in my early teens, I was already dreaming about being an actress.

At sixteen I was putting together a pretty good modeling portfolio.

My high school graduation picture. Wasn't there some sort of zoning law against hair with that kind of altitude?

Miss Roseville, Minnesota, in 1964. I'm not sure about those long white gloves, but what a great car!

The great Florida adventure during spring break of my freshman year in college. No wonder Dad clutched his head in his hands!

The Working Girl. In Minnesota these snowmobiles probably made more sense than Miss Roseville's convertible.

Mr. and Mrs. Bruce Hasselberg at their wedding reception. There was already trouble in paradise.

Mother and daughter. Deidra wisely decided not to wear her hat that day.

Four generations of women: My mom and her mother, Gramma Hazel, join me in doting on Deedee, Easter 1966.

Here's an improvement over that first mother-daughter picture. Deidra is still trying to figure out the camera thing.

Deedee and me in our "made by Loni Anderson" palazzo pants at Andrea's wedding in 1970.

Pre-Hollywood—but definitely post–Miss Roseville.

My sister, Andrea Sams, and me in St. Paul, 1974.

Mom and Dad caught in a customary pose, 1975.

Dad and his number-one fan, mid-seventies.

The Mike Douglas Show, 1979. Mike surprised me with one of the guests that day—I couldn't believe it when my mom walked out onstage!

Deidra and Ross help me celebrate my birthday in 1979.

Here are Loni and Arnold on the *Mansfield* set in 1980. What a nice smile he has—doesn't look much like the Terminator here, does he?

Handsome Gary Sandy, the wild man of *WKRP.* But his date looks quite happy, doesn't she?

Venice, 1987. Looks like a movie called *Two in a Gondola.*

Christmas in Florida, 1987. This is the dress I would wear at our wedding the following spring.

one with words. And I felt intimidated by that intelligence and the power behind it.

He never, ever threatened me—and I never felt threatened *by* him. I just couldn't match him in a fight. I still didn't drink, still didn't swear (Ross was the one who had goaded me that time into saying "Fuck it" in front of the mirror at home), and rarely raised my voice in an argument with him. But the combination of anger and liquor was sometimes overwhelming.

One time, he was swinging for the door with his fist, missed it, hit the doorjamb instead, and broke his hand. Stunned, I just started laughing. I couldn't believe he had done it. And very quietly Ross said, "Loni, please call the hospital. I've done some damage here— you have to pull yourself together and get me to a hospital." In minutes, it seemed, his knuckles had swollen, and the bones had completely disappeared.

So I got a grip and drove him to the hospital, sort of incredulous the whole way there, halfway between irritated and amused. Well, I thought, is the man ever going to hit a door again? Probably not.

One afternoon I was rushing around a shopping center, Fashion Square, doing errands, picking up some clothes for Deidra and me. Laden with shopping bags, I was leaving a store called Country Club Fashions and turned back to say good-bye and thanks to one of the clerks who had been particularly helpful. Next minute, *bang*, I was blindsided by someone coming into the store. Or maybe he was blindsided by me. At any rate, all my packages and bags hit the floor. As I knelt to retrieve my belongings, saying, "Oh, I'm sorry, that was my fault, my fault," he bent down to help, saying, "Oh, no, it was my fault, my fault." I glanced up and found myself looking into a familiar face.

But I didn't know who he was. That is, I didn't know his name. I had seen him on television, and in print, in an advertising campaign that had been running for the past few months, commercials that had turned him into something of a nameless but very recognizable sex symbol. I realized I was staring.

He grinned. "Hi," he said. "Have you had lunch?"

I knew in a split second that if I said no—and went to lunch, or anywhere else, with this man—it would be the end of my marriage. Something had taken my breath away, and I don't think it was the impact of our slamming together in the store doorway.

"Oh, yes, I have," I lied through my smiling teeth. "Uh, excuse me now, I have to be someplace." And I hurriedly turned to walk toward the mall exit to the parking lot.

A little way down the mall, something caught my eye in a store window, and I stopped to take a closer look. And then I saw his reflection in the glass. He had followed me and was standing right behind me. With that grin. He was, not to put too fine a point on it, absolutely gorgeous.

Struggling to avoid eye contact, I turned deliberately away, started walking, and didn't stop until I reached my car. When I was safely inside, I took a quick look around. Nobody. Phew! I felt like I'd just had a major wrestling match in the Garden of Eden and won. I had no way of knowing it was only round one.

In 1977, my dad sent me ten thousand dollars and sent the same to Andrea. "I'm not leaving you girls anything," he said. "Instead, I'm giving this money to you now, because I want to see what you do with it." With what Ross and I had saved, it was enough for a down payment on a house—with a pool, a yard and garden for flowers, a dining room, a fireplace. It was in North Hollywood, on a small cul-de-sac, an easy distance from Deidra's school. When we first saw it, I knew immediately that yes, this was my house. That recognition thing is funny—I had it with the house I live in now.

Andrea and Steve used their money to build a house, and although Dad saw pictures of both places, he never got to visit either of them. His cancer had progressed, and now, after four years of managing it—with experimental drug therapy and sheer force of will—he was failing. When Mom called and said, "Come home," Deidra and I left immediately for Minnesota.

He had battled cancer like everything else in his life—straightforwardly, no complaining, no wimping out. His largest concern was for Mom, who would, he suspected, be adrift without him. But he insisted that Andrea and I stay where we were and live our lives. He didn't want all of us to be fussing over him, and he used his sense of humor to try to keep us from worrying. One phone call he made to me in California characterized that attitude. "I'm pretty tired of this nonsense, and I keep praying for it just to be over," he said. "But you know, I'm still alive here. Someone somewhere is praying very hard for me. I strongly suspect it's you. If it is, please stop it. If it isn't, I'm just going to keep calling around until I find the culprit."

The cancer had gone into the bone marrow, and he was being kept alive with blood transfusions, since his body could no longer make blood on its own. But he'd had enough and decreed that there would be no more transfusions. He had quit smoking eight years before but always absentmindedly reached into his breast pocket (first on his shirt, now on his pajamas) looking for a pack. And now he said, "Hey, I'm dying. I'm going to have a smoke." But he could barely raise his arms, so the nurse would help him.

We all knew the clock was running. Ross came for a few days but had to leave to go back to work. Andrea and Steve, who were living in Sedona, Arizona, came, too, but Andrea, who was in the middle of a difficult pregnancy after a series of miscarriages, couldn't stay long. One afternoon the doctor said to us, "Perhaps we should all leave the room, and each of you can go back in, one at a time, so you and your father can say whatever has been left unsaid, whatever you think is important."

Andrea and I glanced at each other, and at the doctor, and said, "Like what? What kind of things are you talking about?"

He seemed a little uncomfortable. "Well, like telling each other 'I love you' and things like that."

Andrea and I looked at each other again and started smiling, and then laughing. I think the doctor was somewhat offended.

"You don't understand," I explained to him. "We come from the 'I'm-going-to-the-bathroom-I'll-be-right-back-I-love-you' family."

And it was true. We rarely left each other, whether it was to go to the grocery store or halfway across the country, that we didn't say "I love you." And it wasn't just words. We touched, we hugged, we were silly with birthdays and extravagant with Christmas. We told each other all our secrets. It was what we'd learned from Maxine and Andy, it was the legacy we wanted our own children to have. There was nothing left unsaid.

Deidra had brought her schoolwork to the hospital, and as she sat reading in a chair in a corner of his room, Dad gazed at her for minutes at a time with a heartbreaking half smile. At twelve she was blooming, her face beginning to make the transition from girl to woman, her long legs tucked awkwardly beneath her. When I was growing up, I thought my all-powerful father ran the world. But to Deedee, although Gramma ran the house, Grampa was the benevolent one. She had lived under his protection for most of her life; only forty-two when she was born, he had been young enough to be a playmate, old enough to be endlessly patient. "How big a moon do you want, little girl?" he would ask her.

One day in the hospital, Dad motioned me over to his bedside. He's going to tell me something tender now, I thought, or something critically important. This is a significant moment. He motioned me closer, closer, until finally I was right down to his face. "Yes, Dad?" I said sweetly, waiting to hear his wisdom.

"I wish for you with her," he whispered, "every single thing you put me through."

And we just cracked up, both of us laughing until the tears came. Dee looked at us as though we'd lost our minds.

I got a call from Los Angeles about a commercial audition I had done, Pam Cooking Spray, I think. I'd gotten the job, but if I wanted it, I had to return to California immediately. "I don't want to go now," I told my dad.

"All I've ever wanted for you," he said, "is success at what you've chosen. You've been sitting here for two weeks, looking at me. You sitting here and looking at me isn't going to make me live longer. Go back there and go to work; that's what I'm proud of."

Mother didn't want me to go, but I said, "I have to get Dee back into school, I have to go back to work. That's what he wants me to do. I need to make a living, and this is the way it works." And finally she agreed. I told Dad I'd come back as soon as I could.

Almost immediately after Deidra and I reached Los Angeles, Mom called to tell me he had slipped into a coma.

"Should I come back?" I asked.

"He's not conscious," she told me, "and he won't know you're here. There's no way of knowing how long this will last. I'm fine for now, do what you need to do."

The commercial was scheduled to take three days, and of course it took longer. Each night I would call Mom, and she'd tell me, "He's still alive, still in a coma, probably won't make it through the night." Each day more takes on the commercial shoot, more glitches. A whole week went by.

When I talked to the doctor, he said, "He's not on life support, he's not making blood anymore, he's in a coma. He's alive, but I don't know how."

When the commercial shoot was finally done, I got back on a plane with Dee, and when we landed, we went right to the hospital. Andrea, who had been put to bed by her own doctor at this point, wasn't allowed to come back up from Arizona.

I was stunned at how Dad looked; a two-hundred-pounder in his prime, he was now down to a skeletal eighty. His breathing was ratchety, and his beautiful blue eyes were wide open but unseeing. He was completely unrecognizable. I didn't want Deidra to see him like that.

"Can I be in here a few minutes by myself, and you stay out in the hall with Dee?" I asked Mom.

"Yes, but Loni, he won't hear you," she said, and the doctor agreed. I didn't care. And besides, who can ever know that for sure?

I sat down next to his bed. His hand was in a contorted position outside the bedcovers, and I put my hand over it and talked to him for about half an hour. "I'll take care of Mom," I promised. "You took care of all of us; now I can do that. I'll be you." The whole time I was talking, I tried to thread my fingers into his, but his hand was too rigid, so I had my little finger crooked into his little finger. I told him I'd learned all the lessons he had taught me, that I had money and security now, that I would take care of the family, do his work. So it was OK for him to go. And suddenly he moved his little finger, squeezing mine, and one tear rolled down his cheek.

I went out to the hallway and told them what had happened. "Maybe he's going to come out of the coma," I said, trying to give them hope at the same time I was losing it.

The doctor told us to go have dinner, go take our bags to the house. And of course when we got to the house, maybe twenty minutes later, the phone was ringing. He was gone. And I thought, he waited for me. I promised to come back, and he waited.

That first night Mom was almost giddy, because she was exhausted and knew that this responsibility was over. He wasn't suffering anymore, he wasn't in that pain we couldn't bear to watch and were powerless to prevent. The trips back and forth to the hospital, the suspense, were ended. For so long we all knew we had been headed to his death. And we had done it, it was accomplished. So there was an incredible relief, for him and for ourselves—at first. Forever, we found, takes a while to sink in.

I put Deidra to bed, and Mom and I sat in the living room, beginning to make the plans, the phone calls. Long after Deedee had fallen asleep, she suddenly wandered out and said, "Grampa was in my room." She wasn't scared, exactly, just unnerved and half asleep. I steered her back to bed, reassuring her that he loved her more than anybody, so a visit from him was nothing to be afraid of.

I'm still absolutely convinced that he was there. Andrea has always believed that she felt an overwhelming sense of Dad's presence in her room in Arizona that night, too.

The next day we went to choose the casket. Dad had always said, "It only costs a nickel more to go first class." Although he planned and saved, he never pinched pennies—it was always: Let's go, let's do, let's enjoy. So Mom and Deidra and I, we head out there like we're shopping for clothes, we've got that girl thing going. "Oh, that's a nice color." And "Oh, my, look at this one over here." I mean, what's the protocol for casket shopping, anyway?

Right in the middle of the room was a beautiful cherrywood casket with no hardware on it, just beautifully carved wood with a baby-blue interior, the same color as his eyes. This one, we agreed. Absolutely, this one. And of course, it was the most astonishingly expensive one on the floor. When we found that out, we all just hooted. The funeral director looked at us like, well, the grief has really gotten to these women.

It was to be a closed-casket service, so the morning of the funeral, before the service started, we three went in privately to say good-bye. Mom had given the funeral director some pictures of Dad, and so, thank God, he looked like himself. The months had been so ravaging for him, and for Mom. I was glad for the way he looked, for her sake. And I decided that when I got back to Los Angeles, I would immediately make a big collage of all the pictures of Dad that I had, so that the hospital scenes would fade from our minds.

As Mom and I walked out, Deidra slipped behind. When I noticed she wasn't with us, I went back into the room, where they were closing the casket. She was standing there watching very intently.

"Honey, what are you doing?" I asked.

"I had to make sure everything was OK," she said. "I wanted to make sure they didn't hurt him when they closed it."

I had originally planned to stay with my mother for two weeks, easing her through the first days, putting Dad's things away. Two days later we were in the kitchen fixing dinner. My mother's best friend, Rosemary, was there. Deidra was chatting on about some school friend and mentioned in the middle of her anecdote that this friend was Jewish. My mother went completely ballistic! She shouted that Jewish people didn't believe in Jesus and if Deedee liked them, then she didn't really love her grandfather. For a moment I was so stunned that I couldn't even speak.

Dee started crying. "Gramma, are you saying that if I have Jewish friends, I'm doing something bad to Grampa?"

"Deidra, if you have Jewish friends, you're damning your

grandfather to hell!'' shouted my mother. Where on earth had this come from?

"But, Gramma,'' Deedee cried, "practically all my friends are Jewish.''

"Then,'' my mother said, looking wild-eyed, "I guess you just can't *have* any friends.''

That was it for me. I had seen Mom growing tired and more aware that Dad was gone for good, that her dream of their well-ordered old age together wasn't going to happen. I knew she was grieving wildly for him—he had been the love of her life; no one knew that better than I. But now she was taking that grief, and the anger that came with it, and turning it on my child, who was grieving just as much.

"Mom,'' I said, "I think it's time for us to go back to California.'' She wouldn't be alone, she had Rosemary with her. Deidra needed to get away from here, to go back to school and back to a life that didn't have illness and mourning in it. And I needed to get back to Ross and to work.

"But you said you were going to stay two weeks. How can you leave me now?'' cried my mother. "I need you here.''

I shook my head. "No, I can't let you do what you're doing. It's best if we go right now.''

After his funeral, one of my father's friends gave me a note that Dad had written and asked his friend to pass on to me after his death. "I know you're going to make it big one day,'' said the note. "I know you'll be famous. Just know when it happens for you that I always knew it would.'' Oh, Dad, I thought, you were so good at fixing things. Why can't you be here to fix Mom?

She stayed angry with me for a long time. We couldn't even speak on the phone for weeks. Within the year she moved down to Sedona, to be near Andrea and Steve, and started on what we began to call her Merry Widow adventures. Unable to find peace, she was completely bereft without my father and enraged at his death, which had come so early. And with her anger came a bizarre reprise of her girlish behavior—drinking, out all hours, dating an array of increasingly younger men.

"I don't mind when they're my age," I said to her once, only half joking, "but when you start bringing in guys Deidra's age, Mom, I'm going to have to put my foot down."

In the years to come, Andrea and I had many anguished phone calls. "I can't get along with her," my sister said. "And I can't protect her. She's become somebody else. It's like when we lost Dad, we lost Mom, too."

After one visit, Deidra asked me, "Will Gramma ever be normal again, Mom?" I had no idea what to tell her.

I began lightening my hair when I started getting regular commercial work. The photographers would complain that it was so dark and dense, it absorbed all the light and photographed like mud. Over a period of two years, I went auburn, then reddish, then light brown, then strawberry blonde. The lighter it got, the more work I got. OK, I thought, this is working nicely. And Ross had no complaints; he liked it.

Right after that, I was cast as a bimbo on an episode of *The Love Boat*. I had gotten pretty good at bimbo roles—I adjusted my voice and put on that wide-eyed-but-dim look, and bingo! There she was, Dotty Ditz. On this particular episode, Steve Allen and Polly Bergen played a married couple who were having trouble. So I was his fling, and then he went back to his wife, and they lived happily ever after, exit the bimbo.

There was a piano on the set, and when we weren't shooting, Steve would sit down and noodle, and everyone would gather around and listen or break into a sing-along. He is an amazingly talented improvisational musician and composer, and there wasn't much he couldn't play—or wouldn't play, at our request. We were all starstruck. I was so happy to be there, to be working, to be having fun and getting paid for it. Look at me, I thought. I'm singing and dancing, and Steve Allen is playing the piano.

One afternoon I was in the middle of one of my scenes. The writers had really written this girl to perfection, the scene was very funny, and I was really cooking with it. I could see the crew off to the side; some were having to cover their mouths to keep from laughing out loud and screwing up the filming. I was taking the laugh lines and running with them, quite proud of the fact that I was making everybody crack up, crew included. I was pretty full of myself. I *owned* the whole bimbo thing; I had known since *Born Yesterday* that this character was mine.

When the scene was over and we were taking a break, Steve came up to me and said, "Loni, may I tell you something?" He had been supportive and nice—and believe me, stars on those shows weren't always.

And I, fresh from having my ego massaged, said, "Of course, Steve, what?"

He had a very serious look on his face. "You are so funny, and you do that so well," he said. "And you *must stop*. Because if you don't, you'll never do anything else. And no one will ever see what else you can do."

I think it was the best professional advice anybody ever gave me. I started to evaluate the parts a little more, trying to pay attention to where each one might lead me. I would find out who the director was, who the writer was, what they had done before. Maybe Ross is right, I thought, maybe I should start taking my career more seriously.

ABC was about to begin a TV movie called *Three on a Date,* to be directed by Bill Bixby. It was a comedy about couples who win dates to Hawaii; so far they'd cast June Allyson, Ray Bolger, Carol Lawrence, Gary Crosby, Meredith MacRae, Patrick Wayne, Rick Nelson, Didi Conn, and John Byner. They needed someone to play the *Playboy* centerfold and hadn't found a name who was willing to do it. So they had to open up the audition door a little wider—Loni's Luck. I was called in to read a week before shooting was scheduled to begin.

When I walked in, Bill Bixby, Danny Thomas, and Ron Jacobs were there. I didn't exactly get a warm welcome; I was a complete unknown to them. But then, after a long minute, Bill Bixby leaned forward and said slowly, "If you can talk, you've got the part." She was, of course, the proverbial ditz/bimbo—who happily turns out in the end not to be such a ditz after all. I read, and they said, "You're hired."

We got into a car immediately and drove off to the network

to meet the brass. I was thinking, well, even if they veto me, this will have been worth it, because I'm actually going to meet the big guys in suits. One more rung up the ladder! I kept the part. I didn't know until I actually saw the movie on television that in the credits we were all listed in alphabetical order, and there I was, right behind June Allyson.

It was a five-week shoot over the Christmas holidays, and John Byner, who played my date, made me laugh so hard with his impressions that I'd go home with stomachaches almost every night. I would say, "OK, I'm getting sad now, because we're working and I'm not feeling Christmassy here. Would you please do Perry Como?" And Byner would sing a Christmas carol à la Como. Then Johnny Mathis, then Frank Sinatra.

And then he'd do impressions of the cast—he did a wicked June Allyson, much to her great glee. And when Patrick Wayne said, "Do my dad . . . as Donald Duck," John did Wayne as Duck. Or maybe it was Duck as Duke. A sacrilege probably, but oh, so funny. Once, John did an entire scene and all the characters—from the film *Rio Bravo,* which had starred John Wayne, Dean Martin, Walter Brennan, and a very young Ricky Nelson. It was all Bill Bixby could do each day to get us to settle down and go back to work.

June Allyson told me the funniest stories of the old studio days, of Lana Turner and Dick Powell. And Ray Bolger would dance around between scenes, with more energy than all the rest of us had. I would think, I'm really in Hollywood, *my* Hollywood. It was the Hollywood I'd fallen in love with as a kid. Everybody knew this was my first big break, and they were so kind and helpful and patient.

I would get up in the morning and leave long before Deidra woke up for school and get home long after she was in bed. She began to think I was out of town or something. Ross finally brought her to the set one day, and they met everyone, and Ross and I were grinning at each other like fools. This is it, we were both thinking. We're working, in Hollywood.

When I was in junior high school, Ricky Nelson had released a song called "You're My One and Only Love." I bought my first record player just so I could play that record. Over and over and over again. I have it on the jukebox downstairs in my family room right now. And there he was on this set, my teen idol, and I told him the story about that record. He was a sweet, kind man, and still teen-idol handsome. One day, while we were waiting in the lunch line, Rick was standing behind me and started singing the words to "My One and Only Love" in my ear. Merry Christmas to me!

When Rick was killed in a plane crash on New Year's Eve of 1985, I was so stricken, so sad. Because he was too young and too talented. And because the memory of that project is so dear to me. Beginnings, especially good ones, stay in your mind, and the people you share them with hold a kind of magical meaning in your life. After all, you never have another first.

Danny Thomas was another part of that magic. He would come in every day and look at the dailies, smoking that cigar. He would point to me with it, saying, "You, you, you. I discovered you." There are few people as special in this business as Danny Thomas was, or Bill Bixby.

Bix became a good friend to me on that shoot and stayed one for years afterward. He asked me to guest star on *The Incredible Hulk*. I played a killer (who karate'd people to death), and Jeremy Brett, who these days is the brilliant and inscrutable Sherlock Holmes on PBS, played my lover and evil cohort. Everybody thought the Hulk was killing those folks, and it was bad me. What fun. When I called my grandmother and told her that I was going to be a killer, she said, "I can't tell anyone that, Loni, especially my bridge club. What on earth would they think?"

When I was doing *Nurses* in 1993 and Bix was directing *Blossom*, I would see him regularly and we would laugh at our *Three on a Date* memories. And we commiserated—my marriage to Burt had collapsed, and Bix was valiantly fighting prostate cancer, like my dad. Although he had recently remarried, his first wife, actress Brenda Benet, had committed suicide years before, after the death of their son. Mother and son had visited on the *Three on a Date* set, and losing them both had been a terrible tragedy to him. The people Bix worked with, and the work he did with them, meant so much and gave him courage. I think he stayed on *Blossom* until the week before he died. If there are role models in Hollywood—real ones—Bill Bixby was a shining example.

Chapter 7

Before I became totally blonde, I tested for *Three's Company,*
with John Ritter. Joanna Kerns also tested, and so did Suzanne
Somers, who, as we know, got the part. But they liked me and
called me back later to play the girl John couldn't get over. She
was a flight attendant (although we were still calling them stew-
ardesses then). She would dump him, he'd come back, she'd
dump him again, he'd come back. She was not a nice person,
and I quite enjoyed playing her.

In February of 1978 I got a call to go in to MTM and read for
the series that ultimately became *WKRP in Cincinnati.* I'd had
mixed luck with MTM comedies—I got small guest parts on *The
Bob Newhart Show* and *Phyllis* but lost a part on Betty White's
show at the last minute.

Ross had received a script for the new series—and actually got
three callbacks for the lead, Andy Travis, which eventually went
to Gary Sandy. When my agent, Len, called me, I said, "My
husband's got the script; I've already read it. It's window dressing.
She's just another bimbo, and I won't play that anymore."

Len couldn't believe what he was hearing. "You can't refuse
to go in for an MTM call!"

But I stood my ground. "I don't want to play that kind of part
anymore. I'm playing not-so-nice girls now, smart girls, devious

girls, and I'm getting some attention here. I'm not going back to bimbohood!"

Three weeks passed. And then Len called and said, "Hugh Wilson, who is the creator and head writer of this show, and Grant Tinker himself—the MTM boss, Loni, for heaven's sake—say if you're working, fine, but then could you please come in to see them on your Saturday off?"

They were making accommodations for me. "Loni," pleaded my agent. "Please. You can't not go when the head of the production company and the man who created this project want to see you. Worst case scenario, you don't get the part—but they see you, and maybe you get something else later. Show a little respect!"

So I went in on Saturday, with a chip on my shoulder, all ready to climb right up on the no-bimbo soapbox. I started running my mouth right away: This is awful, this is offensive, why do we have to have this stereotype, playing someone like this goes against my feelings about power for women, blah, blah, blah. I did the whole speech and then waited for them to say, "Thank you, don't let the door hit your butt on the way out."

Instead, Grant Tinker quietly said, "Well, OK then, how would *you* do it?"

Nothing like getting your bluff called. "Well-l-l-l," I started, "I think she should look like Lana Turner, and be really, really smart."

And then he said, "Fine, why don't you read the script like that."

"But she's not written like that," I protested. I was beginning to edge up on the maternity-ward whine.

"OK," said Grant, "just ad-lib where you can and show us the attitude, then."

Well, I knew I was going to blow it. I went ahead and did the best I could, but it clanked like a tire iron, because it was dumb blonde stuff, and I couldn't find a way into it. I couldn't find Jennifer Marlowe.

When I was finished, nobody said anything. Well, actually, they did, the standard "Thank you" and "See ya" that every actor recognizes at the end of a dead audition. I'm doomed, I thought. I've talked back, criticized the way something's written, bombed the audition, and blown my chances for all time with MTM. And they were a very large game in town.

I went home and cried to Ross, "I've done such a stupid thing!" And then I called my agent and apologized. "I've blown it, it's over," I wept. If MTM kept a blacklist, I was probably on it now.

On Monday morning they called and offered me the job.

When I went back in and talked to Hugh, he said, "I promise, I'm going to remake her the way you want. The only problem is, it's too late to rewrite for the pilot, so you'll have to play her as written. Just this one time."

Jay Sandrich directed the pilot, and it was an adventure. All eight of us were unknowns—there was no Mary Tyler Moore as our centerpiece, no Bob Newhart. There was only us. The night we taped the pilot, with a live audience out front, we stood backstage holding hands, and Tim Reid—Venus Flytrap—said, just before we went out, "Let's all stop a second, and always remember the way we feel right now. Because there won't be another one like this one."

Afterward Sandrich said to Hugh, "You better fire that woman, she's going to be trouble. She won't play it as written. And fire Frank Bonner, too." Frank, who played Herb Tarlek, was always brilliant in performance. But he completely fumphered around in rehearsal, hemming and hawing, looking for ways to make his character work. He was a genius, and that's just the way he got there.

But Hugh said, "These are the eight people I chose, this is my ensemble. And we'll make it work."

Howard Hesseman—Dr. Johnny Fever—was only supposed to be a guest star, just for the pilot, but he was such a hit, he was on the team, too. CBS picked us up immediately for thirteen episodes, and we were the talk of the network. People who didn't watch TV—or who *said* they didn't watch—watched *WKRP*. By the second episode, Jennifer Marlowe was acerbic, smart, aware. And Jay Sandrich came back afterward and said, "I'm sorry, I was wrong."

That first season, when everyone was talking about us, the series was moved all over the place on the programming schedule. Each time, the fans found us anyway. But for some reason some of the executives at CBS hated us beyond belief, hated Hugh, hated the show, and went to great lengths to kill it. After the first eight weeks we were put on hiatus, but we came back in January of 1979, happily ensconced between *M*A*S*H* and *Lou Grant*.

Hugh Wilson was wonderful to work with and for. We sat around for hours and talked, and some of my own stories began showing up as episodes. The time I did the brunette vs. blonde hair experiment in the Chicago bar, for instance. The fact that I didn't have any casting couch stories. "That's because while your body says yes, yes," Hugh laughed, "there's something about your attitude that says no, no." He even wrote an episode so that we could have Pat O'Brien as a guest star, the mysterious older man who names Jennifer as the executrix of his will.

Our comfortable place on the schedule didn't last—the network moved us twenty-one times in four years. Ultimately, in the spring of 1982, we were canceled the same week we were number one in the ratings.

In 1990 they revived *WKRP*, running it for three more years with the three guys—Gordon Jump (Arthur Carlson, the station manager), Frank Bonner, and Richard Sanders (Les Nessman, the news- and weatherman). Howard and I both made guest appearances. But they didn't have Hugh Wilson anymore. When they asked if I would come back full-time, I said no, I couldn't do that—not without all eight of us, and not without Hugh.

I never had, and never expected, star billing on *WKRP*. It was an ensemble show from beginning to end, and the people I worked with every day became a second family to me. But Jennifer Marlowe was talked about, and increasingly, I was singled out.

I'm not sure that anyone is ever prepared for fame. No matter how balanced or "centered" you are, no matter how rich your fantasy life is—winning the lottery, winning the Pulitzer Prize, winning an Oscar—what happens to your real life when fame hits is a bone-rattling jolt. And within two episodes of *WKRP*'s first airing, everything changed. When I received a congratulatory letter from Steve Allen—and another one from Jack Lemmon!—I knew that something special had happened to me. I still thought of myself as the ultimate fan. And now I had fans of my own, including these two creative geniuses.

Going to the market, picking up the dry cleaning, I would notice that people were staring at me. The first couple of times it happened, I thought it was wonderful—it meant they were watching the show, the series was a hit. And I liked my fans. It was fun seeing them, meeting them, talking to them. It seemed like we were all on a great adventure together.

But I quickly discovered that the choice of when I was the private Loni and when I was the public one was no longer mine to make. Bad mood, head cold, an intense conversation with my husband or daughter, a trip to the ladies' room; it didn't matter. It reminds me of that Irish saying "May all your dreams come true"—which the Irish say is meant as a curse, not a blessing. The flip side, of course, is that when they're *not* noticing you— not passing a piece of paper under a bathroom stall for you to sign, not interrupting you when the fork is halfway to your mouth—it means the notoriety is gone.

I think I was lucky that fame came after some other important things had happened in my life. I had been married, divorced, and married again, this time to a colleague and friend. I had a verging-on-adolescence daughter, whose problems brought me back to earth on a daily basis. I had lost my dad and had constant worries about my mom. And I knew that a TV series wasn't real life, any more than a play was. That doesn't mean I wasn't totally thrilled with the whole thing. And, on occasion, frightened out of my wits.

At one event, a *WKRP* publicity tour in the Midwest, people surrounded the car Gary Sandy and I were in, completely blocking the windows and rocking the car from side to side. And there was an evening at the Hollywood Bowl, a benefit on behalf of the actors' strike. When you hear the expression "mob scene" . . . well, I was mobbed. There were a lot of celebrities there, many more famous and fabled than I had ever thought of being, and I was a little distracted, meeting them, shaking hands with my idols. When it was over, all I wanted to do was walk to my car. Suddenly I was in the middle of a mass of people, hundreds, it seemed, coming at me, grabbing, their voices rising. I was immediately surrounded by six uniformed security guards. As they whisked me away, my feet never even touched the ground.

As the fan mail accumulated and the public appearances accelerated, it was clear I needed help. In 1980 Jeanne Jensen's daughter Linda, whom I'd met some years earlier, became my personal manager and closest confidante. In 1981 Jeanne started helping with the mail and fan club correspondence. Linda started traveling with me as well, and going to events when Ross either couldn't or wouldn't, because once the hype really got rolling, I became increasingly nervous about going places alone.

One day I was sitting in my dressing room, and there was a knock on the door. Linda was there—we had been going over my schedule—and she answered the door. I was behind her, sitting on the sofa, and her five-foot ten-inch frame pretty much filled the doorway. As I heard her talking to whoever was standing outside, her body stance told me something was wrong. I had an intuition not to move, not to make a sound.

"No," she said firmly, "Miss Anderson isn't here. No, I'm sorry, but you can't come in here and wait for her." Evidently that wasn't OK with the person she was talking to, because her voice got stronger, and she moved backward a step. "No, you absolutely cannot come in!" she said, and then she slammed the door. "We have to call the stage," she whispered to me. "There's a guy out there in black leather and chains. He's so creepy looking, you won't believe it. He wants you. He says if he can't have you, then he wants to live in your dressing room."

I don't know how the man got past security. Our soundstage

was right across from the *Hill Street Blues* soundstage—maybe somebody had decided this guy was one of the *Hill*'s perps or something.

After we called for help, the guys from the cast and crew headed down to my dressing room. And there he was, my fan. When they asked him to leave, he started wielding a knife. The security guards finally came on the scene and hustled him out. They did not, for reasons I still don't understand, have him arrested—they just threw him off the lot. Put him outside the gate. Where he waited for me.

Linda and I had gone off the lot during lunch break. When we came back, as we approached the MTM gate, our guy came hurtling out of the bushes, threw himself on the car, and hung on, spread-eagled on the hood with his face plastered against the windshield and his eyes locked onto mine. Linda and I both gasped.

"My God," I said to her, "what should I do?"

"*Gun it!*" she shouted. "And if he falls off, run over him!"

When I pushed the accelerator to the floor, he just flew off the car. I wrenched the wheel around and tore into the MTM lot, laying a strip of rubber behind me, not even slowing down long enough to see if I'd hurt him. At that point I wouldn't have cared if I had killed him.

I called Hugh Wilson and told him how terrified I had been, that something had to be done about security. How, I asked him, had that guy gotten as close as he did? What would have happened if Linda hadn't been there with me and I had answered my dressing room door?

A day or two later, I suddenly realized I was being followed. A car was behind me on the way to work, it was there behind me all the way home. I started taking circuitous routes to and from the studio. I wouldn't stop for anything, no marketing, no getting gasoline; I never got out of the car en route. In public I stayed glued to Ross's side, or Linda's. I couldn't sleep, couldn't concentrate on work, and finally I said to Hugh and everyone on the set, "I'm being followed everywhere, I'm terrified, and I don't know what to do!"

At which point Hugh apologized. It seems that after the hood-riding incident, he had gone to Grant Tinker and told him; I was now being followed by studio security. They didn't tell me because they didn't want me to be even more nervous than I already was. And they didn't want me to know that *they* were nervous.

After the first season, things quieted down somewhat. I got quite a bit of mail (much of it from prisons), and some of those folks have remained steady correspondents. Today Jeanne and Linda still monitor the mail pretty closely, and anything strange or disturbing gets passed along to Mickey Freeman, my longtime publicist, and to security people. But over the years the nutcases have been few and far between—almost without exception, the people who write, especially since my separation from Burt, have been overwhelmingly kind.

The second time I was on *The Merv Griffin Show,* in 1978, was the first time I ever met Burt Reynolds. We actually met on the air—he was already onstage, and I came over late from rehearsal. He was very sweet, and during the commercial break he asked how my husband was handling all the *WKRP* hoopla. He said he knew how hard that could be on a marriage, when both partners are actors and the woman suddenly becomes more successful—he had gone through it himself when he and Judy Carne were married.

Right after that, Deedee and Ross and I were at the Smoke house restaurant in Hollywood, and from where we were sitting, we could see the television in the bar. "Oh, look," I said, "Merv's on. It's the one we just taped." Not a minute later, I looked through the open fireplace (which also had a waterfall—only in Hollywood) and saw Burt having dinner in the adjacent dining room. We smiled and waved at each other, and we both pointed to the TV.

A few months later, I was to be a presenter at the People's Choice awards. Ross and I were sitting at a table with Jerry Reed, and we were laughing away and having a lot of fun. After I had presented my award, I passed Burt's table—he was with Sally Field—and he stopped me. "You're such a lady, lady," he said, taking my hand, and then he asked if my husband was there with me. When I said yes, he said, "I'd like very much to meet him."

I told Ross, who was a huge Burt Reynolds fan, and after the show was over, we happily walked over to Burt's table. He introduced us to Sally (who was pretty reserved), and then he said, "You must be Ross. I've heard so much about you." Now, this was months after we had been on Merv's show together, and yet he remembered Ross's name. He was completely charming, and we both went away thinking, wow, what a nice guy.

From the time Ross and Deidra and I first came to Los Angeles, in 1975, there was a particular neighborhood we often drove around in, promising that if we made it, "we're going to buy a house here—because it has Minnesota streets." There were rosebushes in the yards, and shutters on the windows, and ivy climbing up trellises. Many houses in Hollywood are built on hills and look like they're in danger of tumbling headlong into a canyon at any minute. And, in fact, given a rainy season and an earthquake or two, many of them do exactly that. But the houses in our fantasy neighborhood looked permanent. And four years after we arrived in L.A., we did buy a house there, in Sherman Oaks, on Alomar. It had French doors, several fireplaces, peg-and-groove hardwood floors, and a beautiful guesthouse and swimming pool out back. It was The House That *WKRP* Bought. And in a way, *WKRP* bought our old house, too—we sold it to Gary Sandy.

Around this time, Ross was beginning not to get calls for auditions. This was a man who had started with a bang in the big series dramas. They had all been good parts, with good reviews. But somehow they didn't translate into the success he wanted. One problem was that he looked disconcertingly like someone else who was working quite a bit, Stephen Collins (my old hubby from the Mop & Glo commercials). In fact, Ross was cast as the lead in what was going to be the new *Star Trek* spin-off series. Which then didn't spin off at all (*The Next Generation* came nearly a decade later) and was dropped. And in 1979, when they did *Star Trek—The Motion Picture,* Stephen

Collins got the role that Ross was to have had in the TV series. So the disappointment began. And little by little, the drinking began to sneak up on him.

Hollywood success was supposed to happen for Ross. We both thought so. And if it had, I think I could have made my peace with that. Women do so all the time (whether they're happy about it, of course, is the stuff of bigger books than this one). But when it didn't happen for him—and when what *did* happen, to me, became so huge—Ross began to think that the town had turned on him. Everywhere we went he was Mr. Loni Anderson. He started hating Los Angeles. And it began to feel like he didn't like me much, either.

Of the three of us, Deidra reacted the least (or the most quietly, maybe) to my success. As tenacious in her way as I am in mine, she was determined to have her own life in spite of the circus that was going on around her. When I asked her once about going to private school, she said no, thank you, she preferred to stay right where she was. "Your life might have changed, Mom," she said. "But mine hasn't." Always her own woman, Deedee ultimately became president of the class both junior and senior year, and the first female captain of the cross-country team in the history of her high school.

There were some minor adjustments, however. She had to turn a blind eye to the two swimsuit posters I'd done (which a lot of the guys in her school had bought), and she asked that I please not come to her cross-country meets and distract everyone.

In almost every relationship I had ever had, the men eventually grew jealous of Deidra. She and my career came first and second—or sometimes, to be honest, second and first—but the man in my life always came third, even when that man was Ross. The things the three of us had done as a family, like bicycling or playing miniature golf or jogging or just plain hanging out together, were slowly going by the wayside; if I got it together to carve out time at the end of the day for anyone, it was for Deedee. She and Ross loved each other; now, through no fault of their own, they had become competitors.

For Super Bowl XIV, in 1980, I was invited to be a guest in the announcers' booth during the halftime show, to visit with Pat Summerall and Tom Brookshier. So there we were, Deedee, Ross, and I, in great seats just a few rows down from the press box on a perfectly beautiful sunny day in Pasadena.

Contrary (I'm sure) to the assumptions that CBS, Summerall, and Brookshier might have made about me and football, I was a fan and had been since I was little. There was only one television in my parents' house, and if you wanted to watch it on a weekend, you watched football. We even went to Minnesota Vikings games before the stadium was under a dome; to fend off the cold, we wore those bulky navy blue snowmobile suits that made you feel like a clumsy astronaut.

I had been told that the guys in the booth would give me the high sign when it was time to head up there; all I had to do was turn around and check a couple of times toward the middle of the second quarter, and I would be able to see them wave when they wanted me.

The first time I turned around, my eyes immediately landed on the group of guys sitting in the row directly under the press box. There, in the middle, was gorgeous Mr. X from Fashion Square. Uh, oh, round two.

When last we'd met (or not met, actually), I was an unknown brunette; now I was a platinum blonde with a hit series and way too much press coverage. Although he was still an unknown himself at that point, he was all over the place in television commercials and magazine ads. Every time I caught a glimpse of his picture, I had an instant recall of our crash meeting at the mall and how completely unnerved I had been by that encounter. Now here I was, doing it again. Staring at him. He smiled. And I smiled back.

I turned around to try to focus on the game. Ross and Deidra were unhappy: The Pittsburgh Steelers appeared to be hammering the Rams. I'd better pay attention, I thought, or I *will* be a ditz up in the booth.

I had to turn around a couple more times, and when I did, I tried to make my eyes go only up to the booth and no place else.

But I couldn't do it. Each time I looked at him, he was looking back. And grinning. Once, he even waved.

After I did my stint in the booth and came back and sat down—to see Los Angeles get soundly trounced, 31–19—I didn't turn around again at all. But I could feel his gaze on my back. It felt like a hand.

I met Dinah Shore during the first year of *WKRP*. Our soundstage was adjacent to the one where her talk show was taped, and there was a door between the soundstages; we didn't even have to go outside to go between them. At first I did her show as publicity for the series; soon we were having such a good time that I couldn't wait to go back. And eventually we started visiting back and forth. If she had a guest who wasn't able to be there at the last minute, she would run over and ask me to come on.

Dinah was a lovely woman with a wry sense of humor and a great, roaring laugh. There was an air of adventure and fun around her, a real light in her eyes. If there was a difference between Dinah on camera and Dinah off, it was that her sense of humor was a little looser. Not bawdy exactly, but knowing, wise, smart. She was, to use a cliché that in her case absolutely rings true, a real woman. A great broad. And generous to a beginner, which I still was.

In our off-camera chats, we had some pretty intimate girl talks. This was after she and Burt Reynolds were no longer involved, so I never heard any Burt stuff. He was with Sally Field at the time, and Dinah, I always believed, had her eye on Gary Sandy. And besides, she was such a lady—and Burt was always so dear to her heart—that I don't think she ever would have talked about their time together, or about their friendship afterward.

As long as I knew her, she was always open and fun with me. Before I dated Burt, she would always come up and give me a big hug. After Burt and I were together, she would take my hand instead. I would start to hug her, and she'd step back and put her hand out, making a little distance between us.

Burt was understandably reluctant to talk very much about Dinah. He did say that when their relationship ended, he still loved her, but she told him to leave, that it would be better for him. For one thing, she knew he wanted children, and she was past that. And she had become increasingly sensitive to the twenty-year age difference.

Years later I heard other versions of the split, from other people. But whatever the truth might have been, I believed him when he told me that if Dinah hadn't pushed him, he never would have left her. I think that when she died, Burt lost a truly great friend.

Chapter 8

Along with the rest of the *WKRP* crew, I started doing a lot of talk and game show appearances. We did *All-Star Family Feud* and donated our winnings to Greenpeace, and we appeared on *Dinah!* together and on *The Mike Douglas Show*. I cohosted *Candid Camera* and one of those *Guinness Book of World Records* specials. I was on Dinah's show at least a dozen times, on Merv's nearly as often, and once even cohosted Mike Douglas's show with my mom. I started making regular appearances on Bob Hope's specials. The goofiest thing I did, though, was walk on crushed glass for a *Circus of the Stars*. Everybody kept talking about how I did it painlessly due to the mysterious power of the mind. Hooey, I thought—I was raised Lutheran!

On Memorial Day weekend of 1979, I was invited to the Indianapolis 500, along with Howard Hesseman. We were to attend the charity ball the night before and ride in the pace car the day of the race. When we got off the plane and went to retrieve our luggage, I was horrified to find that mine had gone to Dayton. For a few hours it was touch and go whether my clothes would make it back to Indianapolis in time for the festivities. But Loni's Luck prevailed, and my suitcase, carrying my long red jersey sheath, arrived at my hotel room just in time.

That night, one of the guests at the charity ball was former

President Gerald Ford. I was honored when he asked me to dance, and quite surprised (considering the frequent thumps he took from Chevy Chase on *Saturday Night Live*) to find that he was a graceful dancer and a charming partner. So when our waltz was over and the band switched into a lindy, I asked, "Do you lindy?"

He got a funny look on his face. "I think so," he said. "Maybe if you show me the steps."

So I took him through the lindy, and he got it pretty quickly. After that, the band went into the Charleston.

"What do you think?" I said, grinning up at the President. "Do you Charleston?"

"I do now," he said, laughing, and off we went across the floor.

Just as the number ended, a Secret Service agent came up to us, looking a little sheepish. "Excuse me, sir," he said to the President, nodding to me as well. "But I think it might be best to sit the next one out. The press is here, and, well . . . we wouldn't want this to become tabloid fodder."

The President made a graceful apology, and we went our separate ways for the rest of the evening. A few months later, when I was scheduled to cohost *The Mike Douglas Show,* Mike asked who I'd like to have on as a guest, and I told him I'd like to invite the President's wife, former First Lady Betty Ford. I was thrilled when she accepted, because she had always been someone whose candor and courage I admired.

Once we were both settled in and the show began taping, I said, "Oh, Mrs. Ford, I was privileged to meet your husband the weekend of the Indy 500 race. In fact, we danced at the ball the night before—and you know, I don't know what all those jokes have been about. He's really quite a good dancer."

She looked startled. "A good dancer? My husband?" she asked. "Loni, are you sure you were dancing with the Gerry Ford who is *my* husband?"

After *WKRP*'s second season, during the 1980 hiatus, I played the title role in a TV movie, *The Jayne Mansfield Story,* with a

pre–*Conan the Barbarian* Arnold Schwarzenegger as Jayne's husband, Mickey Hargitay. The shoot was mostly a good time—
Ross's sister, Robin, was my wardrobe person, and Deidra made
an appearance as Jayne's teenage daughter, Jayne Marie. Working
with Arnold was fun, too. He was big and sweet and incredibly
hardworking. But there was much about the movie that made
me take a good, long look at myself.

The movie was based on Martha Saxton's book *Jayne Mansfield
and the American Fifties.* Jayne's story resembled my own in a
couple of ways—we both made it after becoming bottle blondes,
we both had babies early, in teen marriages that didn't end well.
And yes, there were some similarities in cleavage (although she
was rather more spectacularly endowed than I). But the resem-
blance stopped there. I think she was sad much of her life, even
when fame came, and she lost control of her career very early.
Learning as much about her as I did provided a good object lesson
for me.

It also gave me a brutal chemistry lesson. After emptying
endless bottles of evil-smelling stuff on my hair during the
shoot to keep it true to Jayne's white-blonde platinum, I was
horrified to find it breaking off in my hairbrush or falling in
pitiful little drifts to the floor. I had committed hairicide!
Within a few weeks I looked like a miserable army recruit,
with an uneven crew cut where my crowning glory used to
be. For the next *WKRP* season, I wore a hat during rehearsals
and a blonde wig on tape days.

Ross had begun going back to Minneapolis to do plays. Although he was still getting commercials, they couldn't fulfill his
need to really work in the art that he loved. He went back and
forth so often that finally I bought a house there for him, for all
three of us. I didn't want him staying in a motel room all the
time, and I liked the idea of us having our own place in Minnesota.

I wanted him to feel respected and important and to know
that what made him happy was important to me. So I had asked
him to manage the money a year or so before, and I bought our
Minnesota house to show support for his career. But having a

place there only served to keep him away more often, for longer periods of time.

And when he was around, his drinking was a major flash point. A big night for me was a glass or two of white wine or champagne. I never did like the taste of hard liquor, and red wine gave me an instantaneous allergic reaction. Even coffees and colas had never tasted good to me. When Arnold and I did a commercial for Diet 7 Up, it was because that, and water, was what I really drank. And now, around my house, the smell of liquor—and the morning-after coffee—increasingly meant bad news.

Ross wasn't taking care of himself. He had always been so handsome, and now he had . . . dimmed or something. The arguments between us became louder. He left pans burning on the stove, which made me nervous and downright scared Deedee. He said he was going out on interviews and auditions, but he would really go to a bar. At *WKRP* parties I'd glance over, and there would be Ross, holding court, being funny and charming as ever, the life of the party. And then minutes later, the fun would be over—he had passed out. The guys from the show would have to carry him to the car for me.

I was having a triumph, but I couldn't share it, because if I got excited, my husband became even more depressed. I didn't like what was happening to us and didn't want this marriage to end. More than once I asked him to get help, for our sake and for his own. Although the contemporary "recovery movement" hadn't hit Hollywood yet, I knew of people who had been helped by Alcoholics Anonymous, some of them quite famous. And in Minnesota, the Hazelden Center, in Minneapolis, was quite well-respected.

"We could do it together," I said. "I'd even go to Al-Anon."

But Ross was adamant. No AA, he said, because there was no problem.

I kept hoping he would get a job, find pride in his work again—find pride in me again, and in the life we had built together. I had loved and respected him as I had no man except my father, so I kept on looking for the Ross I knew—my confidant, my lover, my partner, the man I had trusted to be my daughter's stepfather. But I couldn't find him anywhere.

During the summer a friend of his, an actress he'd known in school and had been in a play with in Minneapolis, came out to California and stayed at the house with us. She wanted to give L.A. a try, she said, to see what her professional chances were there. We had always had a lot of company, but I was immediately uncomfortable with this one. There was something indefinably strange about her. Just *off*, somehow. How odd, I thought, that this woman would be a friend of Ross's.

One Friday night in January of 1981, I dragged home after a late *WKRP* taping. It had been a tough week, and I was tired, but when Ross was out of town, the tension and the scenes weren't there, either, so it was easy to really miss him—or, maybe, the idea of him. I called him in Minnesota, at our house, and when he answered, I was genuinely glad to hear his voice. And then he said, "You know that girl who stayed with us last summer? I've been having an affair with her. And I'm going to stay here, to work, and to live, in the house. I'm not coming back to California. I don't want to be Mr. Anderson anymore."

I felt like the world's biggest fool, as angry as I was hurt. I had been hoping, praying, that he would get his life together—and all the time he had been building a new one, someplace else. And the fact that he had a mistress —and that she had not only stayed under my roof in California, but had been making love with him in our Minnesota house, a house I'd bought for us—I couldn't abide it. Had they been in our bed here, too, I wondered? Here, while I was working? I couldn't get the images out of my mind.

On Monday morning I filed for divorce. In a day or two Ross called back, contrite. "I was drunk," he said. "I didn't mean it."

"What about the affair?" I asked. "Was all that stuff true?" Say no, I thought.

"Yes," he said.

"Well, then, nothing's changed," I said. "The marriage is over. You were drunk, but you told me the truth."

"Loni, wait. We can work this out. I love you," he said. "I was just trying to get your attention."

"It worked, Ross," I told him. "You got my attention. And you're getting a divorce."

I paid him a two-hundred-thousand-dollar settlement—twenty thousand dollars a year for the next ten years. And he got the house in Minnesota and his car. And a very expensive wardrobe he had purchased the last time he'd been in L.A.

What I was feeling paled next to Deidra's reaction when she found out what was going on. She had loved Ross and loved being a family. Her rock-steady grandfather was gone, her Gramma was being quite nutty, her mother was on posters in boys' bedrooms, in college dormitories, and her entire world had gone to hell. At fifteen, she had more than enough reason for thinking grown-ups were stupid and careless and not to be trusted. We were the worst. She was a very, very unhappy kid.

True to his word, Ross didn't come back to California, although once the anger and the ache had subsided, we gradually grew to be friends again. He eventually moved to New York, where he's consistently done fine work in theater, and two years ago he remarried. When Burt filed for divorce—and the news of his affair with Pamela Seals became public—Ross was one of the first friends who called me. "Listen," he said. "If Burt did this to get your attention, tell the man to give me a call. I'll tell him how that strategy doesn't work out so well."

So there I was, divorced again. Single in Hollywood. I came here married, I thought, I don't want to date again, I don't know how it works here. And if dating stinks in general, Hollywood dating is the worst—the tabloids crawl all over you, completely reinventing your life until you can't even recognize yourself.

So I called my mom and asked her to come live with me for a while. Whatever it was that she had been going through, maybe Deedee and I could help. And maybe, I hoped, she could help us get through this latest heartbreak and upheaval.

About two weeks after the news of my separation from Ross hit the papers, I received a phone call from a man who said he was a representative of Burt Reynolds. Mr. Reynolds, this gentleman told me, had been an admirer of mine for some time and would like to know if I would be interested in going out some evening.

My immediate reaction was that I would never go out with Burt Reynolds, *ever*. He was terrifying. He was Burt Reynolds, for heaven's sake! He was too handsome—in fact, I had just done one of those twenty-question Q&A things in *Playboy*, and when they asked me who the handsomest man in Hollywood was, I said Burt Reynolds. I said, "I've thought so since he was in *Hawk* or whatever it was, and my mother said, 'Come in here and look at this guy, Loni. He looks just like your dad.' "

He was number one at the box office, he was Mr. Tabloid, he talked about his sex life on network television, on *The Tonight Show*. Dinah, Sally, Tammy Wynette, Lorna Luft, Lauren Hutton—the man was a legend. *Semi-Tough, Starting Over,* the *Cosmo* centerfold. Go out with him? "Oh, no," I said, "I don't think so."

And, besides, wisely or unwisely, I was taking a closer look at Gary Sandy.

Gary was fun and funny and cute and perpetually upbeat. Ross said once that the reason Gary had beaten him out for the part of Andy Travis was that Ross couldn't do "good ol' boy," but Gary had it down solid. He was a romper and a stomper, with a hefty temper and a smile that could charm pictures off walls. There may be men in this country who think that I was the reigning *WKRP* sex object, but there are women who will argue—strongly, *passionately*—that Gary Sandy was. The mail that man got! He had a thousand girlfriends, he had women up to his ears. And I used to think, wow, what does this guy have? Because all these women knew about each other, and they didn't care!

For almost three years, Gary and I had spent all our *WKRP* working days together. We had gone on publicity tours together, and game shows, and talk shows. We had weathered the fame thing. We had become good friends and acting partners; we had a great rhythm on *WKRP*. Playing a scene with Gary was like . . . well, it was like play. My life at home had been so difficult for so long; life at work was great.

A month after I filed for the divorce from Ross, I said to Linda

Jensen, "I'm going to go out with Gary. I'm legally separated, I'm just waiting for the divorce to be final, and I'm going to go out!" I had talked myself into a real, live crush. Besides, this would be a good, safe way to start this dating thing. A date with Gary would be comfortable, I thought. It would be friendly.

We went out to dinner. Afterward, he kissed me in the car. And it wasn't comfortable, it wasn't friendly. Instead, it was like experiencing a nuclear explosion in a very small space.

We made love all night long. We went to his house—his house which had been *my* house. (Well, at least I knew where everything was.) I was embarrassed, I made myself blush at how enthusiastic I was, at the things I did, at the fact that we were at it for something like five hours. No wonder he can have four or five girlfriends and keep them all happy, I thought. The man has made lovemaking into an art form! In one night I was completely hooked. Cooked.

Now we had to see each other every day, and I couldn't keep my hands off him. At thirty-five, I was possessed, experiencing something I hadn't known existed and noisily enjoying every second. I felt entitled. And without a single reservation, I admit that I was sexually addicted to him. We would go out to dinner and not even make it home from restaurants; we had to pull over to the side of the road. On a busy street!

We kept it to ourselves as long as we could. I didn't want us in the papers, and I didn't know what the reaction would be at home. But Mom and Deidra had always liked Gary; everybody did. He had been at the house, in and out of our lives, for three years already. We had spend Christmases with his mom and dad, with Ross and Robin and everybody. My friends all loved him— heck, we had the same friends. He lived in my old house, for Pete's sake! And when we went public, everybody said, "Oh, isn't this cute. *WKRP* in love!"

Periodically, I was still getting these calls about Burt Reynolds, inquiring about taking me out. Oh, no, I'd say. I'm with Gary Sandy now. I'm with the *luuvv* machine, and perfectly happy, thank you very much. I remember Deidra and Linda teasing us unmercifully, saying on the weekends, "Do you guys think you'll ever come out of the bedroom today, or do you just want us to slip food under the door?"

He said he loved me, maybe he did. Although I loved him dearly, I wasn't *in* love with him, not the way I had been with Ross, not the way you should be when you want to spend the rest of your life with someone. I was crazy for him and crazed for what we had together. I certainly wasn't interested in anyone else, and he said he was being exclusive at that point. We were practically in each other's pockets all the time, so I don't know when he would've had time to fool around . . . but he might have. I don't know if it would have mattered to me.

In August my divorce from Ross was final, and I was nominated for my second Emmy, as was the show. I heard it on the television that morning, and I went bouncing in to tell Gary. His first words were, "Was I nominated?"

Oops. "Oh, honey, no," I said. "No, I'm sorry, but you weren't."

What a look I got. "Then why are you so excited?" he asked. "You should have come in here and said you were sorry first, and then told me about your nomination."

"Uh, wait a second," I said. "You mean I'm not allowed to be excited about being nominated, just because you weren't?" Was I standing in some kind of flashback? Isn't this why Ross and I were divorced?

Gary got so mad he stomped out of the house.

In 1980, when I received my first Emmy nomination, I had gushed to Mary Tyler Moore (my MTM boss), "Oh, I'm just so excited!"

She looked at me with a perfectly straight face. "Oh, dear," she said kindly. "Pretty never gets the sympathy vote."

I didn't go to the awards that first year. The actors' strike had been in full swing, and few people attended the ceremony itself. There's a very funny scene in Nick Nolte's film *I'll Do Anything* that captures that night perfectly. Ross and I, like everybody we knew, stayed home, made popcorn, and watched it on television. I didn't win; Loretta Swit did, for *M*A*S*H*. It was no wonder that attending the 1981 ceremony meant a great deal to me.

When Gary and I went together to the Emmy Awards ceremony, fans were outside shouting, "Loni, Loni, Loni," and inside, the press wanted interviews. And Gary walked away from me. And then he walked out the door and walked all the way home. This time, Eileen Brennan won for *Private Benjamin*.

So as we went into the fourth year of *WKRP*, Gary and I became the battling couple. Gary yelled, slammed doors, kicked things, stamped his boots. It made for a lot of tension on the set (although he wasn't yelling and stamping there), and the tabloids picked it up. The headlines were kind of general: WKRP NO LONGER ONE BIG HAPPY FAMILY, etc.

And then I started yelling back. I had never been a yeller or a slammer, it's just never been the way I fight. Now, with Gary, I was yelling. And fighting. He was making me nuts. And he was getting nasty. We went to a publicity event in New York, and I got mobbed—backed up against a wall in the theater with people pressing in, pushing, and I couldn't breathe. And Gary was nowhere around. Later I asked him, "Why on earth did you just leave me like that?"

He said, "This is what you want. But it isn't what I want. I'm a serious actor. If this is what you want, you deal with it on your own."

I was confounded. *WKRP* was a force of its own, and Gary had certainly been part of it. He began to belittle everything I was doing. He said I was being a celebrity, not a serious actress, and he was disgusted with me.

I did an Aaron Spelling TV movie, *Sizzle,* with John Forsythe. It was a very stylized Prohibition-era story, complete with flapper costumes and mobsters in Chicago. I got to sing and dance and completely enjoyed myself. And I did a three-hour combination *Love Boat* and *Fantasy Island*—I was the only person who ever came back from a *Love Boat* cruise unhappy, so they had to ship me off to *Fantasy Island* for repairs. So it's not like I wasn't working, and working hard, but Gary thought I should be doing Shakespeare or something.

"What about you?" I challenged him. "You're on *WKRP,* same as I am."

"Doesn't matter," he said, waving away the comparison. "This is just a vehicle for where I'm going, for what I'm going to do. I'm going to do feature films after this. But no one is ever going to take you seriously."

Oh, I was so sick of that line. As soon as I heard it, I heard these words come out of *my* mouth: "Oh, please. I'm the one who got nominated for an Emmy. Twice. Who do you think is being taken seriously here?"

It was a hurtful, below-the-belt thing to say, and there was more at the heart of it than just that fight with Gary. In that nasty comeback was every regret and resentment and sorrow I carried from the end of my marriage. This man, I thought, is bringing something out in me that I don't like.

A few days later, Gary found out that I made more money than he did, and he completely flipped out. I don't know how or why he found out, but it led to an argument the size and sound of which was unprecedented. We were in the yard (I don't remember why), and I couldn't get through to him; I didn't think less of him, what difference did it make, what was the big deal? But he would not listen, he would not calm down. It finally made me so frustrated that I pushed him down on the ground. I just shoved him, with both hands, as hard as I could, and he fell down.

That was the first time I was ever physically aggressive toward someone in anger. I never even spanked Deidra. The one time I ever touched her, when she was about eight, it was because she had sassed me pretty creatively. I smacked her across the mouth and said, "Don't you ever talk to me like that again." It was the only time I ever laid a hand on her in her entire life, and she'll never get over it. I'll never live it down. To this day she still says, "Remember that time I talked back and you actually struck me?"

And I say to her, "Oh, Deedee, it's not as if I slugged you. I slapped your pretty little mouth. Actually, I wanted to plant a bar of soap in it."

But anyway, I gave Gary a full-body-contact shove, and suddenly there he was, completely stunned, on the ground looking up at me. He just started laughing. And then I laughed, too. Because it was funny. Sort of.

But later it scared me. I was completely out of control with this man, both sexually and emotionally, and he was making me a crazy person.

If *he* had gotten the Emmy nominations, if *he* had gotten the raise. If Ross had made it and I hadn't. Everybody would have said, "Get over it, honey. That's just the way the world goes." All I ever wanted to do was work; the star stuff was a happy bonus. Anyone who has been in this business for a while knows that to work—and get paid—regularly is the goal. To do what you love, to have somebody see it, appreciate it, pay for it. That's what I wanted. But all I kept hearing was, "Look what you're doing to *me*." It's the whole man thing. I don't blame them, I think it's the way most of them are raised. But what was I supposed to do about it, hide in a cave? Give back my raises? Apologize deeply, rend my garments, give back my SAG card?

I said to Linda, "Maybe I can't date anyone. Or maybe I'll have to find someone more famous, who gets paid more, who'll see me for me, someone who won't get nuts over an Emmy nomination." And then I joked, "You know, maybe the only man for me to date in this town really *is* Burt Reynolds. Now, there's somebody who would never be Mr. Anderson. I'll never make more money than he does, and I'll certainly never be as big a deal."

In late November Burt was going to be honored by the Variety Club, a show business children's charity, for lifetime achievement. It's a very big deal, a televised black-tie event that honors someone important every year. I've attended the celebrations for Lucille Ball, President Reagan, and Jack Lemmon. In fact, I got to meet Cary Grant, my all-time heartthrob, the evening that Jack Lemmon was honored. Burt's representatives called and asked if I would attend the event honoring Burt, and introduce Jim Nabors. Of course I accepted, and I asked Gary to go with me. When he said, "I'm not going," I was angry, but more than that, I was totally out of patience. This, I told him, was pure childishness.

So I asked Linda if she would be my date, and she said she

would. A few days later they called me back and said, "Burt would like you to invite family or guests, and he will provide you with a table." I invited Mom to come, with her latest beau, and Deedee and her boyfriend, and Jeanne, Linda's mom, and her beau. That should fill out the table, I thought. I was so miffed at Gary that I very deliberately planned what I would wear—a beautiful slinky white gown—hoping that he would see me on television and feel awful.

When we got to the studio soundstage where the event would be held, we discovered that instead of sitting with my own guests, Linda and I would be sitting with Burt's manager, David Gershonson, his agent, Dick Clayton, and all the people who represented him, at another table down closer to the guest of honor's table. Sitting there with Burt were his mother and father, his sister and brother. Gosh, I thought, Mr. Tabloid has a real family!

As the room began to fill up with people whose faces I recognized—Jackie Gleason, Madeline Kahn, Brian Keith, Lucille Ball, Jimmy Stewart—I remembered what I had said to Linda about dating Burt. The last time Burt's people had called to ask me about a date, I had been very adamant about being with Gary Sandy. So I hadn't heard from anybody in a couple of months. I wondered if he was still interested. As I watched the events of the evening, I tried to think of a way to let him know that maybe I could be interested, too.

I noticed that each time a guest introduced a speaker, Burt got up and shook hands or hugged the speaker, saying something private just out of mike range so that the audience couldn't hear. This was a man with a reputation for a wild sense of humor; I knew that whatever I did, it had to be funny.

Now, Burt was always going on and on about how much he wanted to have a child of his own. Every time he was interviewed—in a magazine, on television—he talked about wanting to have a baby. It got to be such a running joke on Johnny Carson's show that one night Johnny even presented Burt with a live baby on the air. So after I walked up and made my little speech introducing Jim Nabors to the audience, Burt came over to hug me—and I instantly knew what I was going to say to him.

"Thank you very much, Loni," he said with a big smile. "That was just delightful."

And then I said, with an air of theatrical resignation, "Well, all right, all right, I'm ready to have your child." As I turned to walk away, he grabbed my hand, pulled me back to him, and whispered in my ear, "When?" We both burst out laughing. Nobody heard what we said, but everybody saw us crack up.

I walked back to my table thinking, well, at least I broke the ice. My heart was pounding. As far as I was concerned, that was one of the bravest, if not the most outrageous, things I'd done in my life. When I sat down, I whispered to Linda what had happened, not knowing whether to giggle or crawl under the table.

From where we were sitting, I could see Mom and Deedee and their pals, and every so often I waved up to them. "Who's that gorgeous girl you keep waving at?" asked David Gershonson.

"Cool it," I said to him. "That's my sixteen-year-old daughter, and my mother's with her."

As the party was breaking up, and I was getting ready to go up there and claim my family, I felt hands on my shoulders. When I looked up, Burt was standing behind my chair. "Thanks so much for being here tonight," he said. Well, since the man had every friend he'd ever had in his entire life there that night, I decided his coming over and singling me out was a good sign.

"Would you please do a favor for me?" I asked. "My family is here, my mother and daughter, and I would love it if you would go up there with me and meet them."

"I'd love to," he said. He took my hand and we walked across the floor, at which point Tawny Little, a Los Angeles newscaster and former Miss America, walked past us and said to Burt as she went by, "I'll be in the car."

Damn. Oh, well, I thought, nothing ventured, nothing gained. I smiled at him. "Nice choice. She's really a lovely woman."

When I introduced Burt to Mom, he said, "Now I know where Loni gets her looks. Although," he continued, smiling down at Deidra, "she's about to be outdone by her own daughter. You know, your mother said something special to me tonight. She wants to know if I'd like to have a child with her—and if that child turned out like you, I can't imagine anything more wonderful."

Deedee was stunned into near speechlessness. "Thank you," she gasped.

And then he said good night to me, and we all said good night to him. As he walked away, my mother turned to Jeanne (they had become friends by then) and said, "I predict they'll be married in two months."

"Mom," I protested, "he's with somebody else."

She shook her head. "Not the way he looked at you he's not."

It had been a pretty spectacular evening, but the next day, of course, I had to go back to work. And there was Tawny Little on TV (with co-anchor Regis Philbin, pre–New York and Kathie Lee), on the morning program I watched every day, and she was talking about how she was happily dating Burt. OK, I thought, that's that.

In the meantime Gary had decided that the solution to our problems was that we should settle down and be together—like forever. With an engagement ring. Although he was almost always angry with me and wouldn't go to a public event with me anymore, he had decided that no matter what, he loved me. The minute I stepped back, he became more ardent.

For Christmas we had a two-week break from *WKRP*. Right at the beginning of the first week of vacation, David Gershonson, Burt's manager, called. We exchanged pleasantries, and then he said, "Would you really go out with Burt?"

"David, tell the truth. Isn't he dating Tawny Little?" I asked.

"Oh, well," David said, "I don't think it's serious."

I took a deep breath. "Look, for almost a year now, you guys have been calling me asking if I'd go out with Burt. And I've been saying no. But I've been thinking, and I just might go, if he'd call me himself. If he's truly not dating anybody else, and he called me himself . . . I'll see."

Two hours later the phone rang. It was Burt.

I've always had a very festive house during the holidays, with decorations, lots of food (I was doing the cooking for Christmas dinner, and all the baking, a holiday ritual I've always loved), and as many people around as possible. Which meant, when Jeanne Jensen answered the phone and whispered, "It's Burt Reynolds!" I had an audience in the kitchen. Mom, Deidra, Linda. I waved good-bye to them all and went to take the call in the family room.

Burt said how nice it was to see me at the Variety Club bash. And then he said, "You know, since even before *WKRP* started, when I saw you on TV hosting that Miss California World beauty pageant, I thought you were the most gorgeous thing I had ever seen. And you're so funny and so talented. I really hope you and I can get together sometime."

I felt like I was back in high school again. "Oh, I think we might be able to do that. In fact, I'd enjoy it a lot."

"I'm in Florida right now," he said.

Oh, shoot. "Well, when you get back, please call me," I said.

"Why don't you come down here for Christmas?" he asked.

Surprised, I started to laugh. "I can't do that! I have a houseful of people here. I'm having seventeen people for Christmas dinner."

"Bring 'em all with you," he said. "We can handle that."

Now I was really laughing. "I can't, I just can't do that. You're going a little fast for me here. I mean, I don't even kiss until the third date!"

He was laughing by then, too. We talked some more, about work, about families. When I hung up, almost two hours later, I thought he was one of the nicest, most fun people I had ever talked to. And a real gentleman. I told my eager household that he had asked us all to Florida for Christmas. Of course we laughed; he couldn't possibly have been serious. Could he?

The next night, he called again, and we talked another two hours. The night after that, he called yet again, and we talked for another two hours. We talked about his career, his friends, my friends, my daughter, his parents, his sister and brother, his niece and nephew, his theater down in Jupiter. There had been nothing to distract us—we weren't watching a movie or being social with other people or having dinner or appearing in public. In about six hours, I had learned more about him than I ever could have done during a date.

At the end of the third night's conversation, Burt said, "Now, we have talked more than any two people could have talked on three dates. Will you please come to Florida? For New Year's Eve?"

It was hard to argue with his logic. "I'll think about it," I said. "I just don't know what to say right now. I have to think about it."

He called again the next night. "Did you think about it?"

I certainly had thought about it but still hadn't decided. "I have to check with my daughter," I said. "I have to ask her, and I have to ask my mother."

"That's just fine," he said. "You ask them, and I'll call for your answer tomorrow night."

In the meantime Gary was coming and going as he had always done, in and out of the house every day. It was the holidays, after all—and his birthday was on Christmas Day. He knew something was up, but he didn't quite know what it was. I was withdrawing from him—in fact, I had been for a couple of months—and maybe he just thought I was testing him, putting him through his paces. He had no way of knowing about Florida, Burt Reynolds, and New Year's.

For weeks I had been talking to Mom and Deedee—my twin consciences—about my feelings about what was going on with Gary. They knew that he cared for me and that I cared for him, but they also knew that we were having our problems, the problems had become worse, and, at any rate, it was not the romance of the century.

"What do you guys think?" I asked them. "Should I go to Florida?" Although we had all been giddy about the phone calls and the possibility of an actual date, I was prepared for them both to say no to the trip.

"You know how I am, honey," said Mom. "Don't miss a party, ever. Besides, he seems like a nice enough guy."

OK, that took care of Mom. "What do you think, Dee?"

She seemed reluctant to answer for a couple of minutes. The past two years had been tumultuous for her, too. She was feeling the loss of her stepfather and the security of the family structure we three had once had together. And this relationship with Gary had her mother behaving like a hormonally mad teenager much of the time. Little wonder, then, that she might've had a reservation or two about sending me off into the wild blue yonder with Mr. Box Office. "I think," she said slowly, "that maybe you should go for it."

"Look, Loni," my mother said. "Between what's been happening with Gary and what happened with Ross last year, you haven't been happy for a long time. What's the worst that can happen here? You spend New Year's Eve with Burt Reynolds. And then you can tell your grandchildren all about it."

She was right, it *would* be an adventure. And maybe, just maybe, it might be something more. So I called Burt and told him yes, I would come to Florida for New Year's. But only for two days.

I had a hard time deciding when and how to tell Gary, knowing that no matter when I did it, he was going to be hurt, and there was going to be a scene. I thought, why does this have to be happening now, on Christmas? On his birthday? My instincts may have been good, but I knew my timing wasn't.

On Christmas Eve we had a big fire in the fireplace, and we were all sitting around drinking mulled wine and singing along to the holiday specials on TV—and all of a sudden here comes Burt on the screen. He was a guest on somebody's Christmas special. And the tension in the room started to run very high, because everyone there, except Gary, knew what my plans were. At the end of the evening, I asked Gary if he could please not stay. I needed to get some sleep, I said, since I had to get up at the crack of dawn and start preparations for Christmas dinner.

At two o'clock in the morning, my gate buzzer started buzzing. It was Gary. He had had a few drinks, and he wanted to come in and talk to me. Once in, he started ranting and raving about Michael Goodwin, a good friend of ours who had been my costar in *Sizzle,* the Aaron Spelling TV movie. Gary had decided that the tension and my cold shoulder toward him was because Michael and I were having an affair. Once I heard that, I knew I couldn't let this go any further.

"Calm down, Gary, it's not Michael," I said. "I've been thinking about this for a long time. We can't be together. You bring out behavior in me that I can't handle, that I don't like, and we're just not going to be what you want us to be. I waited to tell you this, I guess because I didn't want to wreck your birthday. But," and here I took a deep breath, "I'm going to Florida to spend New Year's Eve with Burt Reynolds."

And, of course, all hell broke loose. He shouted, he cried. He wanted to make love to me, thinking he could change my mind that way. "No, no," I said. "Don't you see? You think that's the answer to everything, and it's really part of the problem!"

Christmas Day itself was a nightmare, because Gary was there all day, trying to talk me out of going to Florida. He was sick to his stomach. I'm not sure that anyone had ever broken up with him before; I think it had always been the other way around. It was heart-wrenching, and I felt miserable for him. But not miserable enough to change my plans. At one point he was sitting at my mother's feet, begging her in tears to make me change my mind.

"Gary," my mom said, "we all care about you, and this is a hard thing, I know. But you have to back off, you have to accept that Loni's going to do this."

"Reynolds is just going to eat you up and spit you out," Gary snapped at me. "It's what he does to everybody."

Gary left the house and went to all of our friends, telling them what I was going to do. He went to the *WKRP* cast members' houses, one at a time, and told them, too. And everyone truly felt badly for him. But one of the writers, who finally grew impatient with what was happening to his own Christmas, said, "Gary, you've got to get a grip here. After all, it's not like she's leaving you for Joe Schmoe. If you're going to get dumped for somebody, New Year's Eve with Burt Reynolds is pretty high-class."

Burt had assured me in our phone conversations that he and

Tawny Little were no longer seeing each other and that, at any rate, it hadn't been serious between them. I had no reason to doubt him. I didn't find out until quite a while later that it had been very serious for Tawny. And not until Elaine Hall, Burt's longtime assistant in Florida, published her own book in the fall of 1994 did I find out that Tawny left Florida about an hour before I got down there. She had flown in just after Christmas, and he told her after a couple of days that she had to leave, that he wanted to spend time alone with his parents. So he didn't tell her the truth.

I flew to Miami the day before New Year's Eve day, arriving in the early evening. When I put my makeup on that morning, I couldn't keep my hands from shaking. I hadn't been able to eat or sleep for a week; I had no idea what I had thrown into my suitcase.

Burt met me at the Miami airport with his helicopter and pilot, Logan Fleming, who was also his ranch foreman. He looked so handsome, wearing a soft black leather aviator jacket. He walked right up to me, took my hand, and kissed it. But he never once looked at me or looked into my eyes. "I'm so glad you're here," he said, walking me over to the chopper and helping me climb in.

It had grown dark, and as we flew over Miami, the city lights were glorious. The boats in the harbors and on the Intracoastal Waterway were all decorated with festive Christmas lights. We then flew up the coast, all the way to Lantana, where the *National Enquirer* is headquartered. We circled the *Enquirer* building—with its big decorated Christmas tree on top—and we pretended to drop bombs on the building, imagining what they would do if they knew we were up here, wondering how long it would be before they found out. We were laughing like crazy, and he was holding my hand the whole time. But not making any eye contact. Finally I teased him, "Burt, are you ever going to look at me?"

"I can't," he said, shaking his head. "I just can't. You're too beautiful."

Well, I was totally charmed. Burton Leon Reynolds, Jr., shy

guy. Who knew? The man had real dimples when he smiled, and his brown eyes just sparkled, as though they were lit from within. And *he* says he can't look at *me*. Any doubts I'd had before I arrived in Miami were gone. I thought, if it's just for this weekend, I don't care.

We landed on the tennis court of Valhalla, his eight-acre compound in Hobe Sound, on the Intracoastal. He showed me to my room—the guest room—and after I freshened up, he ordered dinner brought to the house for us. There was no one there but James, the houseman.

Burt said, "Shall I turn on the TV? Is there anything you'd like to watch?"

"But you're the man who talked to me for hours on end," I said. "Don't you want to talk to me anymore?"

"I can't, not yet," he said. "It's going to take me a while to get used to you."

We had a quiet dinner together, and then he walked me to the door of my room, giving me a little kiss good night. We would go to the ranch tomorrow, he said, because he wanted me to meet his parents. And he wanted me to come to the theater.

He was directing a production of *One Flew Over the Cuckoo's Nest,* starring Martin Sheen and Adrienne Barbeau, at the theater he'd opened in 1979, the Burt Reynolds Dinner Theatre. It was an Equity theater, with an apprentice program that operated under the auspices of his Institute for Theater Training. Most of his Hollywood friends had gotten involved with the theater and its programs, either starring in the productions (which were heavily attended by the Palm Beach crowd) or teaching workshops to the young people Burt called his "kids." Sally and Dinah had both performed there; over the years, the list grew to include Tyne Daly, Charles Durning, Vincent Gardenia, Farrah Fawcett, Ned Beatty, Jim Nabors, Stockard Channing, Julie Harris, Kirstie Alley and Parker Stevenson, Elizabeth Ashley, Ossie Davis, Florence Henderson, and Carol Burnett.

The next morning, still on California time, I overslept, and by the time I walked over to rehearsal, they had already started. When I walked in and he saw me, he came right over, put his arms around me, and said, "Come here, I want you to meet everyone." I realize now, of course, that the whole cast must have been somewhat perplexed—they had just said good-bye to Tawny Little!

I watched the rehearsal for a while; it wasn't the only time I would watch Burt direct. I thought then—and still do—that he was one of the best directors in the business. I had seen *Sharky's Machine,* which he had directed, and it was a terrific movie. The critics thought so, too. He had an unerring sense of timing, his own and everybody else's, and when he was directing, he had a great ability to find strengths in his actors, even the inexperienced ones. He was genial and relaxed with his peers and endlessly patient and encouraging with the apprentices. He was, above all, a good teacher.

After rehearsal we went to the B-R Horse Ranch, one hundred sixty acres of real Florida ranchland, complete with horses and other livestock, pickup trucks, barns and tractors, and, at that time, a huge staff. When I met his parents, Burt senior and Fern, they couldn't have been nicer to me. And it was clear that their son—they called him Bud—adored them both. Their approval was important to him, and when they were so warm with their welcome, and told me they were big fans of mine, I could tell Burt was pleased.

We went back to his house to get dressed up for New Year's Eve. We were to see the play—not *Cuckoo,* which was still in rehearsal, but I was in such a daze, I frankly don't remember to this day what the production was. After the play there was to be a dinner and party, with all kinds of Palm Beach and Hollywood people coming.

As we went through the evening, I was definitely floating on some kind of fuzzy pink cloud. Burt never let go of my hand. At midnight, the eve of the New Year, he kissed me. And as the party wound down, we said our good nights to the guests and went back to Valhalla. And that night, he made love to me for the first time.

He was sweet and tentative and gentle, almost as though he thought I was going to break. I was moved beyond words. He's not at all that sex-symbol, macho, thrash-and-bash guy, I thought. The bad-boy movie star image belies everything he is. And his great tenderness was to me, at that time, a kind of blessed relief.

He was the most beautiful man I had ever seen. Dark, powerful, with the broadest shoulders and the most beautifully muscled arms. And his chest, his back, tapering down into that great butt and wonderful strong legs. He was totally worked out, but he wasn't muscle-bound. Instead he looked classic, like the museum illustrations in my art books. Like an ancient statue of a Greek god.

He put on some wonderful music, Frank Sinatra, of course, and Johnny Mathis—I can hear "Chances Are" right this minute—and we danced naked on the balcony outside the master bedroom. Slow-danced. It was without question the most romantic evening I had ever had in my entire life. Just as we were falling asleep, he said to me, "Don't go home tomorrow, lady."

So I stayed. He gave me a beautiful silver squash-blossom necklace, "because you weren't here for Christmas." Each night we were together, each morning I woke up beside him. I went to rehearsal every day at the playhouse, and we walked around the ranch, and we talked for hours. He told me wonderful stories about things he'd done, people he'd known. We talked about my career, and he had advice for me, good advice. I had so much respect for him as a professional, I was grateful for everything he said.

Over and over during those few days, he played the cast album from *Mack and Mabel,* a Jerry Herman musical that had starred Robert Preston and Bernadette Peters on Broadway. Burt was trying to decide if he should put the show on at his theater and play—and sing—the part of Mack Sennett himself. One of Sennett's songs, "I Won't Send Roses," is a bittersweet love song, and its refrain runs through the entire play:

> *In me you'll find things like guts and nerve,*
> *But not the kind things that you deserve. . . .*
> *I won't send roses. And roses suit you so.*

The more we listened, and the more Burt sang, the more special the song became to us.

There were many New Year's Eves to come when he would sing this song to me, at parties, in front of our friends. And many bouquets of flowers, from him to me and me to him, which always included the song's last words: Roses suit you so.

I was definitely in a new world. I felt surrounded, enveloped, by love, by safety. By a comfort I hadn't felt in many years. I kept telling him, "You remind me so much of my dad." The same sense of humor. His laughter. The same sense of power, in the way he moved and in the way people responded to him.

The physical, out-of-control passion I had experienced with Ross and with Gary wasn't there between Burt and me. On the other hand, some of the passion in my life lately—the yelling, the slamming things, the danger, the pain—hadn't been so terrific. And this was so . . . nice. It had a kind of wonder to it. For however long this lasts, I thought, I'm thankful.

I was a day late getting back to *WKRP*—something the girl in *Fiddler* had never been, not in fifty-three weeks. Monday morning, just before he had Logan fly me to the Miami airport, Burt said, "I'll be back in Los Angeles in a week. I'm falling in love with you. I don't want you to see anyone else. I won't see anyone else. We belong together."

I nodded. "OK," I said. It wasn't poetry, but it was the best I could do at that moment.

When we said good-bye at the helicopter, Burt said to Logan, "Take care of my lady. Make sure nothing happens to her."

I could've flown back to California without a plane.

Chapter 9

There are, in the story of any relationship gone wrong, at least two versions: his and hers. And then, of course, there are the versions told by eyewitnesses: family members (loving and not so), employees (happy and not so), bystanders (innocent and not so), and anyone else who wants to make a profit from a couple's joys and sorrows. Once you're in the public eye—once the genie's out of that bottle—there's no way to edit information or to control what people will say about you or think about you or write about you.

Everybody has a story to tell; I can only tell my own. I wasn't going to tell it at all; in fact, if I didn't have children, I might still be responding to questions and queries with an unchanging "No comment," as I did for two years. But when my strong-minded, strong-willed daughter, who has a daughter of her own now, heard this sentence—"And furthermore, Loni wasn't a very good mother"—she angrily broke the silence I had requested of the people who were closest to me. She talked to the press one day, trying to put the record right. And that's when I began to think about doing the same.

I don't know if, in the beginning, I fell in love with Burt Reynolds the man, or if I fell in love with the idea of him. A lot of Hollywood is smoke and mirrors; fantasy, fiction, and special effects are part of how we all live. But whatever was between us in the beginning, it turned into something very real, something that I believed in and trusted, as much as I had any religion. Now, when they ask me all the "why?" questions, the answer is always the same. I loved him without a single reservation.

When I returned from Florida and went back to the *WKRP* set, Gary immediately asked me what had happened. And I said, "I'm involved with him. We're together." And I told him I was sorry that he'd been hurt and genuinely meant it. But of course it didn't help. I knew in advance that nothing I could say or do would help, except to stay with Gary and not be with Burt. And that was not an option for me.

It didn't improve matters when the tabloid headlines hit: BURT AND LONI LINKED IN WHIRLWIND ROMANCE. GARY DUMPED. TAWNY IN TEARS. I had been in a few headlines before—publicity for *WKRP*, my divorce from Ross—but never anything like this. In fact, fear of this very thing was one of the reasons I had said no to going out with Burt in the first place.

In *WKRP*'s three seasons on the air (we were now in our fourth), cast rehearsals had become relaxed and somewhat collaborative, like choreography, with each of us working out our steps with the others. One of us would say, "OK, I'll stand here, and then you can be over there and say this and this." And then we'd do it, and if it didn't work, we would try it another way. We all knew each other so well, we could anticipate the rhythms of a line reading, we knew where the laughs would come and where they wouldn't.

But no more. Gary was seething, and everyone on the set knew it. At one point, when I said, "OK, I'll just walk over here, and then you—" Gary snapped back at me, "*Fuck* you!" First it was under his breath, then he got louder. Finally, Gordon Jump had to step in between us.

"Gary, you just can't do this," he said patiently. "This show is about all of us. We're all in it together. So no matter what's happened, you have to put your feelings aside. Or you have to step out."

When Burt came back to L.A., he gave me a ring, a garnet surrounded by diamonds. "Let's think of this as the beginning," he said. He called me two, three times a day. He would call from the middle of a meeting—he was number one at the box office at this point, and had been for five years, and these were very important meetings he was calling me from, often to discuss nothing more significant than a body part. One of mine. "I called you because I can't stop thinking about, oh . . . your shoulder blade," he'd say. Or "that place behind your knee."

Flowers would arrive in the middle of the day, every day, with notes that said, "Just because it's Tuesday." Or I would get some exquisite jewel, a necklace, a bracelet. Just because.

Burt came over to the house and reintroduced himself to Mom and to Deidra, and after he left, Deedee flopped right down in the middle of the floor and kicked her feet in the air, hooting, "He is so *cute!*" And then she mentioned somebody, Clint Eastwood or Robert Redford or somebody, and said, "Please don't date them and spoil it for me."

I laughed. "What on earth do you mean by that?" I asked.

"When your own mother dates your fantasy person," she said, "it just takes all the glamour away. I mean, you're my mother!"

In February, Burt and I went to Hawaii for a week. He was recovering from a hernia operation, and we were trying to get away, if only for a few days, from the headlines. He rented a little house we called the Grass Shack, and it had a beautiful swimming pool that was filled by the ebb and flow of the sea. There was no staff there; we had a cook come in or went out to restaurants. We saw Jim Nabors and his next-door neighbor, Doris Duke, one night for dinner, and another night we went out with Tom Selleck and John Hillerman, who were filming *Magnum P.I.* in Hawaii at the time. Other than that, we were completely alone.

He was always touching me, holding my hand, touching my hair when he passed, sitting beside me with his hand on my knee. It was the last time we were ever completely by ourselves, and the last real romantic vacation we ever had.

While we were there, he had a jeweler come to the house and selected the most beautiful estate-piece bracelet for me, and a necklace with a Hawaiian fertility goddess charm, all in diamonds. I remember sitting out there on the deck, looking at the sun on the horizon as the ocean filled the pool at my feet, thinking, I just can't believe this is happening. I felt swept away but completely peaceful at the same time. It was as though I had been on a long journey and had finally come to my destination.

When we returned to L.A., I went back to *WKRP*—for the last days, as it turned out, since we were canceled at the end of that 1981–82 season—and Burt flew to Buffalo, to film *Best Friends* with Goldie Hawn. In the middle of that shoot, he asked me to come to Buffalo for a long weekend.

Burt was staying in a hotel suite with multiple fireplaces—it was, after all, winter in Buffalo—and just before I was due to get there, he went around and lit them all. Burt's an arranger—he likes to set the scene, to make things perfect. But he hadn't opened the flues, and, of course, the smoke backed up and filled the suite. As soon as he figured out what had happened, he ran around like a madman, opening the flues and the windows and trying to fan the smoke and soot out of the room before I got there.

When I knocked at the door, he flung it open and greeted me with a big, expectant smile. His face was completely covered with soot, his eyebrows were singed, his eyelashes were white, and the whole front of his hairpiece was melted. Although I knew, of course, that he wore a hairpiece, I had yet to see him without one. But this one was ruined.

"My God," I said, laughing and choking, "what happened in here?"

"Oh, the damn fireplaces all backed up," he said, "and I was trying to get the smoke out of the room before you came. I wanted everything to be perfect."

"Honey," I said, "have you looked in a mirror?"

He went right into the bathroom, and then I heard this scream. And we started laughing so hard, he said, "Oh, hell, I don't even care."

And he came out of the bathroom and grabbed me, waltzing me into the bedroom. Where it was now pretty cold, with the windows wide open and the snow drifting in. Snow and sooty face notwithstanding, he threw me onto the bed and started kissing me ardently. I was immediately as enthusiastic as he was. In minutes our clothes were all over the room. All of a sudden, *cough, cough, cough,* we're both hacking and our eyes are watering. The whole room was filled with smoke again. "There is definitely something wrong with this flue!" he said.

We opened the balcony doors and headed for the terrace, trying to stand outside until the smoke was once again out of the suite, but we didn't last long out there. It was very, very cold, and we were very, very undressed.

When we finally came back in, he pulled out two nightshirts with the hotel name on them that he'd bought before I got there, and we each put one on. He looked at me and started laughing. "I think I should go wash my face now, since I've smudged soot all over your nose," he said. I went in and sat on the side of the tub, watching as he filled the sink, got the soapsuds going, and started making soapy things with his hair, gooping it up in peaks, parting it in the middle, separating his mustache into spiky wings that made him look like the guys on the Smith Brothers Cough Drops box.

When I woke up the next morning, I was alone. No Burt. When he came back into the room a little while later, he was all fixed up. He'd gone to the movie set and tracked down his hair guy and had his hair and burned eyebrows fixed. That night we went to see Richard Harris in *Camelot* and held hands throughout the whole show. The Lerner and Loewe score is so romantic and heartbreaking, we both had tears rolling down our cheeks after King Arthur's last scene. "Boy, what a couple of hard-boiled types *we* are," I said.

In the eleven and a half years we were together, we honored a pact we made that weekend, never to be apart more than four weeks at a time. We knew too well what happens to Hollywood relationships when couples are separated too much. If he couldn't come home, I always flew to where he was working.

When Burt came back from shooting *Best Friends*, it was the spring of Deidra's junior year in high school and my last few weeks at *WKRP*. I had mixed feelings about the end of the series. The cast and crew had been so much a part of my life (with all the ups and downs and turmoil of a family), and I genuinely loved them. But things between Gary and me had only become worse. In fact, Burt never came to a *WKRP* taping, because he said it wouldn't have been fair to put Gary in that position. I knew it was time for me to move on.

Jeanne Jensen had moved into the Alomar house, so that when I was at Burt's, Deedee would never come home to an empty house. On weekends I would go to Burt's place in Malibu (where the tabloid reporters and photographers eventually caught up with us). I was making plans to go to Nashville that summer to do a TV movie, *Country Gold,* and afterward to go with Burt to Atlanta and Charlotte, North Carolina, to shoot *Stroker Ace,* with Hal Needham directing. But before either of us left, we decided to go to Hawaii again for a week, to stay at Jim Nabors' house.

Before we went, Burt asked me if I would live with him.

"Well," I said, "I have a house of my own, and a daughter in school. . . ."

And he said, "Just when I'm in town. Just be with me when I'm in Los Angeles." Since he was shooting two or three movies a year out of town and spent a lot of time in Florida, we agreed that this would be a good way to sneak up on living together full-time.

When I talked to Deidra about it, she initially resented it and said so straight out. She wanted her own mother in her own house. But she also had a steady boyfriend, was winning scholastic and athletic honors, and was beginning to plan for college. She had very determinedly carved out a life of her own. I wanted one, too.

Burt owned a beautiful home on Carolwood Drive in Beverly Hills, about a twenty-minute drive from my house on Alomar. He began making renovations there just for me—a whole new addition containing big his-and-hers walk-in closets and a large bathroom, all of pink marble, with leaded-glass windows. He even consulted my makeup man and had special lighting installed around the mirrors. We called my bathroom "The Little

Jewel Box" because everything in it twinkled.

The day I moved into Carolwood, I was upstairs putting my things away and Burt called up to me, "You have to come down here, I got you something."

"Why do I have to come down to get it?" I asked. "Is it alive?"

"Loni," he yelled, "just come down here!"

So I went downstairs, and he opened the garage door—and there was a hunter green Rolls-Royce with a great big ribbon around it and a license plate that read MISS A. A small gold plate inside was engraved MADE ESPECIALLY FOR LONI ANDERSON. I couldn't drive it for two days, I was so afraid I'd dent it. So I just sat in it and smelled the upholstery. Sitting behind the wheel, which had inlaid malachite to match the car's exterior, felt like . . . being in a movie. At any rate, I was light-years away from my burnt-orange Mustang.

The only downside of Carolwood was the tour buses that regularly came through the neighborhood. They were *so* loud, and we could hear every one of them. Sometimes six or seven buses at once would get jammed up in front of the gate, with people on top of them, taking pictures. Someone was always at the intercom by the gate, pushing the buzzer and hollering, "Hey, Burt and Loni, come on down!" I remember one morning serving Burt scrambled eggs at the desk in his office. The office windows faced the street, and there, suddenly, was someone looking in the window. He had jumped over the wall! We just laughed and shooed the guy away.

I couldn't believe the joy of loving him. Sometimes I would lie awake for hours and just look at him while he slept, he was that beautiful. I loved his forearms and would tease him unmercifully until he rolled his shirt sleeves up. I used to say I was going to have our friend Rick Baker (an Oscar-winning makeup artist, for *An American Werewolf in London, Harry and the Hendersons,* and *Ed Wood*) make a dummy of Burt's forearms, so that when he was out of town, I could still wrap myself up in his arms. "And when you die," I laughed, "I'll just have Rick stuff you."

We were such good friends, and we talked all the time. About life and music and politics and spirituality and the way we both felt about family. He genuinely liked Deidra and began to brag about her to his friends—about her good grades, her levelhead-edness, her "normalness." We talked about books; we would share new writers we had found, and we'd read to each other at night. And we sang to each other, from the musicals we both loved. He knew that musicals were where I had gotten my start in the business, and when I sang around the house, or sang with our friends, he would smile. At those moments, it really was like standing in pure sunshine.

By the time I finished *WKRP,* I knew that Burt took a lot of pills. Proud of his athletic ability and always insistent on doing his own stunts, he had been injured while making *Deliverance* and other films. An automobile accident in high school had caused him to have his spleen removed, leaving a scar that ran the entire length of his body, and college football had done considerable damage to his knees. So he took Percodan for the pain.

He also took Valium, for anxiety, he said. He would be a nervous wreck if he left the Valium anywhere. He would hy-perventilate and clutch his chest, and a look of real fear would cross his face. Was this a heart attack? Nothing would do but that we turn around and go back and get the Valium. He kept little stacks of brown paper bags everywhere, so that when he started hyperventilating, he could grab a bag, put it up to his mouth, and breathe in and out until the attack stopped.

And to settle the constant battle in his stomach between the Valium and the Percodan, he took Compazine.

I knew next to nothing about drugs. True to the way I had been raised, I barely took aspirin. But I did know that those Burt took were prescription drugs and he needed them. It's not like they were recreational drugs; he wasn't having a good time, he was in pain. And some doctor had said it was OK for him to be taking this medicine. After all, he never drank, and he didn't smoke, both of which were pet peeves of mine. He told me he'd done both when he was younger, but no more.

And when he began to get a little possessive of me, at first I thought it was charming. Dad had been possessive of Mom, too.

Gosh, I'd think, look how much he really loves me. But quite soon I discovered that he didn't want me to have a past. With two marriages behind me and a grown daughter, it was hard to deny not only that I had a past, but that it was a sizable one. And he didn't want me to keep in touch with anyone I had ever been involved with, which was a problem: Deidra often went to visit Bruce and his wife, of course, and Ross would be coming to her high school graduation. I had always stayed in touch with both of their families—as far as I was concerned, we were all, for better or worse, an extended family—and I didn't want that to change. And, of course, God forbid Gary's name should come up anymore, in any context.

"B.R., if I wanted to be with any of these men, I'd still be with them. I love you," I argued. But it didn't placate him. He had a past of his own—much more colorful than mine, in fact—but it wasn't one he gave me access to or even admitted to, even though it was out there for all the world to know.

Then he started talking to me about firing Linda and Jeanne, these people who had loved and cared for me. And he didn't want me spending quite so much time with my mother or daughter. Almost imperceptibly, my schedule started getting adjusted, a half hour here, an hour there.

As for his dark moods, well, I was bothered by them sometimes but not worried. I believed he was a serious artist. He had a lot of responsibilities, with a lot of projects going on at once and many people depending on him. He's under a lot of pressure, I thought, and these are the kinds of adjustments that couples go through in the beginning. We'll work this all out in time. He just needs to learn he can trust me, that I'm committed to him, that no one will come between us.

When we went to Hawaii the second time, we stayed at Jim Nabors' house. Jim was on tour, and we were at the house alone, although we got any help we needed from Kalani, a friend and confidant of Burt's and Jim's who owned a limo company and always took care of all of us whenever we were there. The house itself was magnificent but very comfortable, and we had looked forward eagerly to the week alone.

About two days after we arrived, Burt complained of pains in his stomach and then started vomiting. Within hours he was vomiting blood and bile. It was clear to me that he was desperately ill. Burt stubbornly refused to be taken to a hospital, for fear the press would find out and make a big deal of it. Frightened, I called Kalani and asked him to find us a doctor. He quickly managed to locate a physician who not only would come to the house, but promised to keep the name of his patient confidential.

"What is he taking?" the doctor asked me after he'd examined Burt. When I showed him the prescription bottles, he looked concerned.

"How many of these does he take?"

"I don't know for sure," I said. "About a handful, I think. Ten, twelve at a time."

Now he really looked grim. "This is serious stuff. They're addictive, and the Percodan is particularly bad. It's a morphine derivative, with codeine. That's what's making him sick; the chemicals are eating away at his stomach lining. He needs to get off these drugs—now."

He wanted Burt to check into a hospital for a medically supervised withdrawal. "He won't go," I said. "Because of the publicity. We could stay right here, couldn't we? We're on vacation anyway, nobody would think anything of it. Can we do it here?"

"OK, you can do it here," the doctor said, "but the first seventy-two hours are going to be very tough." If we insisted on doing it ourselves, the doctor said, he would stay in touch by phone. He told me what to expect, and he recommended a couple of books, which I asked Kalani to go out and find for me. And he suggested that for my own protection, I might want to lock myself into a separate room at night, because Burt would probably be hallucinating through the first stage of withdrawal. Lock myself in, I thought? That would mean locking him out. How could I ever do that?

Then the doctor told Burt that what was making him sick was what he was taking. And that if he kept taking the pills, he would get sicker and might ultimately die. He had to stop taking them now. And it wasn't going to be easy.

Burt was frightened enough to agree. "OK," he said. "OK. I won't take them anymore. Please help me, tell me what to do."

I learned that withdrawing from Valium can make you feel like your skin is on fire, like things are crawling all over you. So we started with warm baths, emptying and filling the tub over and over, trying to keep Burt relaxed. But he never slept more than a few minutes at a time; if he dozed at all, nightmares would wake him up—something, someone, was trying to get him. He had hot flashes, during which the perspiration rolled down his face and back, and then cold sweats, and I would struggle to get him back into another warm tub. The Percodan withdrawal kept his stomach in an uproar, and it was three days before he could keep even the weakest tea down.

Kalani tried to spell me so I could sleep, but I'd wake to find Burt standing over me, shaking and frightened. I'd put my arms around him, hold him as tight as I could, rock him like I'd rocked Deedee. "We'll get through this," I'd say. "We'll make it."

"Don't leave me," he'd answer. "Just don't leave me."

The fourth day, he was steady enough to keep toast and tea down and to go out into the sun. Then to sit on the swimming pool steps, and then to swim a lap. Then two, then three. He had been in good physical shape, so he came back fast, and we were almost cheering each other as he swam. Look at what we did together! Talk about bonding experiences. He was my man. I had saved him.

When we came back to California, we were closer than any two people could have been. The blissed-out euphoria of the first months had been replaced by something more solid, more grounded. We were glued together not just by what we'd accomplished during that week, but by the knowledge we shared. Now I knew the secrets.

Soon after we returned from Hawaii, during the summer of 1982, I left to do *Country Gold* in Nashville. I wore a dark wig for part of the movie and glitter and spandex for the rest. My costars were Earl Holliman and Linda Hamilton, and we were honored to be able to shoot on the Grand Ole Opry stage and to have some

147

real country music legends performing with us: Mel Tillis, Lynn Anderson, Boxcar Willie. I met Dolly Parton, who joked to the crowd, "I used to look like Loni, until a bee stung me and I blew up!" This was just after she made *The Best Little Whorehouse in Texas,* before she lost so much weight. In fact, she's so tiny these days she gives me the M&M guilts.

Burt came to Nashville during the shoot and took a separate room in the hotel, because he didn't want the papers to say that we were sharing a room. The night before he left, we were having dinner in my room, and I was stunned when he actually went down on one knee and formally proposed.

"Will you marry me?" he asked, with straightforward simplicity.

There could be only one answer. "Yes," I said, without a doubt in my heart.

And then he said, "OK, let's call your mother."

When we called Mom, her first question was, "When do you plan on getting married?"

"Gee, Mom," I said, "we've only been engaged three minutes. Can we just take this one event at a time?"

I had no idea when we would be married, and neither did he. I had barely been divorced from Ross for a year. I wasn't in a hurry, and both of us had full calendars. We agreed to keep this latest development to ourselves, although he didn't keep his feelings to himself, ever.

He told all his friends, "The Countess saved me. Isn't she the most wonderful woman in the world? She's my angel."

That's when the "Countess" stuff started, as an endearment. He had called me "Her Nibs," and "Kid," which came out of the song from *Mack and Mabel,* and now it was the "Countess."

"You'll have to ask the Countess about that," he'd say. "The Countess runs the show." And, indeed, there was almost always a show to run. Parties, traveling, personal appearances for both of us, filming schedules. And we always had a lot of company, on both coasts, with staff to match. Burt was incredibly loyal and loving to old friends, people he had worked with over the years and those who had given him breaks, and they all felt the same about him. Weekends, holidays, and vacations soon included an eclectic guest list: Charles and Mary Ann Durning, Ned and Tinker Beatty, Ricardo and Georgiana Montalban (who were to become Quinton's godparents). Charles Nelson Reilly, and Dom and Carol DeLuise, and Ann-Margret and Roger Smith, and Doug and Diane McClure, Jerry Reed and his wife, Prissy, Esther Williams and her beau Ed Bell, Ernie and Tova Borgnine, and Bernie Casey and his date of the moment. Not all at once, of course, and there wasn't one of them I didn't love. But every once in a while the Roseville, Minnesota, in me came out.

"Buddy Lee," I'd plead, only half joking, "let's just stay home tonight and eat grilled cheese sandwiches."

"Can't do it, kid," he'd laugh. "We're meeting Ricardo and Georgie for dinner, and Dom and Carol. Go get glamorous. We've got a show to put on."

Chapter 10

After I finished the Nashville film, Burt and I traveled together to work on *Stroker Ace*, to be shot in Atlanta and Charlotte, North Carolina. Directed by Hal Needham and based on a novel called *Stand On It*, by William Neely and Robert Ottum (with a script by Hugh Wilson), it was the story of a stock car race driver (played, of course, by Burt), his gang of Southern buddies (which included Jim Nabors and my old "date" John Byner), his money-grubbing sponsor (Ned Beatty), and the spiffy public relations director, played by me. Bubba Smith and Parker Stevenson rounded out the group.

It was to be my first feature film, and I'd be fibbing if I said I wasn't excited about it. Contrary to some people's version of how it came about, I didn't beg, plead, or blackmail Burt for the part—it was his idea, and I had to read for it. I had hopes, of course, that it might lead to good things for me, and if those good things included more features, then great. If not, well, I still had a healthy television career. At the very least, it meant I wouldn't be separated from Burt the rest of the summer.

Initially it looked like it was going to be a good time. Most of the filming was done in and around Atlanta, and Burt and I rented a house on a lake, about twenty minutes from the set. We also planned to spend weekends in a house he had bought some years before, up in the mountains of North Carolina. But right away there were problems.

To begin with, August in the South is hot. Long, hot, blindingly bright sunny days, with humidity that raised hell with my hair and everybody's disposition. The racing scenes were done at the Charlotte Motor Speedway in North Carolina, a "set" that was a real raceway, with real stock cars, real drivers, engines racing, oil smoking, tires screeching, and men, sweating and scratching and swearing. Oh, it was silver-screen glamour, all right.

And one night, after a particularly tough grit-in-your-teeth kind of day, my sweetheart threw himself on the couch, moaning, "Oh, God, I'm so exhausted. Flat-out exhausted. Hey, kid, so what's for dinner?"

I was collapsed in the chair right across the room from him. I had gotten up at four that morning, he had gotten up at five. We had both been on the set all day. It was now seven P.M.

"Excuse me?" I said. "Gee, B.R., I don't know. What *is* for dinner?" Right after that, we got somebody in to cook for us.

We each had our own motor home on the set, with a dressing room, small kitchen, and bathroom. Within a few days Burt started complaining about what was going on in mine. My makeup and hair people were friends, and Robin, Ross's sister, was my wardrobe person, so, of course, we spent a lot of downtime laughing and talking. Gossiping. And Burt would come stomping in with this look and the questions: Who are you talking to? Why are you laughing? Why are you staying in here, what were you doing? Why aren't you over here, by me?

I couldn't understand what was going on with him, why he was such a grump with me all the time. Maybe, I thought, it's just because it's the first time we've worked together. Or maybe movie sets are more serious than what I was used to after the *WKRP* years.

During the shoot, Deidra came to visit for a few days. She had been going through a rough time with her boyfriend, Bobby, and she needed to talk some things through with me. But the very first night she arrived, Burt just snapped and started shouting at her, impatient and touchy about her problems and the amount of time I was spending with her.

The language Burt used, the snarl in his voice, and the speed at which his rage accelerated caught both Deedee and me totally by surprise. In minutes she was dissolved in tears, I was standing between them, and then suddenly he was on the floor, clutching his chest in pain, saying he thought he was having a heart attack.

Burt's assistant Pete had to be called, and once I got Deedee settled down in the guest room, I went into our room to talk to Burt, who seemed to have calmed down a little himself. And that's when I discovered that he was taking pills again. I couldn't believe what I was seeing.

"Honey, why are you doing this?" I asked, struggling to keep my voice steady. "Why, after all the hell we went through?"

"I can handle it," he insisted. "It won't be like it was. I can keep things under control, if you help me. But I need to take them, just while we're doing the picture. After that, I won't need them anymore."

He was under pressure, he said. There were stunts on this picture, a lot of them, and he was once again doing his share. Whatever was going on, something was stirring up the demons.

Later Burt tried to smooth things over with Deedee, but the scene had unnerved her—as it had me—and I decided the next day that maybe it would be better for her if she went back to California.

A few days later, we were driving back from the set to the lake house, Burt's two assistants, Pete and Jim, in the front seat, us in the back, all of us talking about another movie that was being made in the area. I mentioned something about an actor who was in it, something I had remembered reading in the trades about him. Burt said, "Do you know him?"

"No," I said, "I've never met him."

And he said, "You're lying to me. I know you know him, and you're lying to me." He reached over and took hold of my wrist and started to twist it. And he kept twisting.

It felt like my wrist was on fire. I tried not to make a sound, because of the two guys in the car. He's going to break it, I thought. Finally I let out a cry of pain. Neither one of the guys in the front seat even turned around.

When we got to the house, I think I was in some kind of shock. He had broken all the skin around the wrist, and it was sprained and bleeding. Standing in front of the refrigerator, shaking, fumbling with the freezer trays, I tried to get some ice on it. I kept thinking, I'm filming tomorrow.

When I went into the bedroom to lie down, he came in after me and started sobbing. He was begging my forgiveness. And he nursed my wrist for the rest of the night, icing it, wrapping cloths around it, while he cried and apologized. Finally he cried himself to sleep. I never closed my eyes.

I thought it was a onetime thing. He had never physically abused me before, I had never felt threatened by him. Oh, sure, when we fought, he would yell and scream, but once I understood about the pills, I thought that was where all the rage came from. Besides, he was a big, powerful, physical guy, and that's what big, powerful, physical guys do—they yell and scream, and they flex their muscles. So I believed this was a onetime explosion, between a man and a woman who were tired and who loved each other. It was about passion. He was jealous, so he lost control. It happens.

The next day the wrist had to be made up, and I wore a wide bracelet to hide the discoloration. Robin took one look at it and knew immediately what had happened.

"He's crazy," she said, shaking her head.

"No," I said. "He just loves me." He does, I thought. He does love me.

Another night, Burt was finished shooting first, so he drove up to the mountain house ahead of me, with his driver. When I was done, I drove up with my driver, Becky, and Robin came with us. The trip was about four hours, and we were starving, so we grabbed some fast-food burgers and ate them on the way up. When we walked in the door, Burt was fuming. We were late, he said, and extremely inconsiderate for having eaten.

Once I got into the bedroom, he began yelling in such a fury that the veins stood out on his forehead. He came toward me, yelling, with his hands outstretched. He wasn't swinging, he was just coming toward me. And then he lunged.

Almost a head shorter than he is, I had a momentary advantage. I ducked and wheeled around, running into the bathroom and locking the door behind me. At first he pounded on the door, screaming obscenities. And then, finally, he burst into tears, sobbing, asking me to forgive him. Finally, as he quieted down, I unlocked the door and came out. He was completely spent. And so I held him. I didn't know what else to do.

When we finished that shoot, I went back to Los Angeles, Burt went to Florida, and we were estranged. Not in any formal way, no big statements of intent, just . . . estranged. All fall there was great tension between us, and long silences between phone calls. But there was no ease, no comfort, when we did talk.

I had enough to keep me busy. Some voice looping to do on *Country Gold,* and getting Deidra through her senior year. I did a little redecorating at the Alomar house. I read a lot. I took a good look at myself in the mirror and started working out, with Mike Abrums, a trainer Burt had been working with for years.

All my life, when I'm under any kind of stress, I start to lose weight (in the wrong places) and lose muscle tone as well. And I hit the junk food, with a special emphasis on malted milk balls and glazed doughnuts. When you're sixteen, you can rebound from that kind of stuff; once you're past thirty, recovery doesn't come quite so easily. And it shows up on film. I quickly learned to trust the legendary Magic Mike, who's been transforming Hollywood bodies for decades.

When Burt returned from Florida, we started seeing each other again. We were cautious around each other at first, and watchful of what we said and did. But slowly things seemed to get back on track. He was gentle, affectionate. We spent quiet time with friends. I began to relax.

Burt owned an amazing house outside Atlanta. It looked just like *Gone with the Wind*'s Tara, which is why, of course, he called it Tara. It had three stories, a wide wraparound veranda, and big white columns. He decided it might be fun if we spent Christmas—our first one together—in the house and invited some other people to join us. Deidra and her boyfriend, Bobby, Jim Nabors and his friends Stan and Judy, and Jim's Hawaii neighbor, Doris Duke.

I went down ahead of time to begin the preparations. I planned to do all the cooking myself, but I wanted to hire someone to wash dishes and clean up. I took Harry, Burt's houseman from Carolwood, and Lamar Jackson, his longtime personal assistant, with me. Burt said the house was completely furnished and that I'd find everything I needed.

Well, it was furnished, all right. With furniture and nothing else. He had taken the set furniture from *Sharky's Machine* (hardly antebellum period pieces . . .) and moved it all into Tara. But there was not one pot, not one pan. Not a fork. No sheets, no towels, no toilet paper. The cupboards, literally, were bare. Even the mice were stunned. I had three days not just to put together a Christmas celebration, but to put together the house itself I phoned Burt in a panic. "Do whatever you have to do, kid," he said. "Carte blanche. See you in a couple days."

I called Ed Spivey, the head of Atlanta's film commission, and he and his son helped me enormously. I made up an inventory of household goods (six bedrooms) and menus (three meals a day) for the entire week we were all going to be there. With lists in hand (and I think somebody might have had a stopwatch), my team and I hit every shopping center and department store in Atlanta. At one point all of us were in a checkout line with a combined platoon of nine shopping carts. It was like a Marx Brothers movie; when we weren't out of breath, we were laughing hysterically. It was one of the funniest, most exhausting productions I've ever been a part of. And we pulled it off.

By the time everyone got there, the house was a showplace. We even had a real tree, decorated with ornaments Burt and I had bought in the Christmas shops in North Carolina. I was so proud of myself, Helen Housewife, magically producing a Christmas extravaganza for the people she loved. When Burt arrived, he just kind of strolled in, not quite understanding why I was grinning so maniacally. I cooked all the meals (and blessed the two girls from town who cleaned up after me), and we had a fire in the fireplace, and we sang carols and had a wonderful, wonderful time. Even B.R. had to admit he enjoyed himself.

Afterward, Deedee and Bobby and Burt and I drove up to the house in North Carolina for a couple of days, because there was snow in the mountains and we wanted to play. And then we flew to Florida for what was to become our annual tradition—a second Christmas, on the ranch with Burt's parents.

And here things got quite strange again. Once we were all settled, Burt announced that he had decided Deidra and Bobby wouldn't be coming to dinner at his parents' house. He didn't even want them to meet Fern and Burt senior.

"It's too upsetting for them to meet new people," he said.

"Burt, these two aren't 'new people,'" I said, trying to be patient with what I was sure was a misunderstanding. "They're my daughter and her boyfriend."

He shook his head. "No, you have to understand, my parents are too old. Logan will make sure the kids get fed and have a good time. He'll give them a tour of the ranch, they can ride the ATVs or the horses. They'll be just fine." And that's all there was to it.

And I went along with it. I bit my tongue and didn't fight with him. And then I saw how many people were sitting around the dinner table: Burt senior and Fern, Burt's Aunt Edna, his sister, Nancy Ann, and her two children, Nancy Lee and Richie, and Richie's wife, Debbie, and their two-year-old, Brian, and Debbie's whole family. It looked like a *Saturday Evening Post* cover. And it was no place to start a fight.

At the end of dinner, I said to Fern, "I have to excuse myself now. My daughter and her boyfriend are here, and I'd like to spend some time with them."

And she said, "Well, my goodness, where are they? We didn't even get to meet them!"

When I tracked down Deedee and Bobby, I discovered that Logan hadn't fed them anything, and they were famished. Whether he had dropped the ball or Burt had, whatever was supposed to happen didn't happen. We managed to get them some hamburgers, but it was all pretty stupid. I was so angry, at Burt, at myself. And so was Deidra, and she let me know it. I should have either insisted that they come to dinner or not gone myself. She never forgave him after that. He could never get her back, no matter what he did, and believe me he tried everything. He even gave her a car for college, a cream-colored 450 SL Mercedes convertible. But she gave it right back to him.

"The Datsun Mom got me when I was sixteen is just fine, thanks," she said.

Our whole first year together had been a roller coaster, and now 1983 looked like more of the same. Bumpy. Edgy. I hadn't worked since we finished *Stroker Ace*. I had house payments and a daughter preparing for college. I had an agent and a manager and a secretary to pay. I worked in a profession (and a town) in which I had to maintain a certain level of presentation, of appearance. Hair, clothes, visits to a gym or a trainer, a staff. Realistically, an actor's appearance is the product—it has to be maintained. And it's no secret that in Hollywood, women pay a higher price than men do if they *don't* maintain it.

I had received some bad news about my finances. While I was married to Ross and he was managing our money, he had hired a business manager. I assumed Ross was paying attention; Ross assumed the business manager was paying attention. And the business manager was taking us both to the cleaners. Flush with the first big money either of us had ever seen, we had behaved like we were the Mom-and-Pop Acting Shop or something—not an uncommon story in Hollywood. Is there a secret club of accountants and managers who send up the word every time the wide-eyed out-of-towners arrive? "*Psst*, look, over there: hayseed with a series deal."

Not only did the shady business manager pocket a considerable chunk of the money I had earned during the *WKRP* years, he also neglected to stay in touch with the IRS. The only thing we could figure was that although Ross and I had signed our forms, he had never mailed them or the checks that should've gone with them. The result: Between back taxes and penalties, I owed close to a million dollars.

There had been no windfall from *WKRP* for the cast, just our weekly salaries—that series had come too soon for the big syndication deals that made millionaires out of later sitcom casts. The IRS had cut me some slack on the payment schedule, but nobody was giving an inch on the amount. I had to find work.

And now Burt was telling me who I could and couldn't work with, which actors, which directors. I should change agents, change managers, get rid of all the people I'd always had.

Although he had been working out regularly with Magic Mike and wasn't drinking, he had started to get puffy. His meals were always Southern-fried, don't-spare-the-gravy. That, along with the prescription drugs, was working against him.

He was taking pills constantly, and his moods were becoming more unpredictable. For days on end, he would lie in bed, in a darkened room, having massive anxiety attacks. Which he was always certain were heart attacks. But he'd had heart workups before—Dinah had even taken him for one—and no one had ever found medical evidence of any heart trouble. He didn't want me to leave his side, but I couldn't talk him into seeing a new doctor or discussing the pills. He had his Dr. Feelgoods. He wanted what he wanted, and he listened to no one.

He began to get nasty, insulting. He wasn't loving; there was no romance in our lives at all. Our lovemaking was becoming practically nonexistent. And I couldn't do anything right. Once I bought something from Trashy Lingerie and walked into the bedroom wearing it, halfway giggling, halfway anxious about his reaction. I wanted desperately for him to laugh and to hold me.

"What the hell do you think I am?" he snapped. "A stud service?" Some of the things he accused me of that night were more a tribute to his imagination than to anything else.

I knew that something terrible was happening to him. And it was rooting into our life, becoming permanent. One night, I just packed up my things and went back to Alomar. Burt was leaving soon for Arizona to do a film anyway, so I decided to take a break. Or make a break. I couldn't decide which.

I had been scheduled to do a movie in a couple of months, in Detroit. It was called *Fast Eddie*, and my costar was to be my old friend Bob Hays. We had been talking on a regular basis, so he knew what my situation was. Burt and I hadn't spoken for a couple of weeks, and I was in a funk. I was pretty sure we were over.

"You've got to stop moping around," Bob said. "I have to get you out of this house."

"Oh, I don't know," I said. "I just don't feel like it."

"I have an idea," he said. "Come with me to Hollywood Park."

"Well, I sure don't feel much like a picnic," I told him.

He laughed. "Loni, where have you been? Hollywood Park is a racetrack!"

There's a lovely VIP lounge and restaurant at Hollywood Park, with a panoramic view of the track, and we were there as guests of Howard Koch, the producer of Bob's two *Airplane!* movies. When the elevator doors opened and I looked across the room, there was Burt. Not only was he not in Arizona, he was at Hollywood Park. Dinah was with him, and Cary and Barbara Grant.

Bob Hays had just done a play at Burt's theater in Florida and wanted to go right over and talk to him about it. I froze up. "Please don't," I said. "I don't want a scene."

"A scene?" Bob asked. "Why should there be a scene? I just want to thank him for a good time in Jupiter."

I knew that made sense. I also knew that my close friendship with Bob—and in turn, its connection with Ross—had always made Burt nuts.

Our tables were on separate tiers; I could look down and see Burt, he could look up and see me. We spent the entire day trying to look anywhere but at each other. In fact, Burt was so uncomfortable that when he had to use the VIP men's room (he would've had to go right past our table to get to it), he left the restaurant with Cary Grant and went to the public rest room instead. And the two of them, of course, were instantly mobbed. The whole thing was impossibly silly.

That night my phone rang and rang. I would pick it up and hear a click as the other person hung up. After about the tenth time it happened, I called Burt's house.

Before he even got a chance to say hello, I said, "Are you calling me and hanging up?"

"Is he there?" he asked.

"No, he isn't," I said. "He's my friend and took me out because I was moping around the house. Should I be asking if Dinah's there?"

"She isn't," Burt said. "She's my friend and just wanted to get me out of the house."

Then silence.

"Loni," he said, "can I come over?"

It had been a fight, we decided. It had been a fight that had gone too far, nothing more, and we belonged together. We wouldn't ever fight like that again, we both promised. And he wouldn't take so many pills, he pledged. I loved him and wanted to believe him. So I did.

The cast and crew of *Fast Eddie* headed for Detroit for preproduction and rehearsals. No sooner had we arrived than the producers ran out of money. That was the end of *Fast Eddie*.

Just before I left L.A., I had gone in for my annual gynecological exam. And was told I had six fibroid tumors, at least one of which was as large as a grapefruit. I'd had no symptoms, no pain, no swelling. In fact, I was thinner than I'd been in years; my stomach was completely concave. But since the exam the year before had found nothing, it meant that the fibroids had grown very fast, which was cause for concern. My doctor said that although fibroids were ninety-nine percent benign, I would have to have all mine removed. The surgery would be done under general anesthesia, with some hospital time and some recovery time; these days it would possibly be an outpatient procedure done with laser surgery. And the doctor warned me that, depending on what they found, there was a chance they might have to do a hysterectomy.

When *Fast Eddie* didn't happen, it put the surgery and its ramifications on the top of my list. "I want to have children with you," Burt told me. "If everything's OK, I want us to have children."

I discussed the surgery with my doctor and signed a waiver just in case everything was not OK. But I told him what our hopes were, that if I was healthy, Burt and I would like to try to have a child together. After all, I was only thirty-seven at the time.

The doctor had asked me not to work for eight weeks after the operation and to plan on doing nothing more athletic than walking to the mailbox for the first ten days. My mom was going to come up from Arizona to stay with me for a while. And then, just a day or two before I was to go into the hospital, Burt said he was going to Florida.

"But what about my surgery?" I said.

"I just can't handle seeing you like that," he said. "Besides, your mom will be here."

Oh, hello, I thought. Not really good in a crisis, I see. Well, if he's going to be nuts, then fine, I can't handle him, either.

After the surgery—and the happy discovery that there was no need for a hysterectomy—the doctor said that as far as he could tell, I was in perfectly good health and able to conceive. I called Burt and told him, "I'm going to be just fine. We can start on this baby thing anytime you want."

He was ecstatic and decided to send me to Hawaii to recuperate, accompanied by his niece, Nancy Lee, who's just a few years younger than I am. The third week after surgery, Mom went back to Arizona, and Nancy Lee and I flew to Hawaii, where we stayed at Jim Nabors' house and were treated like royalty. When I got home, Burt called from Florida and said, "Now come to Valhalla, kid, and we'll wait on you hand and foot here, too."

True to his word, he spoiled me rotten. He was tender and dear, coming in each night with flowers and gifts. I was beginning to feel like the Princess and the Pea. Sleeping late and reading in the sunshine beside Hawaiian oceans and Florida pools was certainly a lovely way to recover from a trip to the hospital, but now I hadn't worked in a year. In my whole life I had never gone so long without work. *Fast Eddie* had fallen through, and my financial problems weren't going away.

Three or four days after I arrived in Florida, my agent called about a TV movie. Farrah Fawcett was supposed to do it, but for some reason she had dropped out at the last minute. They were a week from shooting; was I interested? I certainly was.

My Mother's Secret Life was about a high-class call girl whose sixteen-year-old daughter shows up on her doorstep. I always called it "The Hooker Mother Story." It meant I had to go to San Francisco, where it was being shot, immediately. There would be a break over Thanksgiving; Burt and I planned to be together in Los Angeles for the holiday.

During our time apart, Burt called me on the set three times a day. Roses came, with the dear, familiar message: Roses suit you so. I loved being back at work and felt healthier every day, more and more myself. When it came time for the break and my reunion with Burt, I was happier than I'd been in a long time, and eager to see him.

We had one terrific night together, tender and romantic. We made love, laughed, and very tentatively started sneaking up on the idea of having a baby. And then, while I was in the shower, he started going through my bureau drawers. I could hear him out there, rummaging around, the drawers opening and closing.

When I walked into the bedroom—we were at the Alomar house, my house—he was pulling things out of my bedside table. My current datebook, the old ones ("lunch with Gary," for instance), old cards and letters, things I'd been stuffing in there and just hadn't thrown out yet. He started shouting at me. Who had I been with? What had I been doing while he was away working?

And then he grabbed me so hard around my upper arms that for two weeks afterward I had angry finger bruises where his hands had been. He shook me, pushed me, and finally slammed me up against the wall.

I couldn't catch my breath. Thank God no one else is in the house, I thought. I tried to talk to him. Didn't he know how much I loved him? How I had missed him? This was a reunion that had been months in coming, because of my surgery and our work separations. I had seen no one else, talked to no one else, been with no one. Why didn't he believe me?

As usual, he soon dissolved in tears and begged my forgiveness. He went out and bought me diamonds. For the next two days, we walked on eggshells, then he went back to Florida, and I went back to work. Where it suddenly hit me: I was in the middle of shooting a movie in which I had to wear negligees, lingerie, strapless gowns. My arms were a mess, and my back was scraped from when he had shoved me up against the wall. High-class hookers don't wear long-sleeved sweatshirts, at least not on television. I had to have body makeup, a lot of it.

I lied to the makeup people. "I tripped and fell down the stairs," I told them. "Thank goodness, he grabbed me as I was falling."

Linda Jensen was there with me and says now that she always knew what was going on and wanted to say something. But she decided that when I was ready to talk about it, I would. And in the meantime, if I needed to keep my own counsel, she would respect my silence.

For the rest of the shoot I kept myself covered when I could, and in the scenes that were somewhat bare, I wore makeup. My feelings were all over the place. It was finally sinking in that this was no onetime thing. It was a pattern. He was in trouble—*we* were in trouble—and I had no idea what to do about it.

Chapter 11

A week or so after I finished filming *My Mother's Secret Life,* Karen Valentine called me at home and said, "I can't wait to see you on our trip to Florida."

I liked Karen and her husband, they were part of the group of people Burt and I saw quite frequently. But I was confused by what she was saying. "I'm not sure what you're talking about," I said.

"Oh, you know," she said. "The premiere for *The Man Who Loved Women.* Burt said he's got the plane chartered and everything, we're all going down there together."

I had absolutely no idea what Karen was talking about and told her so. She was clearly taken aback. "I'm so embarrassed," she said. "I don't know what to say. Are you guys having trouble or something?"

"I don't know what to say to *you,*" I said. "I don't have any idea what's going on."

I immediately called Burt in Florida, where he was finishing production work on *Stick,* and told him about Karen's call. "Honey, am I supposed to be pulling a party together or something?" I asked.

There was a moment of silence, and then he said, "I've been talking to Sally Field. And we've decided to give it another try.

She loves me more than you will ever love me, and she will always be there for me. I know now that I belong with Sally."

So there it was. I don't know who initiated it, or when—maybe it had happened over Thanksgiving, maybe it had been going on for months. Or maybe he had been juggling us both all along. Whatever, it was clear I wasn't going to be a passenger on the party plane. And the other people who *would* be on that plane—did they all know about this?

And then, of course, the tabloids picked up the story and ran with it. He's down there filming, and she's in evidence on the set, everyone is lovey-dovey, and supposedly they're finally getting married. I went to the refrigerator and took out a bottle of champagne, sat down on the living room couch, and drank the whole thing.

No one but my mother knew that he had asked me to marry him and that I had said yes. And no one *anywhere* knew what we had been through a couple of weeks before. What, I wondered, had the last two years been about?

Somehow I got through Christmas. Deedee came home and brought Bobby. The Jensens were there in force: Linda and her husband, Allen Madison, her sister, Patty, and Jeanne and her beau, Al. We put up a tree. And I've always bought presents year-round and stored them away, so being a zombie didn't keep me from being able to give gifts.

There was a big *WKRP* reunion Christmas party—I went with some trepidation. With the state I was in, I was profoundly grateful when Gary Sandy didn't show up to witness it. After what I'd done to him, he might've been justified in gloating.

And then some light glimmered at the end of the tunnel. For some time, Lynda Carter and I had been talking about working together, and now NBC had given Johnny Carson's production company a green light for us to do thirteen episodes of *Partners in Crime*, scheduled for the fall 1984 season. Leonard Stern, who had written for Jackie Gleason's *The Honeymooners* and *The Steve Allen Show*, as well as being the creator, head writer, and producer of the entire six-year run of Rock Hudson and Susan Saint James' *McMillan and Wife*, was going to be writing and directing it.

165

Partners was planned as a high-style female *Hart to Hart*. Lynda and I thought we would have a great time. And the money was very good—I would finally be able to work myself out of the IRS debt. Location shooting was to be done in San Francisco, starting in April. With that to look forward to, I thought, I will get through the rest of the holidays. I *will*.

A few days before New Year's, my phone rang, and it was Burt, calling from Florida.

"I've made a terrible mistake," he said. I knew immediately that I never should have answered the phone standing up—I should've found a place to sit down first.

"Loni?" he said. "Did you hear me? I love you, I want you back."

He wanted me to come down to Jupiter for New Year's, and there we could talk it through, we could make a fresh start. In fact, he said, it was really just like in *Starting Over,* when his character was confused and went back to the old love, then discovered that he really loved "the other one." I, evidently, was the other one.

Quite simply, I was astonished. "Do you have any idea what you've put me through?" I asked. "I have no intention of coming down there."

"But I love you, kid. I know that now," he said. "And I want to make it up to you, if you'll let me."

Do I believe this man, I asked myself? Or do I believe Sally just walked out on him, and now he doesn't know what to do?

"I don't want to see you," I said. "Maybe later, I don't know. I don't know how I feel, but I do know that I don't trust you. For now, you have to just let me be."

The phone kept ringing over the next few hours, but I let the service pick it up. I didn't have any intention of giving him the opportunity to talk me into something I didn't want to do.

I had been a passenger in two serious automobile accidents when I was younger, one in high school, one in college, and both had left me feeling exactly as I did now. Bruised and nauseated. My whole body ached. I couldn't stop going over the past two years, second-guessing everything I had said and done since our first day together. The more I thought about it, the angrier I became. I hadn't felt loved or desired for months. And now this man wanted me to come back to him, to trust him, and to start all over again. I wasn't sure I could do that. I wasn't sure I even knew how.

Mr. X from Fashion Square was no longer an anonymous commercial face. In the eight years since our first heart-stopping encounter, he had become a well-known television actor—let's call him Paul. And in the course of things, Paul and I had become friends, and we soon discovered we had friends in common.

I had never told Burt about the meeting at the mall and the second one at the Super Bowl. They had both happened before we got involved, and Burt didn't like hearing those stories, no matter how harmless and amusing they may have been.

But I did tell Paul about them, one night when Burt was out of town on location and a group of us were all having dinner together. He remembered the incidents but hadn't realized that I had been the woman in both of them, particularly the brunette at Fashion Square. We had a good laugh about it.

"You know," he said, "if you wrote those two scenes and put them in a movie—and then added the part where we became friends later—some critic would say it was too improbable."

After that, it became a connection between us, almost like a secret. I was with someone I loved; he was, too. But we could grin at each other across a room, at a party or a benefit, thinking about the secret. It didn't feel dangerous; it felt sexy and fun.

One afternoon after the Burt-and-Sally-reunion-that-wasn't, Paul and I ran into each other on the street. He had seen the tabloids and heard the gossip around town. When I told him the rest of the story, he put his arm around my shoulder and said, "I'm so sorry that you're going through this. What can I do to help?"

"Take me out to dinner," I said. And so he did.

All that evening I felt like my skin was shooting sparks. As angry and hurt as I had been when I first ran into Paul, the last thing I was feeling as we sat across a table from each other was vulnerable. In fact, I was thinking something along the lines of "I am woman, hear me roar."

I wanted to feel strong, beautiful, desirable. And I knew with absolute certainty that there would come a moment when we would have to make a decision, or perhaps an entire series of them. To linger a little over the wine. To prolong our good nights. To kiss each other, at first with genuine affection, and then with something stronger. To make love. And after that, what?

All he had to do after dinner was put his hand over mine, and it was done. The only decision was "Where?" I couldn't bear to go back to my house, so we went to his.

I can't deny that at first, for me, it was, "Take that, Burt!" But in minutes there was only the man in my arms, and we were the only two people on earth. It wasn't about anybody else. It was about flesh and bodies and imagination and pure pleasure. Somewhere in the middle of the night, with the sheets in a tangle and moonlight streaming in through a window, Paul whispered, "I never thought this would happen. I've pictured it and known it was impossible, and yet here we are. And I'm so glad."

I was pretty glad myself. I was completely out of breath and so happy I could have giggled out loud. In fact, I think I did. He was passionate and generous—there wasn't a nerve in my body he hadn't awakened, not an inch of skin he hadn't touched. Every postcoital cliché rang true: I felt fabulously alive, primitively sexual, seriously giddy. I felt like I could run the Los Angeles Marathon in my bare feet. Or sleep for a week.

The other postcoital cliché, of course, is that no matter how magical the night is, eventually morning comes. The actual morning, when the sun comes up and bodies and bed linens get rearranged. The wake-up-and-smell-the-responsibility morning, when two people look at each other and say, "Now what happens?"

We knew that if I walked away from my relationship and he walked away from his, we would probably be great together. It wouldn't have been difficult to turn this into a real love affair. We liked each other, a lot. We had many things in common and kept finding more. And what had just happened between us sexually had probably gone off Cal Tech's Richter scale. For added mischief, between the two of us we could've given the tabloids a run for their money and merrily tortured a few network executives. At the very least it might have been fun, and there had been precious little fun in my life lately.

But people would have been hurt. A woman Paul had begun to love, a man I had loved for two years and wasn't yet ready to leave behind me. Something that had given us both great joy was capable of causing a huge, painful mess. Could we do that?

No, we decided, we couldn't. We agreed that what had happened between us was a great gift but not a relationship. And so we made a pact: We would never be together again. In the years since, we have seen each other often, he with his family and I with mine. We still grin, and remember. The connection is still there. So is the pact.

If that was infidelity, given the state of my relationship with Burt at the time, then throw me in the stocks in the town square. But it was the only time in all our years together that I ever turned to another man, and I do not regret it.

In February 1984 Burt called me at home and asked if I would please come to Carolwood to see him. We hadn't seen each other since Thanksgiving, although we had been talking on the phone. Negotiating, I guess. I was feeling strong and healthy and pretty independent. It was time for us to decide what, if anything, came next for us.

From the minute I arrived at the house, it was clear to me that he wasn't well. He had lost weight and looked tired. His jaw had been injured when he was working on *City Heat* with Clint Eastwood, and the pain was becoming chronic. Every instinct I had was to reach out to him, hold him, and promise to help him get better. But I waited.

At first we began talking quietly. But then he became more and more agitated, and in minutes he was sobbing. And then, suddenly, he took a gun out of a drawer and held it to his head. "If you don't stay with me," he cried, "I'll kill myself."

Oh, my God, I thought, this has gone too far. It had gone further than either of us had ever intended. I did love him, I had no question about that, and I wasn't ready to walk away from him. He needed me. But I still didn't know if I could trust him. I agreed that yes, we could try to work it out.

"We'll go away," he said. We would go to Acapulco and be alone.

MGM owned a beautiful house in Las Brisas, overlooking the bay, a huge place with servants galore, an endless video library, a screening room, pool, and tennis courts. Burt had made a lot of money for that studio, and they made the house available to him. We flew down together on the MGM private jet.

The setting was magical, and I felt so hopeful when we arrived, believing that the sun, as well as the peace and quiet, would be wonderful for both of us. But Burt was agitated, distracted. After a day or two he called Georgie and Ricardo Montalban and asked them to come down and join us. They were delighted and said they would be down in three or four days. As much as I loved them, I was glad they couldn't come right away.

There were servants at the house during the day, and a cook who left each evening after preparing dinner. One night just before he left, the cook mentioned that in case we wanted a snack while we were watching movies, he had made a batch of fudge brownies and left them in the refrigerator.

Later that night as we were watching a video, I said, "I'm hungry. There must be a brownie in that kitchen with my name on it."

Burt said he was hungry, too. So we put the movie on hold, went into the kitchen, poured two glasses of milk, grabbed the pan of brownies, and went back to the movie. He ate one. I ate one. They were really good. He ate another one.

Burt cuddled up next to me and started kissing my neck. It tickled, and I giggled a little, and then suddenly we were kissing ardently, passionately. And it was clear we weren't going to stop at kissing. We were making love, real love, and I was so happy, I started to tell him something important. Something crucially romantic, or was it romantically crucial? And I just stopped. Went completely blank.

"Sweetheart, what was I just going to say?" I asked.

He shook his head. "I have no idea."

Then he started to laugh. And I started to laugh. We went back to what we were doing. And then the earth moved!

I was ecstatic! What had just happened between us was totally thrilling, totally new, and I was just so delighted I wanted to break into a chorus of "My Boyfriend's Back." "Buddy Lee," I said, "I think we should come to Acapulco more often."

"Honey," Burt said, grinning slowly, "those brownies are loaded."

"*Hmmm?*" I cooed. "What do you mean?"

He was laughing. "I mean grass, Loni. Marijuana. They're full of it."

Oh, my God! "What?" I half shrieked. "Burt, what's going to happen to me?"

As fast as the euphoria had hit, it was gone. I was absolutely horrified, completely freaked out. I had never even smoked a joint, let alone eaten one. I started babbling, and then I lost my train of thought again. Then suddenly I was launched into a crying jag.

Burt patted me on the back, but I wasn't paying any attention to him. All I knew was I had eaten marijuana. Devil weed. I fully expected that body parts would start falling off any second. I crawled on my hands and knees to the bathroom. And then I crawled back and climbed into bed, and that's the last thing I remember.

The next morning I woke up and said, "Where am I?" I had no clue. I looked around, and slowly I remembered. We're in Acapulco. Burt is right here beside me. I wonder what time it is. Uh, oh, it's eleven o'clock in the morning.

Cautiously I checked my vital signs. I felt OK. I had all my body parts. And then I carefully looked over to see how Burt was doing.

Next to me was a peacefully sleeping man, a half smile on his lips and a thin line of brown drool sliding down his chin onto the pillow.

"Burt?" I whispered. Then a little louder. "Burt? Honey, wake up." I shook him, then shook him again. Nothing. He was completely, soundly asleep. Out of it. And on the bedside table next to him, an empty brownie pan. Not one crumb. *Nada.*

And then the panic set in: I am in Mexico, I don't know much Spanish, the servants are in the house by now (they usually served breakfast by nine). And Burt is unconscious. His breathing was regular, his color was good. Well, OK, I thought, maybe all he needs is a couple more hours.

I got up, took a shower, put on my bathing suit, and then tried again to wake him up. No luck. I decided, maybe I'll just have a little lunch, some orange juice, a little toast, and maybe by the time I eat, he'll be awake.

I tried to explain to the servants, in a bad combination of English and Spanish, "Don't go in there, Mr. Reynolds doesn't feel well. Flu, maybe. Don't go into the room." And I said nothing whatsoever to the cook.

When I went back into the room mid-afternoon, he was still out. I didn't know what to do. So I called Linda in Los Angeles and explained to her what had happened.

"Don't panic," she said calmly. "Just keep an eye on his breathing and his color. He's just sleeping it off. You'd still be asleep, too, if you'd eaten all those brownies."

I spent the rest of the day going back and forth between the pool and our room. His breathing was fine. His skin felt the way it always felt, warm, not clammy. That night I told the cook that Mr. Reynolds was still under the weather, no need to fix anything for him, *no problema, gracias.* When I went to bed myself, I listened carefully to his breathing. Very quiet and gentle, in and out, in and out. Easy for *him* to be so damned relaxed, I thought.

The next morning he was still asleep. I called Linda again. Now it had been something like thirty-six hours. "What if this isn't sleep?" I said tearfully. "What if he's in a coma?" The last coma I'd had anything to do with had been my dad's; this wasn't quite the same thing, but it was serious nevertheless. I knew Burt's paranoia about doctors and hospitals and publicity. I touched his face. He felt all right; he looked all right. I decided to give him a little more time. He was just really, really sleeping.

By noon, my jaw was pretty tight, and the Montalbans were scheduled to arrive late that afternoon. Well, I thought, at least Ricardo speaks Spanish. If the world comes to an end here, he will take care of it for me. Everyone in Mexico adores him, and he will be appropriately godlike.

And then, like a prince in a fairy tale, Burt awoke from his slumber. But he was still kind of out of it, kind of high, and kind of amused with himself. He thought it was pretty funny that he had snoozed through a day and a half and scared me out of my wits, and that Ricardo and Georgie were due in a couple of hours. He took a quick shower, drank about a gallon of bottled water, and then cheerfully declared that he was going to the airport to pick them up. I tried to talk him out of it, suggesting that one of the staff could do it. But oh, no, he said, being ever so jolly and competent. He had decided to take one of those canopy-covered jeeps from the house—*Fantasy Island* transportation, how appropriate was that?—to pick them up. I declined to be his copilot, and after I watched him amble out to the car and drive off, I sat by the pool waiting for the inevitable police sirens.

When the three of them returned about an hour later, Georgie climbed out of the jeep and declared, "We are never, *ever* getting into a vehicle with this man again, not as long as we both live!"

I couldn't explain to them what had happened. Devout Catholics, they're very straitlaced, traditional people. They wouldn't have understood the funny part—I couldn't have done justice to it anyway—and they would have been frightened at the rest of the story. But over the next few days, Ricardo began to have a new expression on his gentle, handsome face, one of concern and some consternation.

When Burt had invited them down to join us, he had promised them we'd play tennis and go on excursions, but he was basically out of it for the rest of the week. He was taking pills to recover from his brownies, and we never went farther than the pool.

When we all flew home on the MGM plane, Burt slept the entire way. Ricardo looked out the window. Georgie sat next to me and took my hand.

It was hard for me even to look at her, or to listen to the kindness in her voice, without crying. Georgiana Montalban is one of the most gracious, generous women I have ever known, and one of the most beautiful. Orson Welles once told Burt (and this was coming from a man who had been married to Rita Hayworth) that Georgie was the most beautiful woman in Hollywood, perhaps even more beautiful than another legendary beauty, her own sister, Loretta Young. And what radiates from Georgie's face is a pale reflection of the genuine goodness inside her.

"Loni, we love Burt, and we love you," she said quietly. "We know there's something terribly wrong with him, and we don't know how to help. But you—you just cannot spend your life being his nurse."

All I could say was, "I don't know what to do."

Absent all the other behavior—the mood swings, his unpredictable rages, the fistfuls of pills—the brownie incident might've become funny. It might have been something we could've laughed about in our old age or something. And in fact, during the time that Burt was drug-free in the late eighties, he and I did laugh about it. We'd crack up every time someone asked, "Want a brownie?" But on that quiet trip back from Acapulco with the Montalbans, there was an undertone to the whole experience that made it hard for anyone to imagine laughter.

When we got home from Mexico, he was in serious trouble. The jaw pain had become unbearable, and through the years of pills, his body had developed such a tolerance for pain medication that nothing helped much anymore. He was either in pain, taking more pills, or sleeping it off. He didn't want to go out. The drapes were drawn; he couldn't tolerate noise or light. When he moved his head, he became nauseated. Almost anything he ate made him sick. What was going on with him was a combination of everything: his feelings about his health (which were never good or optimistic), the chemical soup inside him, and the very real pain in his jaw. And a body that no longer recovered quickly from any kind of abuse.

I began working on the series with Lynda Carter, flying up to San Francisco with Linda Jensen on Sunday nights, all three of us flying back down to Los Angeles on Friday night. It was especially hard to get out of San Francisco on Fridays, because at that time the last flight to Los Angeles was at ten-thirty P.M., and often we were on the set until two in the morning. So sometimes I flew in on Saturday mornings and left again on Sundays. Lynda Carter had married Washington banker and lawyer Robert Altman only a few months before, and he was flying from the capital to L.A. on weekends to be with her. What had looked like a good idea for both of us soon became incredibly difficult.

We were two weeks into shooting the opening two-hour episode, which was structured like a movie, and suddenly NBC fired Leonard Stern. Stern had created the series, he wrote it, he was directing it—he was the reason I was there. The series was owned by Johnny Carson's production company, but it was the network that fired Stern; I never did know exactly why.

Although they fired him as director, not from all the other hats he was wearing, he was so angry that he walked out on the whole project. And took the scripts for all thirteen episodes with him. And then his entire writing staff walked, too, in support of Leonard. To make matters more complicated, Leonard was quite disturbed that Lynda and I didn't walk as well. I was so stuck financially, the last thing I was in a position to do was take part in a solidarity job action. When Lynda and I left the set on that Friday night, completely frazzled, we didn't know who would be directing us or even if there would be a show to come back to on Monday.

The week before, my mother had been scheduled to go into the hospital in Arizona for some tests. She had been jaundiced-looking and tired and was afraid she had hepatitis. I had told her that if it was hepatitis, I wanted her to come live in the Alomar house. Jeanne Jensen and her beau, Al, had long since moved into the guest house, and although Deidra was living in her sorority house, she was around on weekends, so we would all be happy to nurse Mom back to health. The tests were to be done on Wednesday. She didn't call Wednesday or Thursday, and then everything hit the fan with Leonard and the writers on Friday. I was halfway home on the plane before I remembered I hadn't heard from Mom.

Linda Jensen reassured me. "Oh, she knows how busy you've been, Loni. She's probably just waiting until you get back home for the weekend to talk with you."

It was nearly midnight when we arrived at Carolwood. Linda asked if she could come in and make a quick phone call. When we went into the house, Burt, who was never up at that hour, was not only up, but dressed and being quite solicitous. He had heard the news about the staff walkouts, he said. "You've had a really rough day, Loni. Come on up and I'll tuck you in." I said good night to Linda, and we went upstairs.

When we got to our room, Burt said, "Honey, I need to talk to you."

I thought, oh, my God, he's going back to Sally again.

"Would you take this Valium, please?" Burt asked, holding out a pill with one hand and a glass of water with the other.

"Oh, for heaven's sake!" I snapped. "That's hardly the way to ease somebody into bad news!" But he was being gently insistent, and it had been such a lousy day. And clearly we weren't through with it yet, he was going to hit me with something. Oh, well, I thought, and took the pill.

"It's about your mom," Burt started.

"Oh, no," I said. "She's got hepatitis."

"No, that's not it," he said, putting his hand on my shoulder. "She's got cancer."

I couldn't believe it. "Where?" I asked.

"Liver and pancreas," he said. "They've told her she's got about six weeks."

Blindly I reached for the phone, but Burt stopped me. "She didn't call you in San Francisco, because she knew you had to finish out the week. And she doesn't want you to call her tonight.

It's past midnight anyway. She wants you to call her in the morning."

And then I turned around and saw Linda Jensen at the bedroom door. She had come in with me, and stayed downstairs to wait, because she knew. I just looked at the two of them. I couldn't even cry. I thought, I'm just going to die right now, because I can't stand the way this feels.

"Tomorrow morning," Burt said, "we will take care of this, together. I want you to try to sleep now, you're going to need all the rest you can get. And I'm going to be here for you, every step of the way." There was a strength in his voice I hadn't heard for months.

When I went downstairs the next morning, Burt, who usually never even dialed a phone himself, had already spoken with Michael Wayne, John Wayne's son, to find out about getting Mom into the John Wayne Cancer Center at UCLA. Michael, bless him, pulled whatever strings were necessary, and within hours Burt had chartered a jet, put Linda and me on it, and sent us to Arizona to get Mom.

When we got there, my mother was in shock. "The doctor just told me to come home and get everything in order," she said.

No way, I thought. No way, not again.

"Mother," I said as we packed her things, "this simply isn't going to happen. Burt's made all the arrangements, you're going into the Wayne center, and we're going to fight this."

By Saturday night we had her checked into the hospital.

My God, I thought the next morning, I'm supposed to go back to San Francisco tonight. When Linda called the *Partners* production office, they told her, "Well, we have to find a new director, it's not really clear what's going on here. So Loni's got a few days' break. Just stay there, and we'll let you know."

The oncologist, Dr. Kristian Storm, had decided to do exploratory surgery on Mom right away, to examine the tumors and see if anything could be done. Sometimes, at least with liver cancer, tumors can be removed and the liver has a good chance of repairing itself.

But not in this case. She had what they described as a sheeting tumor; it was layered instead of clumped and encompassed not just the liver but the pancreas as well. Dr. Storm said he had seen that kind of tumor only on the brain. It couldn't be removed. But they would try chemotherapy, and along with that an experimental procedure he had developed, hyperthermia, in which the body is warmed up to expand the tumor, making it more porous and therefore more receptive to the chemo.

When I talked to Mom after the surgery, I said, "It's your choice. And whatever you decide, I'll be your cheerleader. You've got a whole team of us, and we'll back you in whatever you want to do."

She wanted to fight it. "If they're saying there's a chance. . . ." She wasn't ready to quit.

Andrea flew in from Arizona. She was having a terrible struggle with Mom's diagnosis; she hadn't been able to be there for Dad because of her pregnancy, and all of the emotions from that time were hitting her now, doubling the pain and fear she felt. Deidra was thunderstruck, too. Safely involved in her college life, she might've been able to turn her back on Burt and me, but she couldn't walk away from her grandmother, her "other mother."

As for me, I had gone on autopilot. I had no emotions; I had simply put them away. Feeling was a luxury, or a risk, I couldn't afford. Everything was just too big. My man, my mother, my job, my finances, any kind of security. Plus, I knew what was waiting. We were going to fight this cancer, and we were going to lose. That truth was coming right at us, just like a runaway train, and if I allowed myself to feel it, I would have to spend the next few months on my knees.

Chapter 12

A few days later, I left my mother at the hospital and flew to San Francisco to go to work. Right after I left, Burt went back to bed in the darkened room, returning to what I had begun to think of as his Howard Hughes routine. The strength he had shown at Mom's diagnosis and the hustle and determination he had used to get her into the Wayne center within twenty-four hours were gone. I wouldn't see any of those qualities again for a very long time.

The *Partners in Crime* scene was in complete chaos. We finished the pilot, which was delightful because Leonard had done it, but after that, the hacks-of-the-week took over. From late spring until November 1984, Lynda Carter and I watched as our frothy, sophisticated, reasonably intelligent series became what we called "Kung Fu Warrior Women of the A-Team." What a disaster. Every week, there we were, hotfooting it through San Francisco in designer wardrobes and high-heeled boots, waving guns around and shouting "Freeze!" at each episode's one-dimensional villain. In that revolutionary season of *Kate and Allie* and *Cagney and Lacey,* we had quickly become nothing better than female action dolls with big hair.

On weekends we would flee San Francisco as soon as we could, she to her new husband (when his own increasingly difficult schedule allowed) and I to the two sickbeds that had become my life.

Burt did surface briefly, to get involved with a business venture, a restaurant in Fort Lauderdale called Burt & Jack's. Over the years, there had been a series of disasters with his Po' Folks chicken restaurant chain, failures that ended up in lawsuits and a loss of millions. But Burt & Jack's was primarily owned and run by an experienced restaurateur named Jack Jackson (and in fact it still exists today). The grand opening, scheduled for May, was going to involve a chartered jet and a list of Hollywood guests that included the Montalbans, the Borgnines, and Bob and Heather Urich. And Burt and me.

Although the two of us made it to Florida, we never made it to the restaurant opening itself. When we arrived at the hotel, Burt fell to the floor writhing in such pain that worrying about doctors, hospitals, and bad publicity never even crossed my mind. The doctor who examined him said he was passing a kidney stone and there was nothing anyone could do except let it happen. Ordinary pain pills didn't even make a dent in the pain, let alone allow him to sleep.

"Let's try something new," said the doctor. "Here, take this. It's guaranteed to put a horse to sleep." It was Halcion. The next day we flew back to Los Angeles.

Success with horses notwithstanding, the Halcion didn't put Burt to sleep. He had taken so much other stuff over the years, his metabolism just absorbed this new drug like it was so much sugar. But it did make the pain go, and he wasn't vomiting anymore. Halcion quickly became his drug of choice; he grew so enamored of it, he didn't notice—or didn't care—that he had become a zombie.

Lynda Carter was struggling with the same problems on *Partners* as I was, but throughout the next months I couldn't have asked for a more supportive friend and colleague. We never worked less than a fourteen-hour day, and some days went even longer. Four in the morning became routine. I was down to a hundred and two pounds. My hair was straw, and there were circles under my eyes that looked like manhole covers. I would look in the mirror and think, I am a hundred years old. "Just flood me with light," I said to the camera people.

Claiming a personal emergency and quitting the series was never an option for me. Time had run out on paying off the IRS, and I knew there would be round-the-clock private nurses to pay for when Mom ultimately left the hospital and came home. Finally I went to Johnny Carson in tears, to ask for help.

"I can't get out of San Francisco on Friday nights in time to catch a flight," I said. "My mom's dying, and Burt is ill, and I'm going back and forth between them like a Ping-Pong ball."

There was no way he could adjust the shooting schedule at that point. So he did something incredibly generous instead. Every Friday night he sent his own jet to pick us up. I still flew commercial on Sunday, but Johnny's plane waited for us on Friday nights, no matter how late we were, to bring us home.

They finally got Mom to a point with the chemo treatments that she began to leave the hospital for a few days or a week at a time. In fact, one weekend she even came up to San Francisco and stayed with me, and she went back to Minnesota briefly to visit her family as well. She was weak but game. Although she'd lost her hair, she felt encouraged and optimistic—and after she passed the original six-weeks death sentence, she treated every day like a bonus.

Tony, my old high school boyfriend, had settled in California, and he came to see Mom during one of the times she was out of the hospital and staying at my house. They had a wonderful visit—and, I suspect, swapped stories and commiserated about me.

My college love, Don, who had stayed in touch over the years, also came to see Mom during that time. They had a long talk about how hard she and Dad had been on him that long-ago day when they threatened to take Deedee away from me if I stayed with him.

"We were only doing what we thought was best for the two girls," she said to him. We had all grown up since then, of course, and Don knew that although she certainly wasn't looking for absolution, she did want him to understand. It was odd, and sad, to watch her putting her house in order that way.

My world had become a narrow triangle of Mom, Burt, and work. During the week I got maybe four hours of sleep a night. During lunch hours on most days, Lynda and I did publicity for the show, taping interviews, so very often we didn't even eat. I started taking limos all the time, even in Los Angeles, because I had gotten so robotic, I didn't trust my own driving. I had a driver named Sarge, and he ran me back and forth between my house, Burt's house, the hospital, and the airport. It was like having a large guardian angel.

In the meantime the Burt-and-AIDS rumors had started. Rock Hudson was diagnosed in the spring of 1984, and although he wasn't hospitalized until the following summer (and nothing was made officially public until his death in October), rumors about the cause of his weight loss and obvious ill health began to spill over onto anyone else who even had the flu. There were no red ribbons back in those days, no AIDS benefits. There was only panic, and innuendo.

And tabloid reporters were saying they had seen Burt in AIDS treatment centers all over the country. In Houston, in New York, nurses and doctors were reporting Burt sightings. And, in fact, he *was* in search of medical help, but for TMJ (temporomandibular joint) disorder, the result of the fractured jaw he'd suffered on the *City Heat* set. TMJ, the doctors said, created not only the considerable pain that Burt was suffering, but also the inner ear damage that threw his balance off and made him so sensitive to light. The years of prescription drug abuse and the new dependence on Halcion only added fuel to the fire. He had stopped taking Valium altogether but was taking fistfuls of the others: twelve to fifteen or more Percodan a day, at least two dozen Halcion, and Compazine as a mixer. He was becoming more and more reclusive and was losing weight dramatically.

From the very beginning Burt had said to me, "Don't let me end up like Elvis." Although they had met before Presley's death

In Florida with Burt's mother, Fern, 1988.

Here's a guy with a great grin! Joe Penny and me on the set of *A Whisper Kills,* just before my wedding in 1988.

With the Montalbans, 1990.

The suspender-sporting Reynolds family at Quinton's second birthday party, L.A., 1990.

Longtime pal and personal manager Linda Jensen and my lovely daughter, Deidra, Florida, 1990.

My sister, Andrea Sams, and her dear husband, Steve, L.A., 1990.

Linda Jensen and Linda Jensen's wig on B.R., Christmas in Florida, 1990.

B.R. and the "Kid" at the end-of-the-season wrap party for *Evening Shade,* L.A., 1991.

Big Burt and me, Florida, 1992.

Our gracious Hawaiian island host, Jim Nabors, 1992.

Santa and his helpers, Tahoe, 1992: Steve Sams; my nephew, Erik Sams; and my son-in-law, Charlie Hoffman.

Burt's sister, Nancy Ann, riding shotgun in Tahoe, 1992.

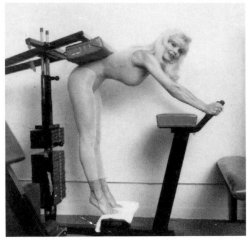

A tribute to Magic Mike's fine (and hard!) work. He keeps this one on his desk!

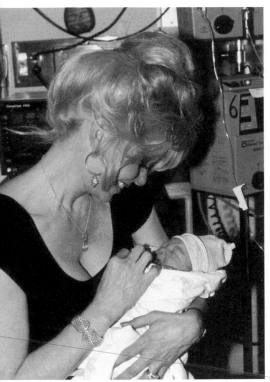

Gramma Loni meets McKenzie Kaye Hoffman about five minutes after Little Mack's arrival, Tahoe, 1993.

Burt with Robin Bickell McLaughlin, her daughter, Leanne, and Q., Florida, 1993.

Building sandcastles in Florida, May 1993.

Geoff Brown, my dear partner.

Geoff and I take Q. and my godson, Cary, to the Monterey Bay Aquarium, October 1993.

"Gramma Jeanne" Jensen and the Q-man in our breakfast room, 1994.

Cary and Quinton scaring Los Angeles, Halloween 1994.

Gramma Loni and McKenzie the Christmas Angel, Tahoe, 1994.

Geoff and me, New Year's Eve 1994.

Quinton (happily missing his first tooth) celebrates Nanny Sybil's birthday, L.A., spring 1995.

Quinton and a birthday party guest.

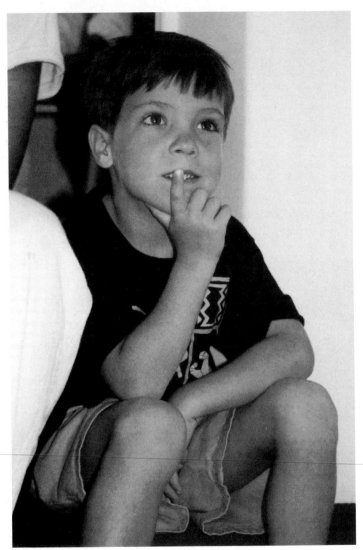

Quinton Anderson Reynolds contemplates the universe, 1995.

in 1977, Burt knew him only slightly. Nevertheless, the similarities were all there. They were both raised in the South, a place where "a man isn't a man until his daddy tells him he is." They were both creative and sensitive and achieved enormous success. Which brought with it wealth and power and people on the payroll who couldn't or wouldn't say no—which in turn gradually led to a dramatically diminished sense of what was real, what was true, and what was healthy.

He was calling me on the set in San Francisco every day, at first three and four times, and soon six or eight times. He was sick and afraid. And he was jealous of anything that took me away from him, including work and, on weekends, my mom. When she was in the hospital, he would call me there. When she was at my house, he would track me down there, too. I would leave him at Carolwood and head for Alomar, a twenty-minute drive, and before I'd even made it over the hill between Brentwood and the San Fernando Valley, he would have called. I would walk into the house, and Jeanne would say, "He's called here twice." When was I leaving, when was I coming back to Carolwood, why was I staying so long with Mom?

One day Georgie Montalban phoned him and said, "Burt, I'm just calling to see . . ."

And he cut her right off with, "Thanks, I'm doing OK, Georgie."

"Burt," she said, "I'm not calling about you. I'm calling about Loni, and her mother."

When he asked me not to leave his house, I said, "Burt, you have to understand what's going on here. My mother is dying."

"So am I," he said. "Look at me. I'm dying, too."

As we neared the 1984 holidays—and the end of the *Partners* shooting schedule—my mother had been in and out of the hospital, up and down with various experimental therapies and treatments. She was getting tired and discouraged. The series was doing OK. Not great, but OK. I started to pray, please, God, no more episodes. Let it be canceled. The financial burden was almost off my back, and I needed to be home with Mom.

One morning in San Francisco, about six o'clock, I was sitting in a chair in my dressing room, getting made up. I was wearing old fake-fur scruffy slippers and my chenille bathrobe and had hot rollers in my hair. And my mother called from the hospital. She was sobbing.

The doctors had scheduled her for seven surgical procedures, one of which was a colostomy and all of which were to take place over the next forty-eight hours. "I can't do this anymore," she cried. "Why aren't you here?"

After I hung up the phone, I called my agent in L.A.

"My God, it's still dark," he grumbled. "Why are you calling me at this hour?"

"Because I'm already at work," I said. "And since you're my agent, you should know I'm getting out of here. I'm going to go in and tell them I'm leaving, because my mother needs me. And I thought I'd better tell you, too, since you're probably going to have to answer to somebody." And then I went off in search of the director and the producers. I had pulled my curlers out but was still wearing the slippers and the robe. Serious star-power fashion.

"I'm leaving now," I announced. "My mother's having seven surgeries, and I'm getting on a plane and going home. I don't know when or if I will ever be back. I don't know what you're going to shoot, or how much it's going to cost you, or how much you're going to sue me for. And I don't care."

Their reaction was a series of film-quality double takes. It was as though everybody suddenly *got* it. Someone rushed over and patted my shoulder, saying, "OK, Loni, you do whatever you need to do, don't even worry about it." Someone else said, "Get a driver to take her to the airport."

I didn't pack anything. I put on jeans and a sweater, wound my hair in a knot, put on a hat and sunglasses, and climbed into the limo with Linda Jensen. We didn't even have plane reservations. When the ticket agent said there was a flight leaving in ten minutes, we both mumbled, "Fine, just get us on it."

The *Partners* crew managed. They shot everything it was possible to shoot with Lynda Carter. They shot background, endless cable cars going up and down hills and fog drifting in and out of San Francisco Bay. I stayed with Mom that week, and through the weekend. She stabilized after the surgeries. And then she started getting agitated about me getting into trouble at work. "I'm OK," she said. "You have to go and do your job."

Just before I flew back up to San Francisco, I had a meeting with Grant Tinker and Brandon Tartikoff at NBC, and with Johnny Carson, too.

"Please cancel the series," I begged them. "I don't think I can go on like this. I don't think any of us can."

And they said, "We'll probably be able to grant your wish. The ratings aren't great." It was the loveliest news I had heard in weeks.

The series was indeed canceled, and Lynda and I limped back to Los Angeles.

And then Burt roused himself long enough to announce, "We're going to Florida for Christmas."

And I focused just long enough to say, "Oh, no, we're not."

"From day one," he argued with me, "we have agreed that we go to Florida for Christmas. You do your thing here with your family, and then we go to Florida. My parents are old; I don't know how long they're going to be around."

"I'm staying here, B.R., and spending Christmas with my mother and my daughter," I said.

A few days later he came back with another plan. "All right, you stay here for Christmas. But you really need a break after all that you've been through. Come down for New Year's. I'll charter a boat and we'll take our friends and go down the Intracoastal to the Keys."

Christmas was bittersweet. I knew it was Mom's last one, and so did Deedee. We all spent the actual day, speaking of bittersweet, with Gary Sandy and his parents, at my old house. It was a gentle, loving day, with everyone trying to be on their best behavior. Burt had called, agitated that I wasn't with him. Mom, frail but functioning, was upset with my New Year's plans. Deidra wasn't pleased with my choice, either. I couldn't win.

The yacht Burt had chartered for the cruise was luxurious, with lushly comfortable staterooms. Any other time I might have been delighted with the whole setup, and a part of the party prepara-tions as well, happy to be surrounded by friends. Dom and Carol, Charles and Mary Ann, Ricardo and Georgie. They were dear, kind, and trusted, and they were very good to me, always. Burt, however, barely came out of his cabin the entire trip. As I sat under the sun and watched the shore go by, I prayed. About Mom, about Burt, about whatever it was I was supposed to be doing: Dear God, help me get through this. Give us all courage and patience, and give me strength. There was no hooting and hollering "Happy New Year!" on New Year's Eve that year; we were all pretty subdued.

One morning at Carolwood, while Mom was still in the hospital and Burt was asleep, with Harry and Lamar standing by down-stairs, I thought, I have a few hours to myself now. I can read a book, or have a really good cry. Nobody's looking at me, nobody wants anything.

I walked into the beautiful dressing room Burt had built for me next to the pink marble bathroom, with the sun streaming in through the leaded-glass windows, and I stretched out on the chaise. For days I'd felt very tired, shaky, and congested. A few months later I was diagnosed with mono; this must have been the beginning of it. As I lounged there, I just drifted, not quite asleep. It was like floating on a raft in the pool. I simply put myself someplace where nothing was wrong in my calm, quiet, orderly life. And the phone rang.

It was the hospital—Mom wanted to come home. Just as Dad had done, she had told them, "No more." No more drug trials, no more chemo, no more transfusions. She'd had enough.

I alerted the nursing service and then called Sarge to come and get me. We went to the hospital in the limo, and as I rode along, my hands folded in my lap, I felt enveloped in a blanket of com-plete calm. Then, just as we had gotten Mom packed up and into the wheelchair, ready to leave her room, Deidra called from school, crying so hard I couldn't understand her. I thought some-one had died.

"Mom, I'm completely doubled over," she said. "I think it's a bladder infection, but I'm in so much pain and my stomach's so distended, I think I'm going to blow up!"

"Just sit tight, honey," I said. "Sarge and I are picking up Gramma to take her home. We'll swing by and pick you up, too."

We bundled my mother into the backseat, complete with the Compazine and the throw-up pan and all the rest of her paraphernalia. Then we drove to UCLA, where I found my daughter bent over with pain, tears rolling down her face. We got into the car, and I sat between her and Mom, one arm around each of them. Dee was writhing, Mom was vomiting, they were both apologizing.

We called my doctor on the car phone, and he referred me to a urologist in his building. "Sarge," I said, "let's take Mom to the house first, and then I'll drive Dee to the doctor's." I was still completely calm.

When we got to Alomar, I jumped out and ran in to alert the nurses to what was going on, and Sarge picked up Deedee and carried her to the Rolls. Then he came back and helped me to walk my mother into the house. As I turned to go, Mom stopped me. She had a strange expression on her face.

"I can't believe you're doing what you're doing, the way you're behaving," she said. "You're just like your dad. And I never, ever saw anyone as strong as he was."

Driving Dee to the urologist's, I replayed my mother's words in my head, using them as a shield against the idea that something serious might be wrong with my daughter. I understood what was happening to my mother; I thought I understood what was happening to Burt. But if something happened to Deedee. . . .

After they'd examined her and said yes, it was a very severe infection, they drained her bladder and gave us prescriptions for heavy antibiotics. She was fine to go back to her dorm as long as she rested. It would take two or three hours for the antibiotics to kick in; in the meantime she could take hot baths if she was uncomfortable. After I dropped her off at the dorm and called my house to make sure Mom was settled (she and Jeanne were watching television), I carefully explained to Burt the kind of day I'd had so far.

"And now," I announced, "I am going to take a bath." But as the tub was filling, the phone rang again, and it was Deedee. The pain was still bad—could she come and stay with me?

She insisted on driving herself to Carolwood, but by the time she got there, it was clear that the pain was very real, and the medicine wasn't taking the edge off. I called the urologist again, who recommended I get her to the hospital.

I told Burt I was driving Dee there, but Lamar took one look at me—I still hadn't had either a bath or a good cry—and said, "I'll drive. We can take the station wagon."

Once there, Dee was catheterized and told she'd have to stay in the hospital until the catheter was removed—three days. And they gave her, a skinny girl who hadn't ever taken anything stronger than aspirin, a Valium.

"I have registered nurses around the clock at my house," I said to the hospital nurses. "Can't I just take Deidra there?"

When we got the go-ahead, the three of us climbed into the wagon, Lamar and me in the front, Deedee curled up in the back, complete with the catheter and the bag taped to her leg. And then the Valium began to kick in.

"Hey, look at my leg," she chortled, kicking said leg up into the air. "Lamar, you have to look at this catheter thing."

And minutes later, in a singsong voice, we heard, "I'm starving, I'm starving, let's find a drive-through McDonald's."

By the time we found a drive-through and got her the requested hamburger, fries, and a vanilla shake, Lamar and I were laughing our heads off. "This is *soooo good,* you guys," Deedee trilled from the backseat. "*Mmmm,* you can't believe how good this is."

When we pulled up to the front door at Alomar, my mother, this frail woman who had to be helped into the house three hours earlier, was standing at the door, ramrod straight, waiting for her granddaughter. "Hi-*eeee,* Gramma," Deedee said, and threw her arms around Mom, almost toppling her.

Mother, of course, was taking plenty of medication for her

pain, and Deedee was higher than a kite. Within five minutes the two of them, dying grandmother and ill granddaughter, were giggling in front of the full-length mirror. Mom had given Deidra one of her old flannel nightgowns to wear, and there they stood, hiking up their nighties and comparing their catheters. It was the silliest, most completely twisted moment yet. And they were unbearably cute. I'm just going to stand here for a minute and look at them, I thought. And that's when my tears came.

One afternoon, Burt asked me to draw a bath for him. I went into the bathroom and twisted the knob on the bathtub, and it came right off in my hand. Scalding hot water shot straight up into the air, and then all over the floor. I couldn't put the knob back on, and the bathroom was rapidly flooding.

I ran out and said to Burt, who was on the bed, "The thing came off, and there's water everywhere, and I have to go find Harry to get the water turned off in the house so we can stop the flooding, and then we'll call the plumber!"

And Burt smiled at me through his fog and said, "Um, sweetheart, how is my bath coming?"

I ran downstairs and called Harry and Lamar, and we all began to run back and forth like the Keystone Kops, upstairs, downstairs, calling the plumber, shutting off the water, mopping up the flood. As we ran around, we kept passing Burt's bed. Each time one of us went by, he'd ask, in a perfectly level, conversational tone of voice, "Say, would somebody make me a BLT? And, uh, is my bath ready yet?"

Harry, who was from Scotland, looked at me conspiratorially and said with his rolling burr, "Miss A, we simply must just ignorrr-r-r him."

Finally, after the plumber had come and the mess was cleaned up, I looked at the man on the bed and thought, you're not here anymore. There is no Burt Reynolds right now.

That was one of the hard lessons I learned about loving someone with an addiction. The person you love really isn't there. And the person who *is* there can't be trusted and won't listen to anything but the siren song his drug makes. The only thing to do is build a protection zone around yourself, to keep the love in and the other stuff out.

During her entire illness, save for the very first day when he helped her get into the Wayne center, Burt had not been to see Mother once. Not at the hospital, not at my house. He was too sick, he said. For some reason I began to focus on this. I had taken care of him as best I could and hadn't asked for anything in return. And finally I just insisted that Burt was going to Alomar to visit Mom.

Well, after Lamar and I got him into the car, he argued and complained, clasping his chest and saying he was having a heart attack because of what we were putting him through. Once we got to the house, he clung to the walls as he walked to Mom's room. "Oh, God, this is so hard for me," he moaned. I just locked my jaw.

Once in her room, though, he straightened right up. He was sweet to her, tender and funny. He did his Burt Reynolds thing. Charmed her, or tried. They talked a little while, about Deedee, about the weather. And after Lamar had taken him home, my mother looked straight at me and said, "Do not ever marry him. You will only have to take care of him; he won't ever take care of you. I cannot die, knowing that you might end up with this man."

She had loved him so much at first, she had been part of our whole romantic beginning. The early days with Burt had been a combination of her two cardinal rules: Make a good match, and never miss a party. Of course she knew that we'd had our troubles, but for so long, she'd continued to hold on to her hopes for us. But not anymore.

One afternoon as I was leaving to go to Mom, one of Burt's Dr. Feelgoods said, "You'd better keep your eye on Burt. He might kill himself."

And I said, "Excuse me, but I have a lot going on in my life at the moment. Why don't *you* keep an eye on Burt."

From the time Mom was first diagnosed, she immediately became the woman that Deedee, Andrea, and I remembered, the woman she had been before Dad's death. That other wild, unpredictable, angry person was gone, and here again was our Mackie, funny, pretty, and impeccable about her appearance and the social graces.

When I went into that house each day, it was a happy place, full of laughter and love. I couldn't wait to leave Burt to go over there. I'd had a hospital bed put into what was our television room, with its beautiful French doors looking out to the pool and the garden. That's where Mom would hold court. Jeanne and her Al were there, of course, and Linda, and Robin. Andrea was in and out of town as her schedule permitted, staying at the house, and so was Deedee with her schoolbooks. It was quiet when Mom needed it quiet, but more often than not, she wanted activity around her. Somebody would be making popcorn or soup, or bringing in new videos, or playing show tunes on the stereo.

Periodically—on her bad days—the nurses would tell me, "Your mother will never get out of bed again." And then we would all go into my kitchen and sit around the butcher-block table and talk about her. About what we were going to do. And then we'd hear the *shuffle, shuffle, shuffle* of Mother's slippers as she slowly came down the hall.

"Oh, hello," we'd say. "We understood you were never getting out of bed again."

"Well, I heard you all whispering out here," she said, "and I didn't want to miss anything. Why don't you all come into my room and talk."

Jan Smithers, who had played Bailey on *WKRP*, had a sister Holly, who was married to a minister, a very spiritual man named Gordon Rattray. And Holly and Gordon started coming by the house to visit Mom almost every day. Gordon was one of those people who, when he came into a room, brought peace and calm in with him. And he calmed my mother. He eased her way.

One Friday morning Burt told me he would be leaving that night for Florida. For a minute I felt like picking a where-are-you-when-I-need-you fight, but I squelched it. The fact was, I didn't need him, and I think he knew it. So I just said fine, I was going to go over and spend the day with Mom, I'd be back later.

When I got to the house, Mom's color was bad. Although she'd lost a lot of weight, she had stayed so beautiful throughout her illness. But today she was gray and listless, fading in and out. I told her that Burt was leaving for a while and that as soon as he was gone, I would come back and stay with her.

"Until the end?" she asked.

"Until the end," I answered, not quite believing that we had used those words.

I left around dinnertime and told her I'd be back in a couple of hours, tops. She nodded. When I got to Carolwood, Burt was still there, poking around, trying to pack. He couldn't seem to get himself organized. I helped as much as I could, but I was impatient. I wanted him gone, and I wanted to get back to her.

After he left, I called the other house. "Jeanne and Al are watching *The Wizard of Oz* with your mom," the nurse said. "And she thinks she might get up in a few minutes and take a little walk around the house for a bit."

I sat down in a chair, trying to catch my breath. It wasn't more than ten minutes. And then I threw some things in a bag and walked downstairs. As I did, a phone upstairs started ringing.

We had long since turned all the other phones off, because Burt couldn't take the noise, but the ringing phone was my own private line, installed specifically to stay in contact with the Alomar house. When I picked it up, Linda said, "Loni, your mom's gone."

On March 1, 1985, at sixty years of age, she died without me, after a ten-month fight. She had taken her little walk, with Jeanne and Al on each side of her, and then had gone back to bed. Not five minutes after they'd said good night to her and headed to the guest house, she died. Did she choose to spare me being there when she died, as Dad had done? Those ten precious minutes— could I have been with her if I hadn't spent them sitting in that chair? All I know is, she had done all her work and done it so bravely. And death is ultimately a private act.

Burt called when he got to Florida, and Jeanne told him that Mom had died. And he hung up without saying a word. When he called back a little later, he told me, "I loved your mother, but I just can't talk about it now."

The funeral was held in Minnesota, so that she could be buried next to Dad. And on the way there the airlines lost her. They removed the coffin at the wrong stop, somewhere between Los Angeles and St. Paul. Once we got over the shock—and once we finally got her where she was supposed to be—it began to seem pretty funny. "This would be her worst nightmare," I said. "The organization queen, with square corners on every bed in a house so clean it squeaked, misplaced on the way to her own funeral."

My grandmother Hazel, then in her late eighties, had come to see Mom when she was still in the hospital. Refusing to be wheeled into her daughter's room, Gramma had resolutely struggled to her feet and walked to Mom's bedside. Now she was going to bury her daughter, accompanied by Andrea and me, and the daughters of Jackie, the other daughter she had buried so many years before.

Up until then Gramma Hazel had always been as sharp as the proverbial tack. Independent and strong, she had been helping to raise her retarded great-granddaughter and was always completely caught up on everything everybody else in the family was doing. But it broke her heart to have outlived her own two girls, and on the way to the cemetery, it was as though we heard her mind break, too. "Now, tell me again, who was it that died?" she asked, looking at us. "It wasn't one of my granddaughters, was it?"

The funeral itself was full of wise, affectionate stories, about Maxine and her Andy, about their girls and the parties and the dancing. About their history. There was a lot of laughter. It was hard to believe that the romance was finally over.

Chapter 13

Although Burt hadn't come to the funeral, we spoke on the phone almost every day, if only for a few minutes at a time. He was quiet, vague, and definitely out of it. A few times when I called him, Elaine Hall, his Florida assistant, would tell me he was sleeping. Dr. Feelgood was there with him, she said.

I had some business matters to attend to, about Mom, and about a TV movie, *A Letter to 3 Wives,* that I was scheduled to do in May with Michele Lee and Stephanie Zimbalist. After those arrangements were taken care of, I decided I would go to Valhalla and take Deedee with me. I would go first; she would fly down and join me in a few days. I could see to Burt; she could begin to get over losing her grandmother.

Logan picked me up at the airport with the helicopter. He was very quiet, like he had something on his mind. We had always gotten along fine, and since I was being pretty quiet, too, I thought he was being respectful of my loss.

There was never a time when Burt didn't either come to the airport with Logan to meet me or meet me on the landing dock when the chopper arrived at Valhalla. But this time Burt wasn't anywhere in sight: Elaine Hall was.

"Where's Burt?" I asked.

"Well," she said, "don't be alarmed. But there are paramedics here."

We ran into the house, and indeed, there were two paramedics, holding our desk chair, with Burt in it. He was having a seizure, his eyes rolling back in his head. Dr. Feelgood was nowhere to be seen.

"We're not sure what to do," said one of the paramedics.

I said quickly, "A hospital. He has to go to a hospital." But I wasn't his wife. I couldn't authorize a doctor, a hospital, or treatment of any kind.

"No, no," said Elaine. "We can't take him to a hospital because of the publicity."

"We don't know exactly what to give him," said one of the paramedics. Somebody mentioned morphine, or adrenaline.

"Nothing!" I said. "You can't give him anything; we don't know what he's taken already!"

Elaine called her own doctor to come to the house, and when he did, he took one look at Burt and said, "Unless this man goes to a hospital immediately, he will die."

We got him into the Jupiter hospital, under an assumed name. Mr. Jeffries.

"What's Mr. Jeffries on?" one of the doctors asked.

I was wearing a hat and sunglasses and was trying to keep my voice down, trying not to be Loni Anderson, wanting them not to see that he was Burt Reynolds. Quietly I recited the drugs I knew about. Valium, Compazine, Percodan, Halcion.

"Who's the next of kin?" someone asked. "Because Mr. Jeffries here is not going to make it. He's gone into a coma."

"No," I said. I had buried my mother only four days before. "That can't happen."

The doctor was looking closely at me. "I know you, don't I?" he asked.

I gave up. I said, "I'm Loni Anderson. And Mr. Jeffries is not Mr. Jeffries. He's Burt Reynolds."

"Oh, my God," he gasped. "I never would have recognized him." Burt, normally about a hundred and ninety-five pounds, was now down close to a hundred and thirty.

195

"We have to do a spinal tap," the doctor said. "With the drug list you've given me, I know where to start. But it's not entirely clear to me what else is going on with him."

And then Elaine explained. "He knew he hadn't been there for you," she said to me. "So he came down here with his doctor to get off the drugs. He quit cold turkey."

He was in major drug withdrawal. Dr. Feelgood had been monitoring him but not, at Burt's insistence, giving him anything. Which he must have known could have killed him.

"He kept saying he had to change for you," said Elaine. "Especially now that your mother had died."

Within minutes they had Burt hooked up to all kinds of intravenous lines, putting the drugs back in to stabilize his system, with a plan to gradually wean him. But they couldn't say when or if the coma would lift.

"I don't believe in comas," I told them. "I think he can hear me."

After they all left the room, I sat down next to him. Whatever fear I felt was gone, replaced by a rage the likes of which I had never experienced in my entire life. "You goddamned son of a bitch," I said, right down in his face. "So help me God, if you die, I will make sure that you *never* get any peace!"

Everything I had kept inside for months, about him, about Mom, was there in that room. I got up out of my chair, stomped around the bed, ranted, raved, and finally I cried. He says he remembers that through his coma he heard me speaking gentle and loving words of support and encouragement. He's badly mistaken.

"This is the stupidest, most unfair, most selfish thing you have ever pulled. Don't you even think about dying, you bastard. Don't you even think about leaving me!"

When I had run out of steam, I sat down in the chair and put my head down on the bed, next to his hand. The doctor came into the room.

"Miss Anderson," he said, "I think you should go home and get some sleep. I can call you the minute there's a change, one way or the other."

I called Linda from home. "Please come," I cried. "He's in a coma, he's going to die." She promised she was on her way. I slept that night in the middle of our bed. Early in the morning I was back at the hospital. Burt had started to surface. Confused and tired and looking like death warmed over.

"He's going to have to stay here for a few days," the doctor said. "He needs twenty-four-hour care. The weaning process will take time, and he's pretty messed up nutritionally. And then he will need to go into a rehabilitation hospital."

Well, that got a slight rise out of our near-death patient. There was no way he was going into a rehab center. He could do it himself, he said. He wanted to go home, to Valhalla, and then back to Los Angeles, as quickly as possible. I argued; the doctor argued. We made absolutely no headway. The drugs might have almost killed him, but the prospect of the press scared him even more.

When Linda arrived, she came to the hospital. "Deedee's coming down here," I told her. "Will you stay with us?"

Burt heard me and became extremely agitated. "No, no, I don't want Deidra to see me like this!" he said. "She hates me anyway. She can't see this, she can't know about this. And they can't stay at Valhalla, either."

In addition to some condos, Burt owned another place in Jupiter, a place we called the Beach House. It came complete with a maid and a cook; it was for the high-powered guests who came down for events or to perform at the theater. We arranged to have Deidra and Linda stay there, and in a day or so, Burt was moved to Valhalla to begin his home-style rehabilitation. Once again I was being whipsawed back and forth between two houses. And Burt didn't want me to tell Dee why.

He truly was going through hell, watching the clock, just barely making it between the regulated doses of phenobarbital. I felt compassion for him: He had gone cold turkey for me and almost died in the process. And he was still very sick. But now he wanted to get back to L.A. Finally I had to tell my daughter what was going on.

"Well, Mom," she said patiently, "if you love him, and if you want to help him, then you have to do whatever you think is best." We decided that she and Linda would stay in Florida and try to salvage something out of the trip they had each made.

We took a private plane back, and I read a new mystery to Burt the entire way to make the time pass. Lamar picked us up at the airport and took us home. And then our real work together began.

In all the stories that have come out since then, Burt is said to have gone through formal rehab in 1985. Even in Elaine's book he "entered a drug rehabilitation program." Well, the "program" was at home in the Carolwood house, and the staff was me, Lamar, and a male nurse, taking our turns on round-the-clock shifts.

During March and April it was hard going. His pain and fear were real—his body had taken an incredible pounding, and his emotions (which he had spent so many years numbing) were all right out there, as though his skin had been peeled off his bones.

When I left for Canada to do the TV movie, he was functioning, but he was still exhausted and frail. When I look at that movie now, it's clear that I wouldn't have won any vitality contests, either. I was still grieving for Mom, and my feelings for Burt were raw around the edges.

I was gone only three weeks. When I returned, things between us began to change. I read to him every day. We played cards, we did puzzles, we played games. I sat by the pool as he swam laps, and at night we watched movies. And we began talking. Or, rather, he did.

He talked about his parents, his sisters, and his brother. I heard wonderful stories about Florida, the Everglades, his childhood friends, his college years at Florida State. About how he had found acting and why it meant so much to him.

For the first time, he talked about Sally, about the time he left me and went back to her. He talked at length about his great love for Dinah, about what she had given him, what she meant to him. He even talked about his marriage to Judy Carne, which we had never discussed. He was telling me, for the first time, the real story of his life. And every barrier was down.

I had pretty much fallen out of love with Burt by the time my mother died. Oh, I cared about him, worried about him, wanted things to be different, but God, I was tired. Every day was just one long slog through the emotional swamp, from morning to night, and he never gave anything back. At one point some tabloid shrink even said that in another life Burt had been my child. But now, as we worked puzzles and told stories, I realized I was living with someone else. A new guy.

I began to understand that Burt had never been off drugs the whole time we had been together, which meant that the person I had now was, for the first time, finally, truly him. The real him. Funny and warm and kind. And I fell in love with him. Not with Burt Reynolds, the star and image, the flash and dazzle of our first months together, with helicopters and jewelry and florist deliveries every day. But with *him*. He didn't have any money, he wasn't working, he looked awful, he couldn't get a job. And I thought he was *it*.

He had found a dentist in San Diego, Dr. Gus Schwab, who over a period of months painstakingly corrected the damage to his jaw. As his appetite came back, I started cooking for him again. Pasta and stews and wicked desserts. We began having company in, one or two people at a time. It was at gatherings like this that Burt's game show (with Bert Convy), *Win, Lose or Draw*, began to take shape—very informal shape—in our living room.

No one in his circle had ever known for sure what had gone on, and even now it was never called a drug problem; it was TMJ. Some friends, of course, didn't come to the house anymore. They had disappeared during the AIDS rumor phase. People Burt had worked with, people he had trusted—people he had given breaks to, lent money to, been a loyal friend to—just vanished. But Georgie and Ricardo were steadfast, and Charles Nelson Reilly, and the Durnings, and Jim Nabors, and the DeLuises. Johnny Carson called all the time, and Ryan O'Neal and Farrah Fawcett came over.

I didn't look for work for a while after the TV movie. I just wanted to focus on him and on what was happening to us. He didn't seem worried about money then, but of course Burt never worried about money. There were investments and property and accountants and lawyers. Money came in over here, and it went out over there. As far as Burt was concerned, if you had a hundred dollars, you could spend a hundred dollars. He never thought about taxes or agents or the future. He lived in the present.

In the fall of 1985, I met with Brandon Tartikoff, who was then head of NBC, and Hugh Wilson. When Brandon and I had last talked, after the cancellation of *Partners in Crime,* he had asked if I would be interested in doing something else for the network—maybe a half-hour sitcom again, something light and funny. At the time I basically said I would walk barefoot across the Mojave Desert for a chance to say words that Hugh had written.

So Hugh created *Easy Street,* where I was the nice young widow who had inherited a great deal of money, and the rest of the family was very snarky and mean. We agreed that we would do the pilot in early 1986. And in the meantime I could stay home with the new, improved B.R.

He probably has never been more handsome than he was at the end of those first six or eight months. He had put on weight, he was pain free, he was smiling a lot, he was relaxed and funny, and there was something about him that shone. The life that radiated out of his face, out of his eyes, just thrilled me. When we made love again after such a long time, it was different than it had ever been. We were *together.*

And once again we had pulled through. I would tell him that what he was doing was brave; he would tell me that what I was doing was saintly. In fact, I did feel sort of godlike. I couldn't save my father, couldn't save my mother. But by God, I could save Burt. With all that I had learned about addiction, I hadn't yet learned that *that* was the biggest trap of all.

We had a lovely Christmas at the Carolwood house. Deidra came, but she kept her distance from Burt. She was an adult, making her own choices, and I understood that she needed to protect herself from the choices I was making.

We flew to Florida for a second Christmas with his parents, who didn't know what he had been through. He never wanted them to know.

My relationship with his parents was always very important to me. When we were at Valhalla, I used to go over to the ranch all the time and visit with his mother. She had broken her hip before Burt and I were together, and over the years, as her health had deteriorated, she had become housebound. So she loved to hear about where we went, what we did, what we wore when we got all dressed up. She told me stories about her young life — she had been a nurse—and how she met and fell in love with Big Burt, and what her son had been like as a little boy. As we talked, Big Burt would wander in and greet me, but he never stayed inside long. He loved the ranch and always had a project going—until Quinton arrived, of course, and then Quinton became the project.

One day Fern told me she loved me, right in front of B.R., and afterward he cried in my arms because he had never heard the same words from her. And it took him years to hear them from his father. It made me endlessly grateful for having grown up in the I'm-going-to-the-bathroom-now-and-oh-by-the-way-I-love-you family.

After Burt made a healthy and feisty appearance on Johnny Carson's *Tonight Show* as exhibit A against the AIDS rumors, the phone started to ring, and he started getting movies again. *Heat, Malone.* They weren't *Deliverance,* he said, but they were work, and at first he was cheerful about that. It was good for his psyche and his wallet to be back at work. But after director Robert Altman took a walk from *Heat,* Burt got into an altercation with the replacement director and punched him. I didn't think of it as a warning flag. I just thought, oh, well, I never expected him to turn into Mother Teresa.

After I did the pilot for *Easy Street,* NBC picked it up for twenty-two episodes. But before I could get started on that, I first had to go to Tahiti, to do *Stranded,* a romantic comedy, with Perry King.

When you hear the word "Tahiti," you immediately picture blue water, swaying palm trees, and serene, tropical bliss. Wrong. This was one hellish shoot. One john outdoors for the men, one for the women. And clinging to every wall and ceiling, large bugs that were our constant (and somewhat aggressive) companions. I had the one air-conditioned room, so that's where they made me up—and the minute I went outside, it all melted. My hair turned bright orange because of the rust in the hotel water. We had no television, no room service. At the beginning and end of every day, an increasingly surly cast and crew gathered in a family-style dining room. And the one telephone in the entire place, at the desk of the hotel, operated somewhat like a short-wave radio, complete with time delays, static, and echoes. Half the time the people in the hotel lobby could hear you much better than the person you were calling.

Burt had become very moody before I left, sulking and grumpy. I put it down to jealousy and nothing more. But once I started calling him from this god-awful shoot—my phone bill for the entire three weeks was four thousand dollars—his attitude didn't improve. If I didn't call, he got mad. If I did call, he got mad. He was convinced that Perry and I had something going. Lucky for Burt that Perry was in love with another woman, actress Linda Purl, or at the end of the first ten days I might've been tempted to hit on him out of spite. What had all these months been for, I wondered, if it still comes down to this?

One night I'd had a fight with Burt on the phone from hell, and Perry had had one with Linda. Afterward we were sitting out on the veranda drinking wine, commiserating about how both our relationships were sort of off-kilter at the moment. "If they could see these bugs," I said, "they'd stop picking on us long distance."

But there was an amazing fragrance floating in the air—the tropical flowers and the saltwater mist—and it was, I admit, pretty heady. So Perry and I kissed. We had kissed each other in the movie for days, of course, but this one was different. This one could have been dangerous. It was almost as though we had decided, well, if they're mad at us anyway, we might as well . . .

"Oh, no." We both laughed at exactly the same moment, backing out of the clinch. "No, we're not going to do this. We like each other, and we love them, and we're not going to screw it up."

Perry had made a commitment to Linda, and I had made one to Burt, and that was all there was to it. It didn't mean we weren't human. But no matter how mad we were, no matter how entitled we may have been feeling, it wasn't worth it. It never is. It's not worth the mess or the pain or the loss of a friendship. Perry's and mine, I mean.

But Burt, of course, never did believe that nothing happened when Perry and I were stranded on *Stranded*.

When I got back, I went to work on the *Easy Street* episodes. It felt like home in the same way that *WKRP* had. The great character actor Jack Elam played my uncle; Lee Weaver was his roommate; Dana Ivey, who has since done wonderful work on Broadway and in both *Addams Family* movies, played my sister-in-law; and Jamie Cromwell played her husband. And Arthur Malet was the superior-to-everybody butler.

The first time out we got the highest ratings anyone had gotten since the pilot of *M*A*S*H* aired, but after that they started moving us around the schedule for the rest of the season. I knew, when that started, that the writing (and it wasn't Hugh's, after the first episode) was on the wall.

For the pilot Burt and Hugh and Dom DeLuise did the audience warm-up, and they were all terrifically funny. But after that Burt never came to a taping again. He was still angry about Tahiti. Perry called the house one afternoon—I think it had something to do with a publicity appearance for the movie—and Burt went ballistic.

"He is my friend," I insisted, "and my working colleague."

"You can't be friends with him," said Burt, and that was all there was to it.

In the fall of 1986 he went off to Rome to do *Rent-a-Cop* with Liza Minnelli. Robby Benson, Richard Masur, and Bernie Casey were in it, too. I had never been to Rome, so on one of my weeks off I flew over to be with him. The trip cost me eight thousand dollars of my own money—except for the first-date New Year's Eve trip to Jupiter, I always paid my own way flying back and forth across the country—and all Burt did the entire time was rant at me: I didn't appreciate him, I wasn't grateful to him for everything he gave me.

One evening, after dinner, I discovered that I was missing a pair of leather gloves. They were expensive ones (in fact, I had just purchased them), and I thought I'd left them in the cab we'd just gotten out of. I wanted to try and go back to find out. Burt became very angry and began shouting. He grabbed me and started pushing me around. We were on the street with other people, Lamar and some others from the movie crew. All men.

"Hey, Burt," they said, not knowing for a minute if he was serious. "Hey, man, lighten up. Get a grip." And he backed off.

I was completely freaked out. Was it the pills again? Was it work? What *was* it? On the one hand, if he had started using again, then we were in trouble. On the other hand, if it wasn't the drugs but rage and anger spewing all over on its own, then we were in a whole *different* kind of trouble.

When I came back to work, I was very tense and not sleeping well. I felt like we were falling backward. Maybe we're coming to an end here, I thought. I even talked to Deidra about it. "I don't know," I told her. "I don't know if we're going to make it."

Burt came home from Rome over the holidays, and we did the double-Christmas routine—with some attendant excitement, since Deedee had become engaged to Charlie Hoffman, with the wedding to come the following July—and then we took another cruise down the Intracoastal, with Liza Minnelli and her husband, Mark Gero, her sister, Lorna Luft, Lorna's husband, Jake Hooker, and their son.

Burt was cantankerous the entire trip. There was no pleasing him. Afterward Liza, who had known Burt for years and worked with him before, said, "I love him like a brother, but I don't know how you stand it." She had battled her own demons; maybe she recognized Burt's.

After *Rent-a-Cop* was done, we went to Venice with Vic Prinzi

(Burt's best friend and roommate from college), Vic's wife, Barbara, and Charles Nelson Reilly. Burt had been invited to Venice as a guest speaker at a young millionaires gathering. I don't recall the exact details, but everybody in this group had to have made a million by thirty or something. Adnan Khashoggi was one of the speakers, as was Admiral Elmo Zumwalt. Burt was brilliant and funny, at the top of his game. And he stayed that way during the entire trip. We stayed at the Hotel Cipriani and took the *Orient Express* from Venice to Paris. It was like a dream, and so was Burt. With one notable and quite weird exception.

At the Cipriani one day, I came out of the bathroom into our room wrapped in a towel. The Cipriani is a luxury hotel, and this was a luxury towel, large and plush, easily covering me from under my arms to my knees. And he got angry.

He said I was immodest, disgusting, that I had deliberately walked in front of the window and that someone might have seen me. "I just can't talk to you about this," he said, and true to his word, he didn't. He didn't say another word to me for two hours.

That night he insisted that from then on I wear something to bed, a nightgown, and said that he would wear something also. I had worn nightgowns before, but not often, not always. Certainly I was decent in my own house, especially when other people were around, but I had always felt perfectly free to be nude in the privacy of my own bedroom and bath. Evidently, Burt no longer agreed.

"If you're completely naked," he said, "it's not mysterious, it's not sexy. I don't ever want to see you naked again."

Chapter 14

There was no doubt about it, Burt was angry. His movie career wasn't coming back as fast or as high-powered as he had wanted. Even remaking something as marvelous as *His Girl Friday* didn't help. When he went into *Switching Channels* (with Kathleen Turner, Ned Beatty, and Christopher Reeve), he took his anger with him. To make matters worse (as far as he was concerned), when I wasn't working on *Easy Street,* I was completely wrapped up in planning Deidra's wedding.

I believed that Burt and I would be separating after the wedding in July of 1987. I was convinced he had started using the pills again, although I hadn't seen him do it. But the tantrums and the silences felt so familiar to me. I talked to Dee and Charlie about it, promising that I wouldn't do anything drastic—or newsworthy—until they were safely on their way.

Dee first met Charlie at UCLA, and they had been together for two years by the time they were married. They are so much alike: both disciplined overachievers, fine athletes, academically at the top of their classes in both undergraduate and graduate school. The love Charlie had—and still has—for my daughter was like a light in his eyes every time Deedee came into the room.

"If you ever get married again," I told her, "I'll give you $11.95 for the license and not another thing. But for this one, the sky is the limit." And I meant it. What a production we put on!

In addition to the wedding itself, I threw two women-only showers. One at Carolwood, with a Venetian theme: a gondola floating in the pool, Italian food, and waiters all costumed as gondoliers. The other was black-tie, at the Montalbans', with champagne fountains and ice sculptures and the waiters all in tails, and with all the family members from out of town. Toward the end of the evening, Ricardo came home from attending a formal event. All the women just swooned. He took some of them on a tour of the house, which is beautiful, and as he was pointing things out, going on about the structure and the architecture, they were all just gazing in awe at Ricardo in his tux and paying no attention whatsoever to what he was saying.

Everybody was at the wedding. Deedee's father, Bruce, brought Pam, his wonderful wife, and their three children, Dee's two stepsisters and her half brother, Jamie. And Bruce's sister, Barbara, who lived in Chicago by that time, came with her husband, Russell. Bruce's parents came as well, and so did Ross's sister, Robin. Family is family to me, no matter what—in fact, when I'm divorced, I always seem to get custody of all the in-laws. But, oh, how Burt struggled with that, and with them. Letting them all into his life meant putting aside self-consciousness and resentments and even history, and he just couldn't do it. He consented to come to the wedding, and he shared the cost of the honeymoon gift with me (we sent them to Hawaii, then on to Fiji), but he didn't want to deal with the rest of it.

"All I care about," he said, "is that you keep Bruce away from me."

So I stuck Burt in the minister's study while I was helping Dee get dressed. He was alone in there, he told me later, when the door opened, and in came a man, a perfectly nice man, and they talked casually for a while before Burt realized it was Bruce he was talking to.

We had wrestled a bit with the who's-going-to-walk-her-down-the-aisle question. Deidra didn't want Burt or Ross or

Bruce. And when I offered, she just rolled her eyes and said patiently, "Mother, if this was your day, would you want Marilyn Monroe walking *you* down the aisle?" And so she walked herself—and quite beautifully, too—down the aisle to her groom.

Burt left the country club reception quite early, which he had already told Dee and Charlie he was going to do. They understood. And after he left, the rest of us proceeded to dance our feet off.

"Was marrying me the worst thing that ever happened to you in your life?" Bruce asked as we whirled around the dance floor.

"No." I smiled up at him. "Because you gave me the best thing that ever happened to me in my life."

The next morning we had a big bon voyage breakfast for the newlyweds and sent them on their way. In my heart I blessed Charlie—and I still do—for being everything Andy and Maxine ever could have wished for their girl.

For the last episode of *Easy Street,* they wrote a lovely romance for me and asked Burt if he'd like to play it. He declined very firmly. "I don't do television," he said.

The TV movie I had done with Perry King had just run, and its ratings went through the roof, so they asked Perry, and he said yes. And when I told Burt one night at dinner that Perry was going to play the part, he very quietly bent a spoon and a fork in half.

When we were first together, I was quite charmed by Burt's jealousy. I figured he could have had any woman he wanted, but he wanted me, and he wanted me to *himself.* But through the years I had discovered that that meant he saw everything and everyone as competition. If I was laughing on the phone with someone, he would come and stand in front of me, just looking at me. "Who is that? Who are you talking to?"

He said to me once, in a fight, that if we broke up, then he wouldn't have to worry anymore about a woman who looked the way I did.

"Looks have nothing to do with whether someone can be

trusted," I said angrily. "It's what's going on inside a woman that you should worry about, B.R. People either behave, or they don't."

We once went to see *Dreamgirls* at the Dorothy Chandler Pavilion, with Georgie and Ricardo. And my pharmacist was there. I kind of waved at him through the crowd, and Burt said, "Who is that? Is that someone you've had an affair with?"

I just looked at him. "Burt, that man has been my pharmacist for the last fifteen years."

But Burt was so steamed, he couldn't even watch the show and kept craning his neck to see this guy, this Don Juan of a pharmacist.

I had decided it was just part of his personality. Like: Deidra's disciplined, Loni's neat and tidy, Burt's jealous. Of everybody. And I was still taking it day by day, wondering how much longer we would be together.

Late in 1987 he said to me, "I wish you'd sell the Alomar house."

"Why?" I asked, surprised.

"Because I always think you have one foot out the door," he said.

"B.R., I live with you," I answered. Could he somehow know what I had been thinking?

"But you always have a place to go," he said, "a place of your own. If you're really committed, I need you to sell your house."

Well, he had a point. I had totally redecorated and remodeled Carolwood by then, and it was, after all, where I lived. Mom was gone, Deedee had a life and a home of her own. Maybe it was time to call my own bluff. So I put Alomar on the market.

In November 1987 I went off to do a TV movie, *Necessity*, with James Naughton and John Heard. It was a chase movie, where I was brunette in the beginning and blonde at the end. Before I left, Burt had begun talking about *Breaking In*, a lovely John Sayles script about an old-pro safecracker and a young protégé. Bill Forsyth, the Scottish director, was going to do it. Burt was back and forth about being in it. It would be such a departure for him: no car chases, no shoot-'em-ups, he didn't get the girl.

But I really hoped he would decide to do it. The part, and the script, was a gem.

He wanted people—meaning critics, I think—to take him seriously as an actor, to see he was more than just his image. Steve Martin told me once, "Nobody does it better than Burt." That kind of casual, funny, leading man/everyman thing that he did. He had something special on the screen, but it wasn't a quality that separated him from the audience or put a distance between him and them. Someone once called him an American Cary Grant—that is, when he wasn't doing the good old boy stuff. But he, like Cary Grant, never got an Academy Award, and it makes him mad to this day. I always thought he should've had one for *Starting Over*—and so did he. And he was never comforted by the list of talented, deserving people who never got an Oscar. He wanted one of his own.

After my fibroid surgery in 1984, I had stopped using any form of birth control, and Burt knew it. I was as regular as clockwork, and we were making love, but nothing was happening. In 1987 I decided to go to a fertility specialist.

Between late '87 and early '88 I had a laparoscopy, I had my fallopian tubes flushed, I had every test—blood, urine, hormones, ovulation, ultrasound—known to fertility research, and I was fine. No reason for me not to get pregnant, they said, and no reason to consider fertility drugs, unless I wanted a multiple birth. They wanted to see Burt next, to fill in the other half of the scenario.

They told me to come in one morning after we'd made love. They ran tests on the semen sample, and the sperm count was very low. It might have been age, might have been drug use, or, as one doctor observed, "For all we know, he could've had mumps at an early age."

The doctor said, "If we could collect semen for three or four months and boost it with hormones, we might have a chance with artificial insemination. Or even, ultimately, in vitro fertilization."

All the way home I thought, this is the test. This will say where we go from here. How can I talk to him about this? I had friends who were coping with this very same issue; I knew what a heartache it was and how sensitive Burt was about the whole question of a child of his own. I wanted to be as careful, as gentle as I could be.

And so I started with, "You know, from all the stress you're under . . ."

And he interrupted with, "And all the drugs I've taken?"

"And our ages, too," I said. "Look, here's what our chances are, and our options. And we're lucky, we have resources, which a lot of couples in this situation don't have."

"No," he said adamantly. "I'm not interested. I don't want to be tested, I don't want anybody standing around counting my sperm, and I don't want to have sex on demand. I don't care if we give *birth* to a child—I just want to *raise* a child."

"Are you certain?" I asked him. "Because I'm willing to do this."

"I'm not," he said. "I think we should adopt."

The week I got the call that I had a buyer for the Alomar house, Burt said, "I want you to marry me."

I was stunned. "Why now? I mean, I've always said I would, but why now?"

"Because I believe you love me," he said. "You're selling your house, and you were willing to go through the whole infertility thing. Deedee's got her own life now, and she's happy, and I just think it's time. Time for us."

He had been building a chapel on the ranch in Florida, and it had been completed the previous year. There had been no ceremonies in it; we would be the first.

I said yes, of course. In my mind I heard my mother's voice, but I hushed it. He had been so sick when she told me not to marry him, and he wasn't anymore. He hadn't been OK then, and he was now, and if she had been here, she would have seen it. I had proved myself to him. He finally believed me.

The minute I said yes, Burt turned into Mr. Adorable. I had two TV movies coming up immediately and didn't know how or when I would be able to organize a wedding at the same time, but he insisted, "I'm going to do it, kid. I'll put it all together. All you have to do is show up in a pretty dress."

We had a prenuptial agreement drawn up to protect me. Burt was always in such financial upheaval—he'd sold the house in Georgia and some other properties as well—and with a prenup no one would ever be able to take anything I owned independently away from me or attach my earnings.

My business manager and his business manager got together and agreed upon the terms. And one of the terms was that if we had a child, the agreement would be null and void. Because that would create a different inheritance situation and would require that a family trust be established.

Later, of course, this proved interesting. While we were in the process of adopting, his attorney said to me, "Now, if you get divorced, Burt doesn't have to be responsible for this child, right?"

I said, "What do you mean? We adopt a child and then it's not his if we get divorced? Whose child is it, then? It's his child, of course he will be responsible for it."

Leaving Mr. Adorable in charge of the wedding, I went off to do *A Whisper Kills* with Joe Penny. My gosh, we had fun on that shoot; I think I felt more lighthearted than I had in years. Those were some of the sexiest scenes I've ever shot with anybody— Joe is hands down the best on-screen kisser in the business, no contest. I think I read somewhere that Melissa Gilbert said that, too!

The wedding date was set for April 29, 1988. At first we thought only family would be attending the wedding, but the guest list started growing, because our friends wanted to get in on it. We had been together six and a half tumultuous years, and these folks had been through the mill with us—they wanted to come to our party.

We asked Mario Caselli, who had been photographing us both for years, to come down and do the wedding, and we told him he could sell the pictures to *People*. But no other press; Mario was it.

Before the wedding I stayed with Burt's sister, Nancy Ann, at her condo on the Intracoastal. In spite of our untraditional lives, Burt and I had wanted the wedding itself to be as traditional as possible, so we decided in advance not to stay together at Valhalla.

Which is why his whole story about how, the night before the wedding, we had a big fight, and I was upstairs crying, and he lost the license, and I was hysterical—fiction, complete fiction. There was no scene; I wasn't there. Here's the deal: *No one who knows, and no one with any integrity, has ever spoken. About anything.* Not Nancy Ann, certainly, who is supported by Burt and is Quinton's loving aunt, and who is embarrassed by everything that has happened since. No, the only time Burt and I saw each other in two days was from a distance, at the ranch, and we waved at each other.

Before the wedding we had a real girls' party, complete with curlers and cold cream and gossip. My sister came down, and Deidra, and Linda and Jeanne. And Elaine Hall, Burt's assistant, who had done so much of the arranging. And Patty Fuller, ex-wife of actor Bob Fuller (from TV's *Emergency* and *Wagon Train*), a brilliant interior decorator and an old friend of Burt's who had become a dear friend of mine. She had known him so long and was so wise about him and was always generous and welcoming to me. She died of cancer in 1993. I guess I can be grateful she didn't live to see what came after.

This wedding was a total blast. The day was beautiful, with a clear blue Florida sky and the mandatory sunshine. Deidra and Andrea stood up for me, and Vic Prinzi and Lamar Jackson stood up for Burt. As Burt's dad walked me down the aisle, they played the "Wedding March," and then Jim Nabors sang "Our Love Is Here to Stay" and the Lord's prayer, all of them songs Burt had chosen.

Each part of the day as it unfolded was such a complete, joyous surprise to me, because the only thing I had done, as Burt had told me to do, was show up in a pretty dress. He had made all the plans. And every few minutes he would lean over and whisper in my ear, "How'd I do, kid?" He was so pleased with himself, and so joyful. Childlike, almost.

When the Reynolds family Bible came out at the beginning of the ceremony, it had my ring, which I hadn't yet seen, resting on top of it. I had always told Burt I wanted a canary diamond, and when this ring appeared, with its large warm yellow stone surrounded by diamonds, I was so astonished that I gasped out loud, and everybody in the church giggled. And then I realized I had lost track of what the minister, Jess Moody, was saying.

"Did I miss my part?" I whispered to Burt.

"No, honey, you're doing fine," he laughed. "But do try to get hold of yourself!"

We were laughing and carrying on so much in the middle of the ceremony that Burt's mom, who was sitting in the front row, said, "Let's get on with it!"

Burt says now that his mother didn't want us to be married— oh, please, she was thrilled, and everybody could see it. There is a video of the whole ceremony, from beginning to end, and of the reception as well, and she was smiling, as was everyone else. Fern used to put her hands on my face and look into my eyes and tell me I was like a daughter to her. She always told me that she and Big Burt were happy, grateful, that I'd married her son. And they didn't even know what he had been through, what *we* had been through!

At the end of the ceremony, when Jess Moody pronounced us Mr. and Mrs. Burt Reynolds and we turned around, everyone in the chapel applauded. And when we got outside, the blue sky seemed filled with press helicopters; there were at least five over-head. We just waved at them.

Burt and I rode to the reception in a stagecoach, and on the way he took my chin in his hands and said, "I'm so happy." And he reallly was, and so was I. I know we're a long way from that now, but I'm sad that he chooses not to remember or admit how truly special that day was.

The reception was held in the hangar on the ranch, which had been completely transformed, with gardenias and green nursery trees and ribbons everywhere. Perry Como and his wife were there, and Ann-Margret and Roger Smith. Robby Benson and Karla DeVito. Bert Convy, who was by now the coproducer on

Burt's *Win, Lose or Draw* on television, sang "Just the Way You Are." And then the apprentices from the theater institute sang "When I Fall in Love" and completely reduced us all to tears.

The food was glorious, too: Gulf shrimp and cornbread and strawberries with chocolate fondue and a heart-shaped wedding cake. Everywhere I looked there was something—a special person, a song, a vase of flowers in the center of a table—that was evidence of what Burt had done to make the day beautiful. And all day long he never let go of my hand. "Mrs. Reynolds," he'd say, and then he'd laugh.

Ann-Margret and Roger Smith took off for the airport in the B-R Ranch chopper, and the other choppers and the press on the ground all thought they were us and followed them like lemmings. Burt and I then escaped in his friend Bernie Little's chopper and flew to Key West, to a private yacht that would take us on a lazy trip through the Caribbean.

On the bed in our stateroom were two costumed stuffed animals—a bride bear and a groom bear. Burt made love to me that night with great tenderness and joy. He felt complete, he said. As for me, I was so happy I couldn't decide whether to levitate or cry. I had every reason to believe that we would live happily ever after.

Chapter 15

I married Burt Reynolds for one reason: I loved him. We loved each other. For Burt, or anyone, to deny that now is a travesty. Throughout everything, I never doubted that the love was there, although it was certainly more obscured on some days than on others. There are ups and downs in every relationship, every love affair, every marriage. But I never doubted that I would be with him until the end of my life—I never would have made that commitment otherwise, and I certainly never would have had a child. Being a single mother again was the furthest thing from my mind.

I told Ann-Margret once that the marriage changed Burt more than anything else in our time together had done. He relaxed, he lightened up. He left little notes on my pillow or on my makeup mirror, or wrote them on the notepad next to the phone for me to find. The flowers came again every day, and the small, exquisite gifts.

When we returned from our Caribbean trip, we began the official adoption application process, through an attorney. We did not buy a baby; we applied, happily and nervously, to adopt one. We had the required home visit from the social worker, the state certification, and all the other necessary paperwork.

Almost immediately, I had to leave Burt to do my third TV

movie in six months, *Too Good to Be True.* It was a remake of *Leave Her to Heaven,* and the cast was just terrific. Patrick Duffy played my writer husband; Glynnis O'Connor, the good sister; Julie Harris, the good mother; and *L. A. Law's* Larry Drake was the family friend and attorney. And I was the bad sister, so twisted that I drowned the pre–*Doogie Howser* Neil Patrick Harris and then set my sister up for my own murder by killing myself and leaving a creative trail of incriminating evidence.

The movie was a hoot to do—and probably as close to a Shakespearean role as I'll ever come! But I wanted to get back home, because there was incredible news from Burt.

"Believe it or not," he said, "they've found us a match." We had a baby on the way.

Deedee and Charlie were living in L.A., where he was coaching football at UCLA and completing graduate work while Dee taught middle school. When I had first talked to my daughter about our desire to have a child—and told her, at one point, that I was ready to give birth to one—she had been upset. She thought that having a baby of our own, and pursuing all kinds of expensive, scientific means of doing that, was a selfish waste of our resources. And she didn't want anything to take away from my feelings about any children she might have. But when she heard about the adoption, and that there was a child actually on the way, she and Charlie both got very excited.

Through our attorney we paid for the birth mother's prenatal care, the hospital delivery and aftercare, and six months of postnatal psychological care. Combined with the attorney's fees, it came to about twenty-five thousand dollars, which from my understanding is about standard. And it was my twenty-five thousand. There was no *B. L. Stryker* series yet, no *Evening Shade.* But I had sold my house and done three TV movies in a row. As far as I was concerned, it was pure joy money, and I never looked back.

The weeks leading up to this baby's arrival were so funny— we were two of the goofiest expectant parents you could imagine. Happily, Burt had made the decision to do *Breaking In,* and he was up in Portland, Oregon, on the shoot. We talked every day on the phone. Any word yet? Have you heard anything yet?

I flew up to visit him, and all we could talk about was the baby, the baby, the baby. The birth mother went into false labor a couple of times, and we just about jumped out of our shoes. Were we ready for this, we asked? Did we have everything the baby needed? Could we *be* everything the baby needed?

Just before the due date, Burt freaked. He had been so excited, so endearing, and then he just kind of seized up with expectant-fatheritis. He said that he thought maybe the baby should live out in the guest house, with the nanny. Because he wasn't used to having anybody around, he said.

"Calm down, sweetheart," I said. "We don't park babies in the outbuildings. This baby will live under this roof, and there will be toys on the floor, and it will be disorderly, and you will be just fine. Years from now, when there's a girlfriend or a boy-friend in this child's life, *that's* who can live out in the guest house."

I don't think, in all those years when Burt had wanted a child, that he thought it was about having a baby. I think he thought it was about having a *boy*—like Tom Sawyer would just arrive at his house, skipping the messy part altogether, and proceed directly to the backyard and begin throwing a football.

Linda Jensen was pregnant, and her baby was due when ours was. And Quinton came to us on the same day that Cary, Linda's little boy, was born, so they share the same birthday. The day Quinton arrived, a look came over Burt's face that I had never seen there before. Awe and stark terror and wonder. Quinton's eyes were huge and brown, and he stared back at his father as though they had been looking at each other forever.

We asked Ricardo and Georgie to be his godparents; the ceremony took place in Los Angeles, in Jess Moody's Baptist church, with a Lutheran minister officiating. Talk about covering all your ecumenical bases! Linda's son was christened there on the same day, and Burt and I are his godparents.

At first Burt was scared to feed the baby, scared to diaper him, didn't want to hold him, didn't want to drop him. He wasn't not interested in this little boy; he just wanted to be perfect at anything having to do with him. And with Quinton you had to be prepared for anything, at all times. The child was a firecracker from the very beginning.

He crawled at five and a half months, he walked at eight and a half months, he was out of the crib and on the loose before he was a year old. If a baby can have a motto of his own, Quinton's was "Let's get going!" I've always said he was born with the jock gene—his indulgence of choice will probably be athletic equipment.

Except for one TV movie a year—three weeks away and that was it—I basically quit work after Quinton came. I didn't have that luxury when Deedee was little and had always regretted it. Now I had it, and I was glad. And when Burt began doing *B. L. Stryker,* a series of six TV movies of the week in rotation with new episodes of *Columbo* and a Lou Gossett, Jr., series, he sold the Carolwood house and we moved the whole household to Florida bag and baggage. He was happy to be nearer to his parents, who were enthralled with Quinton, and he wanted to concentrate on the series, the theater institute, and the apprentice program.

Even Dee and Charlie made the move: They lived in Orlando, Charlie coached football at the University of Central Florida, and Dee taught junior high and high school history. The apprentices were in and out of the house and working on *Stryker* in Jupiter (where Quinton and I visited the set every day), and we always had company from Los Angeles. Valhalla soon began to resemble a Florida version of Walton's Mountain.

One day in 1989, I was in the Jupiter Hilton with Quinton, and I was shopping for a bathing suit. I noticed that in addition to the hotel guests (some of whom were trying to be inconspicuous while they watched me shop), there were all these men in suits and sunglasses walking around the hotel with very serious looks on their faces. Now, Jupiter isn't a place where you often see a lot of grim men wearing suits, and I was mildly curious, but I was also preoccupied with my shopping expedition.

And then one of the men, followed by two others, came right up to me. "Excuse me, Miss Anderson?" he said politely.

"Yes?" I said.

"Please excuse this request, Miss Anderson," he said. Here it comes, I thought. He wants an autograph.

"I'm truly sorry, Miss Anderson, but I'm afraid I'll have to ask you to leave for a bit," he said politely. "You see, President Bush is upstairs in the hotel—he's been visiting his mother here on Jupiter Island—and it's time for him to leave now. But we can't sneak him out of the hotel safely as long as you're here attracting so much attention."

Well, we all know how intense bathing suit shopping can be, but I didn't think it was worth a face-off with the Secret Service. Besides, they seemed to have called a Code Loni. So Quinton and I trundled home, with plans to come back another day.

A few months after Quinton arrived, I said to Burt, "Now that we have this baby and now that I'm not working, we can have another child. And I could do it now, I could give birth to it. We could do artificial insemination or in vitro. We've made a new life, with time for Quinton, which means we can easily make room for another one."

He broke down and cried. "No, no," he said. "No doctors, no surgery. If anything happened to you, if we tried this and you were hurt somehow, it would be my fault, because of the drugs. Nothing must happen to you." He didn't sound like a man who had never wanted to be there, who was looking for a way out. He sounded like a man who loved and cherished his wife.

Soon after, Burt and I decided to go ahead and try to adopt another child. Working again through an attorney, we were happy to learn that there was a little girl on the way. I got another car seat, another stroller, and we started talking about names. Once again, I paid the attorney and the medical expenses. I was going to have another daughter, Quinton would have a sister. It was a done deal, in both my mind and my heart. And then, three weeks before she was due to arrive, Burt abruptly changed his mind.

"There's too much going on right now," he said. "I just can't do it."

Four years later I discovered that at the same time Burt turned down the second baby, Pam Seals had begun appearing as an extra on the *B. L. Stryker* set.

Quinton's first nanny, Nanny Betty, was primarily a baby nanny, but Master Q. had clearly decided that he wasn't a baby anymore. So Nanny Joan came to live with us, and he quickly proved too much for her, too. That's when John and Janet Spring arrived.

John, who had worked for Donald Trump, originally came on board as manager of Burt's house staff in Florida, and Janet, a nurse, became Quinton's full-time nanny when he was two. They were British, and initially Burt and I liked and trusted them both.

They were affectionate with Quinton but firm. At first I liked their conservative approach; much as my parents had done for me and then for Deidra, they were providing consistent limits for Quinton, with the kind of energy and focus that Burt and I sometimes lacked either because of our work or because we simply adored the ground the child walked on. And unlike us, they could take Quinton out for jaunts in public without causing a publicity stampede or encouraging roving nutcases. In spite of my own fears for his safety, I wanted Quinton to have a normal life, or at least as normal as it could be, and it looked like the Springs would help us to give him that.

In late 1989 I did an episode of *B. L. Stryker* with Burt—I played a mysterious con woman. We played off each other, flirting like our characters did, and he had as much fun doing it as I did. Or at least I thought so. Now, when I watch that video, I can slo-mo one specific section and see Pam Seals as an extra in the background.

A month or so later I went off to Rome and Luxembourg to do a TV remake of *Three Coins in the Fountain* with Stepfanie Kramer and Shanna Reed; according to my "good friend" Elaine Hall's book, Pam spent some time in my house while I was away.

Stryker, which we thought had been doing very well, was canceled after its second season, in 1990. Burt was pretty distraught about it for a while, until something else came up—a new comedy series, with the *Designing Women* team, Harry Thomason and Linda Bloodworth-Thomason.

The character of Wood Newton, a Southern small-town high school football coach, had Burt Reynolds written all over him, and *Evening Shade* came into our lives like a true blessing. It meant moving back to California, which was a small effort to make in exchange for gifted actors like Hal Holbrook and Marilu Henner, Charles Durning, Ossie Davis, and Michael Jeter. It was an ensemble production, and Burt would wear many hats: Not only would he act on the series, he would coproduce and sometimes direct.

From where I had been sitting since our wedding, we had been living a good life, with a healthy marriage and a wonderful child. And now we were moving back to California—into a rather palatial mansion Burt had rented, on five acres in Bel-Air—to be among our old friends and colleagues, who would treat my husband with the respect and admiration I believed he deserved. Toward the end of *Stryker,* I had started to see some familiar signs—moodiness, sudden bursts of anger—and I was hoping that the move and the new challenge would head the danger off at the pass.

Although John and Janet Spring came to California with us, I was quickly out of sync with them and they with me. Something had happened to Quinton during their time with him, and it was beginning to make me uneasy.

I knew that three- or four-year-old boys in quest of their independence routinely give their mommies a bad time, but this one was making me jump through hoops. He started sassing me, in what was rapidly becoming a British accent. He would run toward me and then stop suddenly, looking over to the Springs almost as though he were asking their permission. He didn't want to be hugged or cuddled, he didn't want to accompany me anywhere or settle down for a story.

It wasn't just little-boyness; he seemed almost afraid to show affection to me in front of them. The weirdest thing was that when the Springs were off duty and Jeanne Jensen was the weekend nanny, Quinton was his normal self—energetic and ram-bunctious certainly, but cuddly and fun to be with.

The relationship between parents and the people who care for their children—and in particular between mothers and caretak-ers—can be a delicate, difficult negotiation. Questions of love, loyalty, and authority are hard enough for adults, but they are true torture for kids. I knew that Quinton was getting caught in the middle. The happy baby had become a petulant, naughty toddler.

As he began to misbehave with frequency, the Springs got rougher and rougher on him. They shoved him, they shook him, and they called him awful names—turd, moron, idiot—in angry voices that grew louder as they grew angrier. If I had ever treated Deidra like that, or spoken to her like that, my parents would have come after me with garden tools!

I tried talking to Burt about it but saw very quickly that there was little purpose. He was up to his chin in the new series, and more to the point, since he had never raised a child, he simply did not see the problem. As far as he was concerned, there *was* no problem, unless it was that "Loni is being unreasonable."

It wasn't until Burt's dad and sister came out to visit us that I finally found my allies. My father-in-law, although a traditional strict disciplinarian who believed in physical punishment, was appalled at what was going on and equally appalled that nobody was paying attention to my concerns about it. So he and Nancy went to Burt and told him what was happening with his son. Big Burt's word was law: *Whoosh,* the Springs were gone.

After their departure, Jeanne Jensen reported that she'd heard Janet say nasty things about me, not only in front of Jeanne, but in front of Quinton as well.

In retrospect I've often wondered if Burt was trying to use them somehow, to set me up—to be discouraged by my son's behavior, to feel rejected by him, and ultimately, perhaps, to abandon him. At least two people heard him say that Pam Seals would eventually be Quinton's mother. And after our separation, one friend heard Pam tell Quinton, "You better get used to me, I'm going to be your new momma."

After the Springs were gone, Sybil McCrorie, Scottish god-send, came and tackled our short, cantankerous problem. And under her good guidance (which continues today), my sunny Quinton returned.

Until *B. L. Stryker,* and except for his frequent appearances on talk shows, Burt had never wanted to go back to doing television. TV wasn't art, it wasn't theater, it wasn't serious, it wasn't big enough for him anymore. But after *Stryker,* and from the very beginning of *Evening Shade,* Burt made himself at home on TV.

There are movie stars, sex symbols, whom we may look at and fantasize about, but in reality we don't want them anywhere near us. They're too formidable or frightening or complicated. We can't imagine them living next door to us, let alone in our house. But with Burt, as with performers like Candice Bergen and Ted Danson, there was an approachable quality, a vulnerability be-neath the zinging one-liners and the good looks. And the writers on *Evening Shade* used that quality for maximum effect. Burt Reynolds–as–Wood Newton could've lived right down your street. He inhabited the part, and as the show gathered momen-tum and became a big success, he seemed very happy about the whole thing.

His investment in the series was financial as well as creative and emotional: As many series stars now do, he had a percentage, along with Linda and Harry and the network. In addition, to resolve some of his constant financial troubles, he had borrowed four million dollars from CBS against the eventual syndication of the series; that is, when the series was eventually sold as a package and the episodes could run on other channels, Burt would then repay the loan from his share of the proceeds from that sale.

Right from the start *Evening Shade* felt like an adventure we were on together, because now he was in TV sitcom territory, my old neighborhood. And unless I was working myself, I never missed a Friday night taping. Burt always made sure the audience knew I was there, proudly introducing me from where I sat. He asked my opinion of line readings and scenes. He'd move me down a few rows and ask me to watch a rehearsed scene from one vantage point, and then move me up and over so I could see it from another angle. Rence Valente, an associate producer, once told me, "He looks for you all the time, for your approval." And more often than not, he got it. There wasn't one moment that I didn't feel I was a partner in the whole process.

The night he won his Emmy, I would've given up twenty Emmys for him to get that one. The funny thing is, he wanted to sit way in the back of the auditorium, to make a quick escape if he lost. *When* he lost, because he was absolutely certain he would.

"No," I insisted. "Your name is on this chair down front, and that's where you're sitting. Because if they announce your nomination, and then announce that you've won, and the camera goes there and you're not sitting in that chair, we won't have a tape to show Quinton. I'll never forgive you if you win and you're not sitting where you're supposed to be sitting."

He grumped and he groaned, but he finally went down front and sat in the designated seat.

That particular Emmy ceremony will probably always be notable for Kirstie Alley's acceptance speech (for *Cheers*) in which she thanked her husband, Parker Stevenson, for "giving me the big one." But Burt went her one better by thanking me for "giving me the two big ones." Backstage, he spoke very movingly to the press about what the Emmy meant to him, what I meant to him, and how I had saved his life.

Chantal Westerman, the entertainment reporter for ABC, said I should've gotten the Wife Award that night, because when Burt won and the camera cut to me, a guy in the control booth said, "All I want in my life is for a woman to look at me the way Loni Anderson looks at Burt Reynolds."

After the ceremony we went to Chasen's for a celebratory dinner with everybody from CBS. Burt barely let go of my hand the whole evening. And then we came home and stayed up all night long, with the Emmy on the bed beside us, and watched the news coverage on TV, on all the networks and on E! What vindication it was, for both of us. He had finally received the acceptance and praise of his peers, and I felt that everything we had been through had been worth it.

"The man adores her," everybody said. "He worships the ground she walks on." He was always having my portrait painted, usually from photographs. Oils, acrylics, and watercolors, they were displayed everywhere, on walls on both coasts. Up until we were married, he had commissioned three; after the wedding there were four more. There's even a nude that I didn't pose for in the beginning but eventually posed for in a bikini—I was so proud of what I had accomplished working out, and the guy wasn't getting the muscle structure right!

At first, of course, it was flattering and romantic. But as time went on, it began to seem strange. He couldn't see a wall, in any of his offices or dressing rooms, without wanting to put an image on it. There were pictures of me, of the two of us together, and eventually of the three of us together, absolutely everywhere. I had family pictures, too, and photo albums going all the way back to grade school, but this was somehow different. I had this feeling of being enshrined—or entombed, maybe. Like being pinned in a butterfly collection.

In early 1991 I was cast as thirties vamp Thelma Todd in the TV movie *White Hot: The Mysterious Murder of Thelma Todd*. Todd was a comedienne and restaurant owner who had an affair with mobster Lucky Luciano, played in the movie by actor Robert Davi. At twenty-nine she was murdered, a crime that's still unsolved to this day. My costars were Paul Dooley, who's Brett Butler's boss on *Grace Under Fire* these days; Linda Kelsey, my old friend from the University of Minnesota showboat; and Scott Paulin, who played the detective/narrator.

That period of history, and its Art Deco style, has always been one of my favorites. It seems uncluttered and elegant to me, with its angular furniture and jewel-tone glassware, and the women's fashions draped to the body or beautifully cut on the bias. In my alternative universe, I've always had a fantasy in which I live alone in a perfect Deco apartment, in a high-rise building (maybe it looks like the Chrysler Building in New York City), where the doorman says, "Good evening, Miss Anderson," as I come through the doors. Everything in my perfect abode is white, with only occasional accents of black or claret—some interesting sculpture, maybe, or plush throw pillows. No children ever come there, and no men live there, although I would have a lover, of course. He'd be about twenty-five, wildly inventive and energetic. My rules for him would be: Don't talk, look wonderful, make great love, and then please leave. And once a week or so I would go to Paris for lunch. In a gorgeous silk georgette dress that I bought in Paris when I was there for lunch *last* week.

That place isn't real, of course—it's just a fantasy I go to when I'm in pain. Real life is infinitely more complicated and interesting: Little boys spill orange juice on the carpet, I need my roots done every two weeks, the *National Enquirer* is pawing through the garbage. But after the Emmy, I would have ample opportunity over the next few months to long for the solitude and serenity of that fantasy. Because Burt had started using drugs again.

During the summer hiatus from the series, he went on the road with his own one-man show, *An Evening with Burt Reynolds*. He had always been a good storyteller—and, with his history in Hollywood, he had more than a few good ones to tell. He put together pictures of his family (including Quinton and me), his friends, and his acting colleagues, and combined them with his film clips and slides. The entire show was cued by computer, and he had a sizable technical staff, as well as Elaine Hall, who traveled with him. It was an expensive undertaking—and they lost money—but when he was first creating it, I believed it was a perfect coming-together of everything he did so well.

The performances and the audiences were both wildly erratic. One night Burt was brilliant, the next he was awful; one night the audience was bad, the next night terrific. He began throwing temper tantrums and in many cases wouldn't start at all unless the theater was full. He would get out of sync with the computer and his tech staff, or wander around in his narrative until what was happening up on the screen had little or nothing to do with the anecdote he was telling. One story that made the rounds had his pills sewn into his jacket lining for easy access or falling out of his pockets onstage. When I visited him a couple of times while he was on the road, he was moody, distracted, and seemed genuinely irritated every time he glanced up and saw me looking back at him.

When he returned for the second season of *Evening Shade,* the rage returned with him. He would come in the door at night already in a dark mood that was all too familiar to me. He would check all the phone messages, look at my calendar, go through my mail. He'd pick a fight, agitated about a complaint that wasn't specific, and then it would escalate until he was incoherent. "You people . . . !" he'd shout, or "Everybody always . . . !" or "Nobody knows . . . !"

He started up again about Perry King. Or John Gavin, or anyone I had ever been in a movie with. I would try to walk away from a fight, and he would storm after me, knocking the furniture out of the way.

Soon I started hearing about arguments on the set. He didn't like something Linda Bloodworth-Thomason had written, or he didn't like the way a scene was blocked out. He would stop rehearsals, leave the stage, go to his dressing room. His workdays started getting longer, to accommodate the delays his behavior was causing.

One day he came to me quite upset, saying, "The *National Enquirer* wants a story from me. They say if I don't talk to them, they'll run a piece that says you've had plastic surgery."

"Oh, for Pete's sake," I laughed. "They can say I've been lifted from my toes to my hairline for all I care. I don't care if they say I'm a man! It doesn't matter, we don't need to cooperate with that rag on anything." And I thought that was the end of it.

A day or so later he came back and said, "Loni, I have to give them a story. They know who Quinton's birth parents are, and they're threatening to print it."

That hit all my panic buttons. "Oh, B.R.," I said, "we can't let that happen. Of course you have to give them something."

And so to keep the *Enquirer* from using whatever it was they had, he cooperated with them on some bogus story about his ongoing business difficulties.

What they had, of course, was Pamela Seals.

When Burt's old behaviors and the paranoia started up again, I never gave a minute's thought to the possibility of another woman; in fact, I would have bet my life on that being the very last thing I had to worry about. Infidelity just wasn't on my radar, which was alert for signs of addiction behavior and nothing else. He had married me; we were parents to a child. Oh, he was a legendary flirt— we had that in common—but he never was sexually voracious, not even in our earliest, most passionate days. He said later that we didn't make love for months or years before we separated, but that's not true. It might not have been great, it might not have been as frequently as I would have liked. I might've been disappointed on occasion, or perhaps he was, but we did have a physical relationship. When he was clean, we made love a lot; when he wasn't, we didn't. Anyone who has ever had a partner with a drug or alcohol problem knows that sex is erratic; that's textbook behavior. And what someone who loves an addict knows is, you don't take behavior personally. Or at least you try not to.

Chapter 16

I've always been very disciplined, both physically and emotionally. No matter what, I just soldier on. Maybe it's that Midwestern Lutheran thing, but whatever it comes from, I've always been grateful for it.

Once Burt introduced me to trainer Mike Abrums, regular physical workouts became very important to me. How I looked was part vanity, of course, but it was equal parts common sense and emotional survival. As long as I stayed strong and healthy, I could always get work, keep up with a young child, and withstand whatever else was going on in my personal life. Initially Burt had valued that discipline in me, but more and more he saw it as a negative reflection on him. "Miss Perfect," he would snarl. Because it was becoming increasingly clear that the part of me that had adored him had gone on hiatus.

I had begun treating my husband like a child, a loved but unruly child. I patronized him, I talked down to him. I ignored his insults and walked away in mid-conversation. I didn't laugh at his jokes, I rolled my eyes when he said outlandish things. I thought he was becoming pathetic, and I treated him with increasing contempt. I knew I was doing it—sometimes it was almost as though I were standing back observing my own behavior—and I didn't like the way it felt.

But when the cameras caught me looking at Burt with the adoring-wife look—the Nancy Reagan gaze, we called it—I wasn't faking it. When we were out in public, at charity events or with our friends at a restaurant, he was at his best. He was *on,* he was charming, handsome, funny, open, gallant. And charming to me as well, and gentle and affectionate. When he would take my hand in his, or put his arm around my shoulders, I would look up at him and think, here he is, here's Buddy Lee. And for that moment we connected, and all the old feelings came back in a rush.

The minute we were in private again, however, that man disappeared, and the angry, abusive person with a bad temper and a fistful of pills was standing in his place. Some of the names were familiar to me, a couple were new. Percodan, Valium or Ativan, Vicodin, Compazine, and Didrex, an amphetamine. And now, Prozac.

To make matters worse, there were increased rumors of drinking on the set. Someone at *Evening Shade* had opened a bottle of Evian and found vodka instead. Sybil discovered vodka in Evian bottles at home; even Quinton got a mouthful once, his big eyes watering as he gagged reflexively. We were in a downward spiral. I would look at the man in our house and think, who are you and what have you done with my husband?

The work of a daily series is arduous, of course. The day begins very early and often runs very late, and the schedule can be unforgiving. There was no question that Burt was exhausted, and the chemicals were making a bad situation worse. Quinton barely saw his dad at all; I would call the studio each night so he could at least say good night over the phone. As for weekends, once Burt got home on Friday nights, he would go to bed and stay there, with the shades drawn, for both Saturday and Sunday. If Quinton wanted to visit, he had to do it in that dark room. No bouncing on the bed, no talking above a whisper.

"Daddy's so tired," I would tell Q. when he wanted Burt to come outside, to play or sit in the sun beside the pool. "He's been working so hard for us."

Every so often Burt would arrive home laden with presents:

jewelry and flowers for me, toys for Q. The more guilty he was feeling, the more gifts would come in the door for us. I used to fantasize taking all my clothes off and surrounding my nude self with everything he'd ever given me. "This is what I have instead of you," I wanted to say. "Take it all back."

One night he brought in a toy truck for Quinton. When he handed it to him, Quinton shook his head and threw the truck down on the floor. "I want *you, Dad!*" he shouted. He was four at the time.

In 1992 Marilu Henner, Burt's "wife" on *Evening Shade* and an old friend as well, took an incredible (and loving) risk and suggested that he seriously consider talking to a therapist. The therapist she recommended was her own, Dr. Ruth Sharon, whose practice is in New York. And wonder of wonders, he took her up on the recommendation.

Burt had always resisted any clear-cut admission either that there were problems between us or that he had a problem with substance abuse of any kind. "Denial" is a mild term for what greeted me whenever I raised the possibility of getting help— no twelve-step stuff for him, and definitely no shrinks. But Marilu not only convinced him to talk with Dr. Sharon, she spent the first few sessions with him, almost like a coach teaching someone to swim. And then he came to me and asked if I would be part of the therapy process with him.

"I'm having so many problems," he said. "But I want to work on them, and I want you to feel about me the way you used to. So please, let's do this together."

I threw my arms around him, I was so relieved. It felt like a prayer had been answered.

Although Dr. Sharon's office is in New York, Burt had special phone lines put into our house in California, so that we could speak with her once a week—together—as well as see her in person whenever we were in New York on business. This is how Marilu had handled it, and she and Burt talked to the doctor from their *Evening Shade* dressing rooms. It might sound like an awkward arrangement, but I was so grateful that we seemed at last to be on the right track, I wouldn't have cared if we'd had phone lines to the planet Saturn.

Once the phones were in, once he had arranged the whole routine, Burt introduced me to Dr. Sharon over the phone, and after that he never spoke to her again. He didn't even make excuses; he simply said, "I don't want to do this anymore," and that was the end of the discussion. Just as he'd found me a trainer—his—and then stopped going himself, he found me a therapist—his—and stopped that as well. I stayed with it.

I never said to Dr. Sharon, at any time, "How do I get out of this marriage?" I didn't want to get out of it; I wanted it to work. But, I told her, I felt like I was emotionally shut down in the lust department; the switch was in the off position. It had nothing to do with wanting anyone else. I didn't. I didn't *want,* period.

"I still love him," I said, "but I don't desire him. And what's worse, I don't respect him. I don't have a husband, and I don't have a father for my child. I want the husband and the father back again, and I want those feelings back again, too."

"But you can't make a marriage work all by yourself, Loni," she said. "Can't we get him back on the line?" I couldn't even get him to talk to me about it anymore, so Dr. Sharon called him any number of times at the *Evening Shade* studio, leaving messages on his private line. But he never returned her calls.

When I told her about the drugs, Dr. Sharon was quite alarmed. She arranged a three-way conference call, bringing in a colleague of hers who was a specialist in pharmacology and toxicology. He didn't know who I was; all he knew was that I was Dr. Sharon's client, and my husband was taking these pills and mixing them with vodka. As the two doctors listened, I held the bedside bottles in my hand and read the names off the labels. There was an audible gasp on the other end of the line.

"What you can expect," said the toxicologist, "is that one day your husband just won't wake up."

That night, when Burt came in the door, I went to him. I had been rehearsing my speech all day and was determined not to cry and not to raise my voice.

233

"I talked to a doctor today, about all the pills you're taking," I said quietly. "And he says that if you don't stop, you're going to die. B.R., Quinton's not even five, and he won't remember you if you die. He won't have you, I won't have you. And if you die because of this, nothing else you've ever done will count. They'll only remember that you died of a drug overdose."

All I got in return was a stone face. "I'm fine," he said. "There is no problem."

When the old troubles had surfaced again, Linda Jensen said to me one day, "What would you do if Mr. Right—the real Mr. Right—walked through the door?" It was a girlfriend kind of question, the speculative, silly kind of way old friends try to circle around a big problem.

"If I haven't fallen for anybody else by now," I said wearily, "after everything we've been through, at the age I am now, how likely is it that Mr. Right hasn't come and gone already? One fling in nearly twelve years and I'm still here, married to Mr. Almost Right. That's all there is to it. Mr. Trouble, Mr. Occasionally Adorable. And I'm staying, no matter what." With Dr. Sharon's help, I thought, I will figure this out, and we'll get through this somehow.

My commercial agent, Nina Blanchard, had been approached by someone with a small cosmetics company who was interested in having me put my name on a beauty product I had used and liked. I've had a checkered career with cosmetics: I'm allergic to a lot of things, to lanolin, to fragrances in facial products. When I wear perfume, which I only rarely do, I spray it in the air and kind of walk through it, hoping something will land.

But this particular product had worked well for me—I didn't break out, there weren't any rashes, or any problems at all. So we decided, well, all right, they could use my name, and in return, I would receive a percentage of the sales.

A short time later I was sent a videotape of some Minnesota news program that had done an exposé of telemarketing scams. The scheme worked like this: In the mail you received a notice saying you had absolutely won a huge and wonderful prize—a

trip to Hawaii or a boat or a TV or a four-wheel-drive vehicle.
To collect your prize you had to call a certain phone number.
And when you called it, you heard, "We will send you your
prize. All you have to do is buy this Loni Anderson skin care
line, for five hundred and some dollars. So give us your credit
card number or send us your check."

It turned out that without my knowledge, the cosmetics company had sold the product to the telemarketing group. The "prize
winners" did in fact get a product (after they sent in their money),
and it was the one I had approved and put my name on. But the
big prize, the Jeep or the trip, never materialized. When the
people tried to track down their winnings, they reached discon-
nected numbers or storefronts where nobody was doing business
anymore. That made it interstate commerce fraud—and my
name had been used as the bait. At which point the FBI came
calling.

I thought I had been protected. It was clear that I hadn't been.
Nina Blanchard called to suggest a solution. "I've been represented for a while by this old, bluestocking Los Angeles firm,"
she said. "They're not entertainment lawyers or fly-by-nights—
they handled the J. Paul Getty estate. Let's talk to them and see
if they can't clear this mess up for you."

She made the appointment for me, and we arranged to meet
with the attorneys at her office. When I walked in, there were
two lawyers at the desk, and one of them was Geoffrey Brown.

God knows I have been blessed with handsome men in my
life, both on-screen and off, but I was embarrassed to find that I
couldn't take my eyes off this one. Soft-spoken, a little over six
feet tall, with a touch of gray at the temples and the bluest eyes
I'd ever seen. I had to concentrate hard on what he was saying,
because I just wasn't listening very well. He had a quiet air of
authority and a reassuring sense of humor, which I desperately
needed, since I was certain I was going to end up on a wanted
poster in the post office. As he spoke, I checked his left hand to
see if he was wearing a wedding ring. And then I caught myself
and kind of laughed inside. Well, I thought, the old girl's not
dead yet.

We all agreed that Geoff's firm would represent me and handle the case through its conclusion. In fact, when Burt and I were in Florida during the next *Evening Shade* break, Geoff flew down and stayed at Valhalla with us and sat in with me as counsel when I met with the FBI. The fraud matter was soon resolved. I was cleared of any involvement with it, and that's where the whole thing ended.

Geoff and I became friends then. I liked him, admired him. I know what I'll do, I thought, I'll fix him up with somebody. I had so many single friends, women I really loved. And I decided he was such a great guy, we couldn't let him get away. I knew he was from Pennsylvania, I knew he'd gotten his law degree from UCLA, but I didn't know another thing about him. I didn't even know if he was involved with anyone—I never delved into his personal life. I just kept giving him the phone numbers of all my California girlfriends.

Things at home were becoming increasingly impossible; the violent arguments were constant, the physical confrontations were happening more often. Big explosions, accompanied with physical force. Burt never hit me, but he was in my face. Quinton witnessed the yelling and screaming, and once he threw himself at Burt, crying, "Don't you ever yell at my mommy again!"

Burt's mother, Fern, had died during the previous summer, while he was filming *Cop and a Half* in Florida. She had lived a long life—she was ninety-two when she died—but her death had shaken him badly, and he was having a hard time with his grief. It was a pain I understood very well, and I tried to comfort him, as did the people he was working with, but he was having none of it.

One night Burt came home from the set and was in mid-explosion before he was fully through the door. "I can't stand to come home and look at your face," he snapped. "All day long I'm at work, and people respect me there. They listen to what I have to say. Then I walk into this house, and I see what you think of me."

"What do I think?" I asked. "What do you see?"

"I see that I'm not the man I want to be," he shouted, "and not the actor I want to be. I'm not the father I want to be. I'm not *anything!*" And then he grabbed me so hard I saw stars, and he threw me up against the wall. All I remember is flying through the air, hitting the wall, and then a blank.

When I came to, he was beside me on the floor, sobbing. Begging my forgiveness. And I finally realized how vulnerable I was. For years I had believed I could handle Burt, get away with more. At that moment I knew for certain that I couldn't.

I said to him, "You know, if you kill me, it won't matter how sorry you are, because I'll still be dead. And you will be in jail. And being sorry won't get you out."

After that, when I saw those rages coming, I thought of all kinds of ways to circumvent them. I tried telling him jokes, I tried laughing wildly. Once, I even deliberately pushed myself into hysteria, so completely incoherent and babbling that he stopped yelling abruptly and just stared at me.

"What the hell is wrong with you?" he asked. Inside I was thinking, oh, God, I should get an award for this, I really should.

I knew that Burt had had surgery on his knees and that they were bad. Once, in the middle of his grabbing me, I kicked out and connected with his knee, and he dropped like a stone to the floor. But he was six feet tall, two hundred pounds. I'm five-foot six, a hundred seventeen pounds on a good day. It was pretty clear to me that I was outclassed.

Another time, he was working himself into such a fever pitch that I just slowly started taking off my clothing, one item at a time. Not to seduce him, but to stop him. He was so private, so averse to that kind of display, that when I was entirely naked, he simply turned and walked away, shutting the door behind him. As I sat there watching him go, with my clothes all over the floor, I thought, *hmmm,* that looks like a surefire tactic.

One night, after an *Evening Shade* taping, Burt was having heated words with Doug Jackson, one of the producers. The cast was taping public service announcements, and Burt, angry that Hal Holbrook's was going to be taped before his, stormed off the set and into his dressing room. Doug followed him. As the argument escalated, I could see what was coming. Seconds before Burt lunged at Doug, I just hurled myself at him from behind, grabbed his arms with all my weight, and hung on with every ounce of strength I had. He kept right on moving, yelling and trying to swing at Doug, and dragging me across the floor behind him. We finally got him calmed down, but it wasn't a pretty scene.

In the months after we separated, he would throw a punch at former *Cheers* star John Ratzenberger, who was guest-directing an *Evening Shade* episode. He would hit his longtime friend Jim Hampton, who was directing and writing for the show. He would hurl a chair at young Jay Ferguson, who played his son, and the chair would come very close to leveling Kathie Lee Gifford instead. The *Evening Shade* crew would attempt a drug-and-alcohol intervention, and Burt would walk out on them. In short, he would bring the whole house of cards down on his head and on the heads of many talented, dedicated people as well.

During my years in Hollywood, I had developed close personal friendships with two women who had become indispensable to me: Sharon Sanders, my manicurist, and Germaine Morgan, my hairdresser. Every woman knows the kinds of secrets, both serious and silly, that are often shared during hair-and-nail sessions, and these two had heard more than a few of mine. Both of them had worked with me on location (Germaine especially, since the *Mansfield* haircide incident) and over the years had become part of the bicoastal girlfriend gang. Some time after my marriage ended, I found out that Clarence Goss, our cook, had gone to Germaine and Sharon and told them what was going on in the house. He told them that he was keeping a constant eye on me and that they should watch out for me, too. And he had gone to Linda Jensen and said, "Get her out of there." Because I was in danger.

Deidra and Charlie had relocated from Florida to northern California, to Lake Tahoe. We saw them less and less; they weren't sure exactly what was going on, but they knew something was, and that it was bad.

Deidra had been out of love with Burt for a long time but tried to keep her feelings to herself. As she said to me later, "How many times can you say to someone, 'I don't like your husband,' and still be friends with them? Not very often."

For his part, Charlie had stuck with Burt a little longer than Deedee. Burt was usually genial around Charlie, and they both enjoyed the guy/jock things. But little by little Charlie had figured it out. And after we spent Christmas of 1992 with them and Burt never came out of his room (except for a public appearance to hear Harry Belafonte and parade Quinton around like a trophy in front of photographers), he was history for Charlie as well.

When Deidra and Charlie's first child, my granddaughter McKenzie Kaye, was born in March of 1993, Burt said to me, "Are you ready to have a little girl with me now? Do you want your girl now?"

"B.R., right this minute I'm celebrating my granddaughter," I said, quite stunned at what he'd just said. Only minutes before I had called Bruce Hasselberg to tell him that we shared a granddaughter, and this intersection of old history and recent drama was making me dizzy. "But another baby . . . are you sure that's what you really want?"

"Yes," he said. "I'm sure."

"We'll talk about it when I get home." How, I wondered, could I have so much joy in my heart at the arrival of Little Mac and still have so much room for pain?

In May of 1993 *Evening Shade* was on hiatus, and the entire household went to Florida for the break. Burt was beginning production work on *The Man from Left Field,* his TV movie with Reba McEntire.

Along with everything else that was going on between us, Burt had decided that what I really needed was a new house. He would sell Valhalla and start all over again, building us a brand new place, because, he said, "I want to see you be all excited about something, kid, and be happy again, like you used to be."

He had picked out a lot in Admiral's Cove, a beautiful new Florida community on the Intracoastal canal. When he took me to see the lot, we invited our friends Bobby and Diane Goldsboro to go with us, and there was some discussion of their buying a lot next door.

He had even found an architect. "I promise, everything you've ever wanted will go in this house," Burt said. There were blueprints being made, decorators being consulted. Then the nice architect made a critical error.

"You shouldn't even have to pay for the lot," he said to Burt. "The people who live across the canal should pay, because after all, they'll get to look at your lovely wife." At which point all hell broke loose, the deal fell through, and that was the end of the dream house.

I had to make a quick business trip back to California for a few days with Linda Jensen. I had signed on to do the next season of *Nurses,* which I was very much looking forward to, and there were some final preparations—wardrobe fittings, contracts, and so forth—for us to take care of. The last incident of physical violence, just before I left for L.A., was the one that should have sent me screaming into the streets, and to this day I don't know why it didn't. Burt had shoved me around, bouncing me off the furniture and yelling and finally pushing me to the floor. Then, as I watched, he opened the drawer in the bedside table, pulled out a gun, and tried to hand it to me, saying, "Here, why don't you kill yourself and do us all a favor!"

Burt had grown up with guns, but after Quinton came, I asked him to put them all away, out of the house, out of the child's reach. And he swore that he had done it. Now here he was, standing over me with a gun in his hand. And I thought numbly, this is it, this is as bad as it gets.

The next morning he was contrite, as usual. "I haven't been a very good husband," is the way he started the conversation. "It's the pressures of *Evening Shade,* and now there's all the work to do with this film. But we don't spend enough time together, and now you're going to be working, too. After your business in L.A. is done, let's go up to the place in North Carolina. It could be kind of like a second honeymoon. Maybe we can find a way to put this marriage back on track."

Quinton, Sybil, and Clarence would be going back to California, so it would be just the two of us. Maybe I was punch-drunk at that point, or maybe there was just enough naïveté left, just enough hope, to believe that this time he meant it. "OK," I said.

The morning before Linda and I left for L.A., I first went with Burt to visit our friend Patty Fuller, who had been bravely undergoing cancer treatment for many long and difficult months. Her prognosis was very bad, and she had left the hospital for the final time, wanting instead to be at home with her three children. After the visit, as we were preparing to leave, she looked at us with such an intense expression on her face, saying, "It's so good to see you two together. It always gives me hope."

I thought my heart would break on the spot—I didn't know what, if anything, Patty knew about our troubles. Was she trying to remind us about what we had shared? Or was she saying good-bye?

I was planning to return to Florida the following Tuesday. The Saturday night before, Burt called me at the house in Bel-Air. "The editing isn't going well here," he said. "So we're not going to be able to go to North Carolina after all."

"Oh," I said. "Well, since that's the case, and since everybody else is coming back here next week, why don't I just stay here and wait for them? If we can't go to the mountains, and you're so busy in the studio, it's silly for me to make the trip back there."

"No, no," he insisted. "Just because we can't go away, that doesn't mean I don't want you here with me. You can be in the studio with me while I'm editing. I like to be able to ask your opinion about things. Please, come back. We'll be alone, and we can talk things through."

I agreed. The next Tuesday, Charles Nelson Reilly rode in the limo to the airport with Linda and me, just to keep us company. He called Burt from the VIP lounge, on the cellular phone that Linda carried in her purse, and we passed the phone back and forth between us, each of us chatting with Burt, who had, he said, been buried in the studio and was very much looking forward to my return.

After we hung up, Charles said, "Boy, Burt really misses you when you're not there. He says he can't wait to see you."

On the flight down, I was so preoccupied that I couldn't read my book. I found myself hoping that maybe we would be able to talk about a formal rehabilitation program. I knew I couldn't handle his demons alone anymore.

When I got back to Valhalla, everything seemed pretty normal. Quinton, Sybil, and Clarence were getting organized for their trek back to L.A. on Thursday. Jeanne Jensen would be accompanying them, too, after which Burt and I would be alone. On Wednesday Q. and I kind of futzed around all day by the pool and with his toys while Burt was in his editing studio. When he came in that night, we all had dinner together, and then, before Quinton went to bed, the three of us were laughing and rough-housing on the big bed in our room. We were making what we called Reynolds' Sandwiches, where Quinton would be in the middle, and Burt and I would squeeze in on either side of him, or I'd be in the middle, and Burt and Q. would be on either side of me.

After a while Sybil came in to retrieve Quinton, and he went off to bed. Soon the whole house shut down for the night, because of the travel plans for the next day. Burt and I began to get ready for bed. After I'd washed my face and brushed my teeth, I came back into the bedroom and asked Burt, who was already in bed, if he wanted me to read to him for a little while, and he suddenly said, "No, I can't stay here."

"Oh, do you have to go back to the studio tonight?" I asked.

"No," he said. "No. I haven't been a very good husband, and I think I need some time alone."

I said, "You mean, you and I alone, right?" Because he had specifically asked me to come back to Florida so we could be alone and talk things out. Isn't that what I'd heard?

He shook his head. "No, I just don't think I'm any good to anyone right now. I think I'll go and stay at the ranch for a couple of days." He had gotten out of bed and put his clothes on, and now he was walking back and forth in front of the bed.

"B.R., I don't understand," I said. "Should I wait for you here then?"

"You can do whatever you want to do," he said. "I just have to go away."

I had the strangest feeling inside of me. Anxiety, unease. Something was off. And so I just asked him straight out. "Burt, is there someone else? Are you leaving me?"

"No, no," he said, shaking his head again. "There is no one else. There never will be. You're the love of my life, kid. You and Quinton, you guys are my life."

He went to the door, and then he said, "Just know this, just know how much I love you." And then he started down the stairs. Alarmed, I grabbed a robe and followed him.

Scott Jackson, his assistant, was down there waiting for him. I was confused for a minute. Scott didn't live at our house, he had his own place. What was he doing here? And the car was out front. Burt had obviously summoned him and the car.

Burt turned around at the door, looked at me, and said again, "I love you." And then he walked out.

As Scott turned to follow him, I said, "Scott, do you know what's going on here? Is he leaving me?"

Obviously uncomfortable, Scott said, "Oh, you know . . . he just needs some time." And then they were both gone.

I ran back upstairs to Sybil's room. "I'm not sure," I said, "but I think Burt just left me."

"What?" She was completely astonished.

"Did something happen the week I was in Los Angeles?" I asked. "Was there some kind of scene or something?"

"No," she assured me. "Everything has been fine here, Loni. He's been busy, but that's all. He's probably just in one of his moods."

I called Clarence down at the gatehouse. "Do you know what's going on with Burt?" I asked him, telling him what had just happened.

"No," he said. "I sure don't. Hold on, Miss A., I'm coming up there."

For hours, it seemed, the three of us sat in the kitchen, huddling around the counter, trying to figure out what was going on with Burt. These people were members of our family, they knew him as well and saw him as often as I did, yet they were mystified, too.

It was nearly two when I went back upstairs and looked at the bed. I can't get back in there, I thought. So I went downstairs and called Linda, who lived in Port St. Lucie, about forty-five minutes away, and told her what had happened. "Something's really wrong here," I said.

"It's a mood, Loni," she said, trying to reassure me. "Don't panic, don't worry. I'm sure he'll be back in the morning, just as soon as he gets it together and realizes he's being a jerk."

As we talked, I was walking around with the long phone cord trailing behind me, and I began to notice there was furniture missing, from the living room, the dining room, and the den. Chairs, a couple of paintings, a side table. I had decorated that house, I knew perfectly well what was supposed to be where. Sybil had come downstairs, and as we went from room to room, I was telling Linda about the empty spaces we were seeing where things used to be.

"I'm coming first thing in the morning," she said.

I didn't sleep the rest of the night. I didn't cry or read. I just lay there, watching the clock move, waiting for it to be daylight. Eventually Linda arrived, and Jeanne. And then Nancy Ann, Burt's sister, dropped in because she wanted to say good-bye to Quinton.

"Where's Bud?" she asked.

"I don't know . . . I think he just left me," I said.

She looked at me like I was joking. "Oh, Loni, no. He's probably just in one of his moods again," she said.

Right after Nancy left, the front gate buzzer went off. Linda answered it and said to me, "It's Burt's lawyer, Loni. Shall I let him in?" I started to tremble, and I couldn't get any words out. I just nodded.

"Burt's been up all night, and he knows what he wants," the lawyer announced. "He wants a divorce. And there are two sheriffs outside the gate waiting to serve you with the papers. I just wanted to inform you. Are you going to let them in?"

He handed Clarence a plane ticket for me, to go back to L.A. with the rest of them that very same day. He'd even gotten me on the same flight, in first class with them. Obviously this had all been in the planning stages for weeks. This time, I thought, he's truly gone insane.

"But why didn't he just tell me?" I asked.

I let the sheriffs in. I didn't cry. I was stone. Quinton was upstairs with Sybil; I wanted the sheriffs out of there before he came down. I said to Linda, "I don't know what to do, I don't know what my rights are. I don't have a lawyer here in Florida. I mean, I had one, I thought, but I guess he's Burt's lawyer now. I'm supposed to be leaving the state with my son. Today. Can I do that?"

And sure enough, as we read through the documents, we discovered that no, according to the papers, I was not allowed to take Q. out of the state. And we were all scheduled to go in just a few hours.

"I'm not leaving here without my son, Linda," I said.

"I'm calling Geoff Brown," Linda said, reaching for the phone. "It looks like he's the only lawyer we've got."

Geoff was as stunned as we were, but he didn't want to give me any advice. "I will find you a divorce lawyer, Loni," he promised. "I'll find you the best one I can, as fast as I can. And I'll call your publicist and the limo company, so we can get you off the plane at this end."

"But, Geoff, she's actually been served with these papers," Linda said.

"Well, they can file them with the court anytime after they're served," he said, "but they probably haven't had time to do it yet, so don't worry about the publicity or the press."

In less than an hour, all the lawyers were on the phones, with faxes flying from California to Florida and back again. Burt's lawyers were waiving this, waiving that, saying that yes, I could leave with Quinton. They wanted me out of here, they wanted us all gone.

I went upstairs to pack. After Burt had sold Carolwood, although a number of my things went into storage and some were in the rented house in L.A., many had been moved to this house. Personal belongings, clothing, jewelry, photographs. But all I could think of was getting out. Running.

A little while later, I had just finished my shower, and I heard helicopters. They sounded very close. And indeed, when I looked out the bathroom window, I saw someone dangling from a helicopter on a rope ladder. A photographer. And there I stood, wrapped in a towel.

"My God!" I called out to Linda. "It's the press! Look, there are the TV call letters on the side!"

Minutes later, our phone started ringing: The headlines were on CNN. The lawyers had filed the papers with the local court immediately after I was served, so it was all public record, and everybody, it seemed, had gotten the word. There were news vans at the front gate, there were five helicopters over the house. Are they the same five that had hovered over our wedding? I wondered.

Quinton was thrilled at the air show outside. "Mommy," he said happily, "look at all these choppers!" Television reporters were calling from California. The minute Linda put the phone down ("No comment!"), it would ring again. All our friends, asking, "Is this a joke?"

My friend Deidre Hall, from *Days of Our Lives,* who had played *Win, Lose or Draw* with us, called from L.A. "Loni, what on earth is going on down there? Did you know this craziness is on CNN?"

I kept trying to reach Deedee in Tahoe, worried that she would hear the news from someone else. Finally I tracked her down at school and quickly told her what was going on. She simply couldn't believe it. "I can't talk now, honey," I said. "I'll call you just as soon as I get home."

There wasn't time to talk to anyone; we had to get out of there. Linda was frantically making phone calls: to Bob, our Florida limo driver, and Dave Gregg, the security guy from The Gardens mall in Palm Beach, who we'd always used to help us at the airport. Geoff was making the same kind of calls on the

West Coast, to Cel Castro, our L.A. limo driver, who has all these huge, football-player sons; we knew we'd need the whole Castro team when we landed at LAX.

When the car drove through the front gate, with our little band inside—Linda, Jeanne, Clarence, Sybil, Q., and me—an entire phalanx of press vans and photographers was out there waiting, and the helicopters were still thundering above us like something out of *Apocalypse Now*. They were with us all the way to the airport. And somewhere on the B-R Ranch, I knew, Burt was hiding out, completely turning his back on what he had created.

He had thrown me to the wolves. And Quinton. To the wolves. This little boy, whom he said he loved so much, and me. We were his life, he had said only the night before. What a director. He had always been such a wizard for setting the stage, for organizing an event—well, he had certainly organized the hell out of *this* one. And he had clearly been working on it for a long time.

When we arrived at the airport, there was a complete mob scene. Quinton was getting scared. I hadn't cried, and I hadn't raised my voice, but my entire body was rigid, and since I was holding him, there was no way the tension in me wasn't being transferred to him as well. The photographers were all yelling his name. Quinton, Quinton, look over here, Quinton! Quinton, can you give us a smile?

"Mommy, why are all these people here?" he asked, trying to hide his head in the curve of my neck. We were surrounded by people, shouting, shoving microphones in my face. I could barely think.

"Well, Quinton, because they love you so much," I whispered into his ear. "And you're leaving Florida today, so they're all here to tell you good-bye."

The airport personnel shepherded us into the Delta VIP lounge, where we had a forty-five-minute wait for our flight. I sat at a table with Linda, who would stay behind, Jeanne, and Sybil, while Clarence and Dave Gregg took Quinton over to the window and tried to entertain him, pointing out all the planes landing and taking off. I've since heard that Burt tells a story that has me at the airport locked in a clinch with the "security guard from the mall, who had become more than a special friend." What a pathetic joke.

Now that I'd left Burt and Valhalla behind, I knew I was going into some kind of real shock. As I sat there, I couldn't say anything, I couldn't feel anything. I wasn't even sure I was actually there. Is "audioanimatronic" a word? Or maybe I was a hologram.

Once on the plane, I looked out the window or read stories to Quinton. The poor little guy had diarrhea throughout the entire flight west. Sybil made endless trips to the bathroom with him, and in between, Q. went from her lap to my lap to Jeanne's to Clarence's and then back to me again. The little boy had all his people around him, but he knew very well that his people were not OK.

There was reporters on the plane, which I didn't realize until halfway through the flight when a woman came over, knelt down beside me, and said she was from the *Enquirer*. She had been in first class with us the whole time, just watching us, I guess.

"Do you have anything to say?" she asked.

I shook my head. "No, I don't."

"Well, if you want to talk anytime during the flight, just let me know," she said.

I looked at her in disbelief. "I won't," I said. She went away.

I couldn't eat, couldn't think, and there was no room to pace. I can't believe he did this, I thought. I can't believe it. Somewhere over Kansas, I remembered that Patty Fuller's funeral had been that morning.

When we landed in Los Angeles, Cel Castro and his large sons hustled us out of the plane, past the press, out of the airport, and home. The five-acre estate was completely gated, so once there we were a good distance away from any interference.

The phones were ringing off the hook. Ann-Margret and Roger Smith had called, thinking it was some kind of mistake. Robert Goulet called, asking, "Is he going through a mid-life crisis or something? A very late mid-life crisis?" Bobby and Diane

Goldsboro called, as did Michael Jeter from *Evening Shade*. What, they all wanted to know, was going on? All I could tell them was, "I don't know."

The next morning I had to tell my son that his dad had decided he wouldn't be living with us anymore. In all my life I had never imagined anything harder than taking my child through the minefield of that first divorce discussion. And when Quinton's eyes got big with confusion and he asked, "Why, Mommy?" I had to give him the same answer I had given everyone else. "I don't know."

Chapter 17

For weeks on end I never went out of the house. Although I ate a lot of ice cream—it was the only thing that would go down—I lost fifteen pounds in two weeks. I didn't cry, didn't break. I had a little boy who was watching me carefully for cues. He and Sybil had to stay pretty close to home; we were afraid that if they left the house, they'd be followed and Quinton would be photographed. In fact, the *Enquirer* did follow them to Quinton's school and published a picture of the school that clearly identified it—and its location. And a helicopter buzzed the estate one day when Q. and Sybil were out on the tennis court. Press was lying in wait outside the gate; we'd walk down to the mailbox, and there they were, shouting questions through the fence.

Mickey Freeman, my publicist, phoned me and said, "I just got a call from the *Globe,* which said there's a cocktail waitress involved here somewhere."

And I said, "What? Don't be ridiculous."

I met with the divorce attorneys that Geoff had found for me; they came to the house. At first they wanted to file criminal charges against Burt, because he had fraudulently brought me to Florida under the pretext of taking a second honeymoon and putting the marriage back together, when actually it was so he could file suit there—because the community property laws in Florida would be more financially favorable to him than the ones in California.

Since Quinton had lived most of his life in California, and since I didn't want to be on the end of Burt's yo-yo string, running back and forth with custody battles, I petitioned that the custody matters be heard in California and countersued for divorce there, too. It was decided that the divorce action would be heard in Florida and custody in California.

The day after I left Florida, Burt invited the *Enquirer* reporters to the ranch. A week later the story was printed: We had discussed divorce for hours, he said, it was a mutual decision, and there was no other woman. He even said he'd talked to Quinton about it. There are always items like this in the tabloids, things in the wind, and you just have to dismiss them all or you'd go mad. But this was something else; he *gave* them this story.

A couple of days after the story appeared, I received two phone calls. One was from Terry Warren, the young theater apprentice with whom Burt ultimately accused me of having an affair; the other was from a young woman, a former apprentice, whose name I don't want to use here.

Terry asked, "Don't you know about Pam?"

"I don't know what you're talking about," I said.

"Loni, he's had this other woman all along," Terry said. "In fact, I met her before I met you. We all knew about her from the first year of your marriage. And the reason I know this, which I am not proud to admit, is because I set up her hotel rooms, I entertained her when she was in Los Angeles or Florida and Burt couldn't be with her because he was with you. She was always with one of us, or pretending to be with somebody else. She was always where you were, only a few feet away."

The young woman former apprentice corroborated this, that they'd all known about her, that she had come to all of their classes and had done so almost from the beginning of our marriage. Not as a theater apprentice, but as Burt's shadow.

She had always been part of our lives. She had been in the

Jupiter Beach House. At one point Burt owned condos on both Florida coasts, in Pompano Beach, Miami, and Indian River. Maybe she had been in all of them. She'd been in my houses, in my bathroom, in my bed. Maybe she had gone through my clothes. Maybe she even wore them, I don't know. It's not like being raped, of course I can't say that, but it is like a thief coming into your home and taking your most private, precious things. And then it turns out that your husband is intimately acquainted with the thief.

She was often in the audience at the *Evening Shade* tapings, two or three rows behind me. Burt would blow kisses, said one of the cast members, and no one knew if they were to her or to me. She traveled with him on the one-man show tour bus, right after the first year of *Evening Shade*. Elaine Hall had helped arrange that, I discovered.

In fact, after all was said and done, Charlie and Deedee said, after they saw her picture in the paper, they remembered meeting her backstage at one of the one-man show performances. Tampa, maybe.

And a celebrity who shall remain nameless called Deedee and said, "I respect your mother too much not to tell you that there were a number of their friends who knew about Pam, and in fact Burt and Pam stayed at their houses."

Burt's former business manager kept trying to reach me, leaving messages that he had information about Pam Seals, about financial arrangements. I never talked to him, but we learned later that there were checks made out to her going back at least three years.

The insults just kept coming. Burt had brought her to Los Angeles for the Emmy ceremonies the year he got his nomination. He had installed her in a hotel room—in fact, at the very moment he was thanking me, with tears in his eyes, and me with tears in mine, Pam was cozily watching the ceremony with Vic Prinzi, the best man at our wedding, who was keeping her company that night.

Everybody knew, everybody knew. Our best man, the kids at the theater, Elaine Hall (who had been part of the girlfriend posse), some of our friends, some of the *Evening Shade* crew, Scott Jackson. Even Clarence knew, shortly before the end.

And then came the second *Enquirer* story. Burt and Pam together, in Los Angeles, with makeup and hair people fixing her up for a photo shoot. Burt even tried to get Mario Caselli, who had photographed our wedding, to do the pictures, but Mario declined. Charles Nelson Reilly posed for the story, Vic Prinzi posed. And there they were, the happy couple, in a hot tub, under a banner headline: MEET THE WOMAN I LOVE. "Burt Reynolds as a lover is every woman's dream," said Pam Seals, in an unending series of television ads she did—and was paid for—for that issue of the *Enquirer*. We rented videos during the period the ads were running, to keep Q. from seeing them on TV.

At one point someone wrote, "We'll be glad when the war between Burt and Loni is over, and we don't have to read about it anymore." What no one knew or believed was that it was a war with only one army fighting. I wanted the noise and the flow of ink to stop as much, if not more, than anyone else. When I look back on it now, I think that our divorce was part of the first wave of the tabloidization of the legitimate press. Gennifer Flowers, Michael Jackson, Tonya Harding, Woody and Mia, and Burt's secret love life. First we'd read it in the *Enquirer,* then days later it would show up in *Newsweek.* He said, she said. But they were wrong. I *never* said.

Every day was a new pain, a new humiliation, a new lie. I was talking to Lamar Jackson one afternoon, when I'd had just about enough. "There isn't a shower long enough to wash the filth of him off me," I said. And yet I still didn't cry. I knew that wasn't right. Why, I asked myself at night, can't I cry, and at least get it out of the way?

Anyone who lives with the constant threat of earthquakes—as Californians do—knows that there's absolutely nothing you can do in the middle of one except hold on until the ground beneath your feet stops shaking. And by then the damage is done. After that the next steps are to make sure you have all your body parts and to start to clean up the mess. So it was that I began to apply earthquake psychology to the chaos around me, all the while keeping my eyes open for the inevitable aftershocks.

Just as with *Nurses,* production for the next season of *Evening Shade* was about to begin, so within days after our return to Los Angeles, Burt rented yet another house there, and he and Pam took up residence. Although we did not speak directly, the attorneys made interim arrangements for visitation so that Quinton could see his dad. I knew that's the way it had to be, but I hated it when Sybil and Quinton would leave, and I watched the clock until their return.

Q. and I went up to Tahoe for a few days to visit Deidra and Charlie and my granddaughter. I had hoped for a respite from the circus, but the press was there, too. My daughter and her family have a home of their own and a life of their own, a life which is determinedly not show business, and yet there it all was, in their front yard. At one point a reporter even tried to break into their home, going from door to door, checking the locks, pounding on the window. Lying down on the floor so that I couldn't be seen from outside, I called the concierge at Harvey's casino, where we had made security arrangements on previous trips to Tahoe, and hired a private security guard for the house.

Deedee and Charlie were angry at the lies that were being told and asked me if they could say something to the press. All my friends had reacted the same way, as did my sister, Andrea, and my Minnesota cousins, Aunt Jackie's daughters, Sharon, Claudia, and Maxine.

Lynda Carter and Deidre Hall both called, each saying, "Loni, please let me go on television. Somebody's got to say something on your behalf!"

Burt's sister and her children called me from Florida, horrified at Burt's behavior. Nancy Ann is almost totally supported by Burt, but she's never been afraid to criticize his behavior or be a friend to me, as well as a loyal aunt to Quinton.

Nanny Betty and Nanny Joan both called, asking what they could do to help. Even my ex-husbands called, both saying, "Who do you want us to talk to? When can we talk?" And in fact, Russ did ultimately appear on *Jenny Jones* and *Hard Copy*.

But I asked everyone not to respond. "I don't have to defend myself," I said, "and you don't all have to be drawn into this. Just ignore it." I kept waiting for the ground to settle under our feet.

I heard that Burt was telling our mutual friends they weren't allowed to speak to me anymore. And some of them didn't. But others stood fast. Diane Goldsboro had to sneak over to the *Nurses* set to see me, but she did it. Doug and Diane McClure came and went very quietly, not wanting to attract attention but not willing for Burt to force them to choose sides. Even Lamar Jackson, who was caught in quite a difficult balancing act, and Karen, his then fiancée, stayed in close touch, as did director Alan Levi, who had come to Florida to direct a *Stryker* episode, and his wife, my friend Sam Currie.

Ricardo and Georgie stood fast as well. In fact, it was Ricardo who said, "You have to write a book, Loni. Don't let him have the last word. At least if you write the book, it will come from love."

In the midst of all the chaos, I noticed that the cars seemed to be disappearing. Clarence would take one out, to get the oil changed or to get a new inspection sticker, he said. All perfectly legitimate excuses. But then the car wouldn't come back. First the Cadillac, then the Ford Explorer wagon, then the Jaguar. All these cars had come as gifts, with big bows around them; the Explorer in particular had been a very vocal gift to Quinton from his dad. One by one they each rolled down the driveway, never to be seen again.

"Clarence, he's asked you to take the cars away, hasn't he?" I asked one day.

He looked uncomfortable. "Miss A., I don't want to get in the middle of this," he said.

"Well, I'm sorry about that," I said, "but if you're driving them from here to there—and then leaving them—you're already in the middle of it."

My lovely green Rolls—the one with my nameplate in it, which had moved to Florida around the time of *B. L. Stryker*—was never seen again, either.

Not long after that, Clarence left us and went to work solely for Burt. He was a nice man and had always been good to me, but we were both in increasingly awkward positions—and now, it seemed, he had joined the ranks of people I couldn't trust anymore. Before he left, however, he warned me, "Don't go against him. I'm afraid for you."

In addition to the vanishing cars, we also had the problem of the disappearing art and antiques. When Burt had started *Evening Shade* and we'd rented the Bel-Air house, we had brought some things out of storage (where they'd been since Carolwood was sold) to make it homier for both of us when we were there. But now Scott Jackson was coming in every few days with a list of things that Burt had decided he couldn't live without.

"You know, Scott," I said dryly, "this is becoming quite strange, especially for Quinton. The walls are getting more bare by the day."

Martin Simone, my attorney, finally put his foot down. "Until the court decides otherwise," he said, "these are joint possessions. There's been no property settlement yet, and Burt simply cannot keep making raids on that house."

So we had all the locks changed, and the gate clickers. In the meantime, many of *my* dearest things were still in Florida. It would be months before Linda Jensen and Sybil were given clearance to fly down to Valhalla and go through the house with Scott Jackson, and then I paid to have my possessions shipped back to California. Someone alerted *Hard Copy* about the move, and they taped the whole thing, asking the Mayflower guys about what was in the boxes. My picture collage of my dad arrived with its frame badly bent and all the glass broken, nearly ruined, yet surrounded by other things suspiciously intact.

As the *Enquirer, Globe,* and *Star* stories kept on coming, the information in them—or, rather, the misinformation—was being repeated not only by the TV tabloid shows, but also by the "serious" media. I received calls to be interviewed by Maria Shriver,

Connie Chung, Diane Sawyer, Joan Lunden, Katie Couric. And while I considered the offers, I couldn't see what would be gained. I was still reeling from what had happened—how on earth could I have explained it to anyone else?

"The only person I could comfortably talk to at this point," I said to Linda, "is Princess Diana. What do you suppose the odds are that we could get together for lunch?"

However, I did agree to do some press as part of my new relationship with *Nurses,* on the condition that no one ask about my situation with Burt. *The Today Show*'s Katie Couric was the only one to break her word. One interview I gave was to Vernon Scott, a journalist and friend from the early *WKRP* years, for that September's issue of *Good Housekeeping.* And Mary Murphy of *TV Guide* ran a piece, too.

In both magazine articles, although the authors may have commented on Burt's behavior or the specifics of our separation, I did not. I spoke only of my own sorrow and disappointment at the end of my marriage and my recent and genuine pleasure at being involved in *Nurses.*

When Army Archerd, the venerable Hollywood reporter, called me for my comments, the only thing I said to him was that I had been surprised by the divorce action. And then, although I had never met or talked to her, columnist Liz Smith wrote a piece in which she expressed her dismay at Burt's co-operating with the *Enquirer.* When the Archerd and Smith columns appeared in print, Burt let it be known through channels that he believed I had contacted Archerd and Smith as part of a publicity campaign against him. And he became convinced that NBC (the network *Nurses* appeared on) was in on the diabolical plot as well.

In spite of the fact that I wanted to stay curled up in the fetal position, I had to start doing "maintenance" work on myself, to get ready for *Nurses.* One Monday night, Sharon Sanders came to the house to do my nails. Just as we got settled in, Lamar buzzed the gate and asked to see me. When he came in, he handed me a thick white envelope, saying, "This is from Burt." And then he left.

Inside the envelope were sixteen pages, handwritten with a black marker, full of exclamation marks and underlined words. I read first one page and then the next in disbelief. It was the most vicious, vindictive, threatening object I had ever seen—if it had been alive, it would have been festering.

In obscene and abusive language, the letter basically mapped out a plan of attack—on me—that would go into effect unless I appeared with him at a press conference, "full of laughs and holding our precious Quinton," ready to back his story that the divorce was a mutually agreed-upon decision. He had eavesdropped on Linda Jensen's phone calls, he said, and intimated that he knew deep dark secrets about her. In his opinion, I had collaborated with Army Archerd and Liz Smith, and now, he said, "It's war . . . World War III, like you've never seen." The letter said there would be a three-part *Enquirer* article by John and Janet Spring, accusing me of having affairs with three married men. There would be a similar story by Terry Warren. And if all that failed to convince me to cooperate with his version of events, Burt then threatened me with something called the H-bomb, saying, "If you ever doubt I'm too much of a nice 'gentleman' to destroy you, and *everything, every person,* that respects you, you're wrong."

If his intention was to frighten me, it worked. Not only was I terrified, I was, at last, in tears. It was as though I had turned over a rock, and something—someone—unrecognizable had come out from under it. Within seconds I was hysterical, sobbing, walking around the room in circles, flinging myself on and off the furniture, sitting, then standing again, pacing, shouting. Who *was* the man who had written this letter? What was this big lie that had been my life?

Sharon tried to comfort me, but I couldn't stop crying. Sybil had been upstairs putting Quinton to bed, but in minutes my sobbing had brought them both down to see what the matter was. Quinton ran into the bathroom and brought out some potpourri to me. "Here, Mom, here, this will make you feel better," he said. Sybil wisely took him back upstairs.

I cried for a good two hours and was completely sick to my

stomach by the time I finally stopped. When Linda called Lamar and asked him what he had been thinking, why on earth he had been part of getting such a letter to me, he was dumbfounded.

"But, Linda," he told her, "when Burt handed me that letter, he said, 'this will make everything OK with Loni.' " He had honestly thought that what he was carrying was a love letter, with a possible reconciliation offer.

Within weeks of the letter, Burt made his legendary appearance with Chantal Westerman on the prime-time version of *Good Morning America,* wearing a garish eggplant-purple suit I had never seen in his closet (believe me, if I had, I would've removed it), challenging me to take truth serum, saying I was a bad mother, accusing me of having lovers and low self-esteem, saying that we hadn't had sex in three years. I couldn't decide which was more astounding: that he would tell such a shrieking lie, or that he would tell it on national television.

Sometimes I think men who have other women tell their mistresses that they don't make love to their wives. "Well, I may have to live with her, but I promise you, I don't make love to her." Isn't that something they say? I think it's right up there with, "My wife doesn't understand me."

Well, in this case, neither was true. I understood him perfectly well, and we did make love. There were the fights and the drugs and the tense times when we kept our distance from each other. But in fact, the last time we made love might've been about three weeks before we separated.

As for low self-esteem: Thanks to my parents, that had never in my life been one of my problems. Nor had I been upset over not working regularly, as Burt claimed on *GMA.* Except for doing one TV movie a year, it had always been my intention to stay home with Quinton during his baby years and not look for more movies or a series until he started school. I would not have brought a child into our home under other circumstances. Burt knew that, and supported it, as I supported his revived career in *Evening Shade.* I had turned down offers in the interim; I went into *Nurses* because Quinton would be starting kindergarten.

Through my publicist's office, all I said in response to Burt's charges was, "I do not intend to engage in a media war. I have to consider the welfare and best interests of my little boy."

The oddest thing happened after that interview. I got letters from fans or was approached in the street by well-meaning people, and what they all seemed to be saying was, "Even if you did tell Quinton not to muss your makeup or wrinkle your dress, we understand, because of course mothers have to do that sometimes, and we love you anyway." That's all very nice, I thought, but I *never said those things* to my son. It was totally bizarre to be forgiven for something I never even did.

After Burt's *GMA* appearance (which Linda Jensen quickly began to refer to as "the Barney episode") came the Terry Warren *Enquirer* story, complete with his byline. Terry, who had moved from Florida to California, was now married to Kelly, who had been his girlfriend from the very first time I met him. He had called to warn me about the story and said he was told that as long as he didn't deny it, he would be well paid, and Burt would help him with his acting and singing career.

The gist of the piece was that I had been sexually involved with Terry, Burt had discovered us together, and it was only then that he had become involved with Pam Seals. In the meantime Terry, of course, had told me that Pam had been in the picture for a long time.

Of all the coverage, all the stories, it was this one that pushed Deidra over the edge, because she had known Terry, as a friend, and knew the truth. And so, when a reporter from the *Star* came by and knocked on the door, Dee practically pulled her into the house.

"Everyone in Burt's personal life is on his payroll," Deedee said, "because that's the way he can feel he has control. Terry Warren was a protégé of Burt's, hired to keep my mother out of Burt's way. There were countless times when we would all go out to dinner, but instead of Burt joining us, Terry would come."

She told the reporter about all the split Christmases, about the many times Burt had stayed behind in his room at Valhalla and left me to take gifts to Fern and Big Burt alone. She told of my years of excusing Burt's erratic behavior by telling her, "He works so hard and is so tired." And she passionately defended my mothering of Quinton (and her) and my determination to fight for my marriage.

"She is a very patient woman," Deidra said. "And after two failed marriages, she wanted to make this one work. She made a commitment to him the day they married, and she was willing to honor that commitment, no matter how difficult it was."

As I was reading my daughter's words—and feeling grateful that she hadn't "obeyed" me and turned the reporter away—I thought of all the years we had spent growing up together, and all my doubts and fears about having done right by her. Although I was glad my parents hadn't lived to see this divorce debacle, I missed them more than ever and wished that they could have seen the kind of woman she had become.

As each travesty revealed itself, I began to see what Burt was doing. I didn't understand it, but I saw the tactic. It was as though the only way to make his affair OK—the only way to justify throwing me out—was to make me the bad guy. The unfaithful wife, the bad mother, the distraught, unemployed actress. The marriage that had been "an empty shell" for years. It was all so convoluted, like a maze you wander into and then can't find your way out of. Why, if he hated me so, hadn't the man simply come straight out and asked me for a divorce?

For years I had heard one story after another about Burt's fear of confrontation with the women in his life. Oh, he wasn't reluctant to mix it up with a director or a stagehand or a writer, but he was legendary for not being able to end a relationship with a woman in a straightforward fashion. I knew this because many of the women themselves told me their end-of-Burt stories, both before we separated and afterward. It was as though we all belonged to the same support group or something. At parties, at wedding and baby showers, at the hair salon, the story would begin, "Now, don't get me wrong, Loni, I love the guy, but this is the way he is. . . ."

When he was involved with Lucie Arnaz, he left one morning saying he was going off to Hawaii but would leave his car with her. And he just never came back to get it, she said. Finally she trooped over to his house to see what was going on—and there was Sally Field.

Adrienne Barbeau told me that she went out to her driveway one morning, and there, stuck under the car's windshield wiper, was a note from Burt ending their relationship. And Susan Clark told the one about the time Burt took her down to Florida to meet his parents. She thought she was his fiancée; in fact, that's the way he introduced her to Fern and Big Burt. But when they came back to California together, they made love at her apartment, he left, and she never saw or heard from him again.

My favorite story was Lorna Luft's. She first met Burt when she was in her early twenties, when he was making *Lucky Lady* in Mexico with her sister, Liza Minnelli. They began a romance right then, and he assured her that when it came time for the premiere, they would attend the gala event together.

Lorna, who is a talented cabaret singer, then went out on a road tour with Sammy Davis. When she returned to L.A. for her birthday, she was reading a newspaper in the back of her limo and discovered a picture of Burt and Dinah attending a *Lucky Lady* screening. She heard nothing from him after that, although he'd been invited to her birthday party. The day after the party, she opened her front door, and there on the stoop was a box. Inside was a small jeweler's case—with a card that read, "Happy Birthday, Lorna, love, Burt"—and inside the case was a ring. A big, masculine-looking ring, large enough for a man's hand. One of his rejects, she decided. She scratched out the message on the card, scrawled the word *WRONG!* across it, packed the whole thing up, and drove over and stuffed it into Burt's mailbox.

A few days later he tried to make up with her—first by saying that he was a stupid jerk, and then by sliding into a charming "Burt's-trouble-with-women" monologue the likes of which he'd done so often on Johnny Carson's couch. Lorna just smiled, merrily started humming the *Tonight Show* theme, and walked away from him.

They continued to be friends, of course, as evidenced by the trip she and her husband took with us down the Intracoastal one

New Year's. "He wanted me to cook pies," she said, laughing. "But I wanted to go to Rolling Stones concerts."

Patty Fuller, who knew all the parties—and often must have felt like an air traffic controller—said that Burt was dating both Lucie and Lorna as he was getting ready to leave Dinah. And when he did leave Dinah, he simply changed all his phone numbers and didn't contact her for a very long time afterward.

The most recent story came from Tawny Little, who— as luck will have it—is the mother of a little boy in Quinton's class. And not only are they classmates, they're best friends. Tawny and I have become friends as well, putting history behind us as you have to do when you're trying to keep up with six-year-old boys and running into each other at Parents' Day. Tawny told me when she was dating Burt, he broke up with her for Sally; then he came back to her; then he became involved with Dolly Parton; then he came back to Tawny; then came the fateful New Year's with me, and she never heard from him again.

Some of the stories are sad, some are funny—and who knows how many are still unaccounted for. I guess I could be overwhelmed by the sheer number of members in this particular club. But you have to admit—there are worse sororities a girl could belong to.

Chapter 18

In the weeks after I fled Valhalla, I slowly began to lean on Geoffrey Brown. He not only came with a clean slate, he was also even-tempered and calm when absolutely everything else in my life had gone spinning. He had quiet advice and answers to my questions. I trusted him.

The night Burt's letter arrived, we tried to reach him but got only his answering machine. I left a fairly incoherent message, and in minutes, it seemed, Geoff was at the house. He tracked down Martin Simone, and they both agreed that this letter, which went immediately into the law office safe, was serious business. At the very least it was a threat of character assassination, which could then become part of a custody fight for Quinton; at its worst, it was a physical threat. More to the point, it was a clear statement of a campaign, a battle plan. Martin strongly recommended that we hire a private investigator to start putting the puzzle pieces together. What was Burt prepared to do to fight this "war" he had declared on me?

It turns out that Burt himself had hired a private investigator months before he ever filed for divorce, to try to prove that I was having affairs. One affair in particular was supposed to be with Harry Lippman, an old beau from college who was now an attorney, married (to a woman I knew) and living in California.

Harry and I had stayed in touch sporadically over the years, exchanging the occasional holiday greetings and promising to get together. I had even invited him and his family to a pilot taping once. Finally, after playing telephone tag for some time, we did meet for lunch, about a year before I was served with divorce papers. At which point Burt's investigator started following Harry, opening his mail, watching his house around the clock (waiting for me either to go into it or to come out of it), checking up (quite illegally) on both our telephone records. And the telephone records showed a number of calls. Of course, what they didn't show (as they might have done, in the old days before answering machines and voice mail) was that it took eight or ten calls before we actually spoke to each other to arrange the lunch date. First Harry left a message, then I left a message, then he left a message, then I left a message, and so on. One wonders what Sam Spade would have made of all of this.

When Harry's law office was broken into and the thieves took only a new, untailored suit of his and a secretary's portable radio, yet left behind more than two hundred thousand dollars' worth of computer equipment, it made everybody jumpy. Was this the work of incompetent thieves or somebody looking for something specific? In addition, somebody had alerted the *Star,* which sent a photographer to stake out Harry's law office.

When Burt's private investigator was unable to come up with anything prurient about my relationship with Harry, Burt grew quite angry with him and demanded that he falsify the reports. It was at this point that the p.i. approached Martin Simone and told him what had been going on. He also told him I was a very boring person to follow—all I did was work, work out, and go to lunch with the girls.

A story linking me to Harry showed up in the tabs, as did other stories linking me to other men, all of them groundless. A stuntwoman who worked for Burt and lived rent-free in our guest house went on a tabloid television show to report that in front of Quinton I had talked about having sex with someone in the back booth of a restaurant.

Once our private investigator started coming back to us with bits and pieces of information, many events of the past few months began to make a bizarre kind of sense. For instance, Linda Jensen's phone calls had indeed been "eavesdropped" on—from a surveillance van. And I'd had an agent for some time whose name was Pam. When I'd say to Burt, "Pam called today," he'd flinch or gasp. What an odd reaction he always has to her, I thought.

Then there was that time he was "forced" into giving a story to the *Enquirer* when it threatened to reveal the names of Quinton's birth parents. The paper had obviously known about Pam; Burt's "giving" them the story about his business plight was his way of keeping them at bay. No wonder the man had behaved like a crazy person—he was telling Pam Seals it was over between us at the same time he was arranging to build me a dream house, talking about second honeymoons and adopting more children, and paying a private investigator to dig up divorce evidence. What we had been witnessing was a human being experiencing spontaneous combustion.

I continued to talk with Dr. Sharon each week (as I still do today), working my way through the pain and the mess. It is ironic to me that the woman who helped me through Burt's leaving is someone I had developed a therapeutic relationship with *because* of him. I don't know what I would have done without her during this period, not just for my sake, but for Quinton's as well. He needed me to be steady, and steady seemed to be right up there with "able to leap tall buildings at a single bound."

Aside from going to the *Nurses* set every day—where people were being extraordinarily kind to me, in spite of the fact that extra security had to be posted at the studio gate and on the set, because of the press—I didn't go out in the world much. I was tense and jittery. I was grateful for my friends and family and their support, but it was getting harder and harder to talk about Burt, to try to understand his motives, his behavior. The more I learned, the more Byzantine it all became.

Like spies in a Cold War novel, Clarence and Sybil sometimes met at Denny's restaurant to compare notes. Sybil reported that the old life-size cardboard cutout of Ed Sullivan that we'd had for years now had Loni pictures taped to the face, with darts stuck in it. That was right around the same time that the damaged collage of my dad arrived from Florida. And when Burt bought Quinton a set of drums—to be set up and played at *my* house, not his—he told Sybil, "I want to drive her crazy."

Like clockwork there was a crisis almost every day, a TV tabloid story—John and Janet Spring selling their Burt-orchestrated lies to *Hard Copy,* for instance—all of it calculated to undo me. The poison-pen letter had arrived on a Monday night, and I had had to go in to work on Tuesday morning, puffy-eyed and ragged, looking like I'd been chased through the desert by bandits. And this wasn't a prime-time soap I was working in, it was a *comedy.* I was supposed to show up every day ready to be *funny.*

Most of the time Burt had six attorneys hard at work, hammering away at me on two coasts. It seemed like they were filing documents every other day, and no one appeared to have any incentive to resolve things. When Linda Jensen criticized the way Burt had set me up that first day at Valhalla, complete with the press mauling, one of his lawyers said to her, "It was nice of Burt to give Loni all that good publicity, letting her leave Florida that way. It made her look like a good mother."

At the very first meeting the two sides actually had together in Los Angeles, with Burt and me both present, there was a preliminary discussion of working through an arbitrator, trying to settle matters without having to go through the costs—and headlines—of a court battle. But the meeting disintegrated when Burt first lunged at Martin and then screamed at me, "You never loved me!"

We could have fed small countries with what these kinds of scenes (and the knotted thinking behind them) were costing us both in billable hours. My own legal bills ultimately came close to half a million dollars; Burt's had to be a million or more. Whenever he talks about the money he spent getting rid of me, I wish he'd be a little clearer about what was Loni money and what was lawyer money.

In addition to Martin Simone, I ultimately ended up with a bicoastal battery of lawyers myself. Bill Stolberg, in Fort Lauderdale, ably represented me in Florida, as did Tom Wackeen, in Martin County, where Jupiter is located. And then we needed Victor Karcinel, a forensic CPA; that is, he digs around and finds out where the financial bodies are buried. Because, of course, Burt was talking about declaring bankruptcy.

As attractive as I thought Geoff Brown was in the beginning, there are a lot of attractive people out there, and I wasn't interested. The last thing I was feeling was desire for a man—unless it was that wildly inventive and energetic twenty-five-year-old fantasy in the imaginary black-and-white Art Deco apartment. But gradually, as Geoff continued to be a protector, and a calm, competent one at that, I began to pay more attention to him. And then I noticed that I would get flustered when he called or when I knew he was on his way over with some papers for me to sign. When he smiled at me, I had difficulty smiling back and felt myself blushing. I've got to get out of the house more, I thought.

After two and a half months of this, I realized I had developed a real crush on Geoff. I was kind of fascinated at the very idea of it—me with a crush, a woman in her late forties who has just had her life torpedoed by an apparently unhinged husband. This is just silly, I thought. I don't know anything about this man's personal life, or if he even has one, and I can barely get the sentence "Would you like to stay for a glass of wine?" out of my mouth.

I didn't like being alone in the house. The occasional press van was still outside the gate; each time they seemed to have gone away, another tabloid headline would bring them back. People were always trying to get over the fence. Who knew who they were: press, tourists, gawkers, stalkers? So one weekend, when Quinton and Sybil were going to be at Burt's, I called Geoff at his office, on impulse.

"Quinton is going to be away," I said, "and Sybil's going with him. There's nobody here, and it's making me very nervous. Could you . . . could you come and baby-sit me?"

"I'd love to, Loni," he said, "but the firm dinner dance is

tonight, and I have a date." Well, I thought, so much for that.

He seemed genuinely concerned for my discomfort about being alone, though, and made sure that I would call someone else—in this case, Jeanne Jensen—so that I wouldn't be frightened.

That same weekend, Lamar called saying that Burt wanted more items from the house and that on Sunday, Scott and a "bunch of guys" would be coming into the house to get them.

Here we go, I thought. Martin Simone had said no one was to take anything else out of the house. Jeanne and I were alone. What was I supposed to do, hold off a "bunch of guys" with my hairdryer? On Sunday, I called Geoff again.

He came over, and while the three of us waited for the raiding party, Jeanne and I showed Geoff some of the fan mail I'd been receiving since the divorce story had first broken. Many of the notes were kind and supportive ones. But others were straight-out marriage proposals—from men eighteen to eighty, all over the country. Guys who worked on farms, who worked in investment banks, who drove trucks, who owned their own companies, all expressing a variation on the theme of "Trust me—I'll take care of you." The letters from young men often included snapshots of bare (and buffed) torsos; the older men left out the pictures but included detailed financial information instead. Some of them were completely genuine and dear; others were so outlandish that when I read them aloud, all I could do was laugh helplessly.

When Jeanne said her good nights, Geoff said he'd stay awhile longer. To pass the time, we decided to watch the video of *Stranded,* the comedy I'd made with Perry King. Geoff had never seen it, and I was in the mood for more laughs.

We sat right next to each other, and I never even brushed up against his arm. He didn't put his arm around me. I thought, well, he's a terrific guy, and he's been a good friend who's stood by me, but there's nothing between us. I'm just not his type, that's all, and this crush is a figment of my damaged imagination.

To make it worse, the whole thing was a false alarm. The raiding party never arrived, and I felt totally foolish.

When he left to go home, I walked him to the door, and then I just kept walking out into the dark, onto the driveway. It was a beautiful night, with a clear and starry sky not often seen over Los Angeles these days. When I remarked on it, Geoff looked up—and when he did, I snuck over to him as close as I could, so that when he looked down, there was my face. It was like the scene between my mom and dad, when she put her face right up to him and left him no choice but to kiss it. Or back off and say no. Geoff chose to kiss me. And then he kissed me again. And then he stepped back.

"You know," he said quietly, "you've been going through a great deal these past months. And I'm seeing somebody. Loni, we have some serious talking to do before this goes any further."

We spent many hours and days after that first kiss discussing where we might—or might not—go from that moment. My emotions were still raw, my life was still in upheaval, and Geoff was thinking more clearly than I was. In fact, he knew more about my life at that point than I did: He and Linda Jensen had become collaborators in keeping many of the headlines—and many of the missives from Burt's attorneys, which went directly to Martin Simone—away from me, so that I could get up and go to work each morning without being totally obsessed with whatever the crisis of the day was.

In addition, it was becoming clear to everyone (especially after I told my family and close friends about the episodes of violence, as Dr. Sharon had advised me to do) that I wasn't trying to recover just from the divorce, but from everything I had been through in the months, and even years, before those papers were ever served. Geoff had no desire to be an intensive-care knight in shining armor, and he didn't want to be a rebound romance. My tendency to romanticize relationships (and in truth, I *did* see him as that knight) had to be brought down to earth before we could go any further.

And, of course, there were my children to consider. Geoff, who had been married briefly in his twenties, had no children of his own, but coming into my life meant being part of what I shared with Dee and Quinton. Although Deidra was an adult, with a family and life of her own, she had always been protective of me —and not a little critical of my ability (or inability, as she saw it) to make good choices about the men in my life. "Normal" is one of her favorite words. "I want things to be normal," she says. "I want your life to be normal, for your own sake, as well as Quinton's. Even McKenzie . . . well, McKenzie better be normal!"

As for Quinton, he was a little boy who had been through a great deal, with more to come. He had already been in therapy for some time. Contrary to Burt's rendition of events, he had never discussed his divorce decision with his son, and it was left to me—and Q.'s therapist—to explain the separation, the divorce, the living and visiting arrangements in both California and Florida, and the immediate presence of Pam Seals in Burt's (and therefore Quinton's) life.

Quinton was very angry with Burt in the beginning, not just because he sensed that I was, but because he wasn't seeing him much once we came back to California. Burt spent so much of his time in Florida, and Quinton never liked the traveling back and forth between coasts; he is happiest when Burt lives in Los Angeles. In fact, he's still trying to figure out whose house is whose: He wants things to be convenient, and he wants the grown-ups to make that happen. Which isn't unreasonable for a little kid to want.

For a while Sybil provided a loving continuity between the two households, but even that was to change. One morning, in Burt's kitchen, he said to her in exasperation (whether in response to headlines or lawyers' bills, I don't know), "I'll be glad when the divorce is final, and this is all over."

When Sybil responded with a heartfelt "So will I!" Burt flew into a rage. He shouted at her, he screamed obscenities (while Quinton was within earshot), and finally he picked up a chair and threw it across the room at her. Quinton burst into tears, and Sybil was completely terrified.

Thereafter, she would not go to his house anymore (and became, to Burt, part of the cadre of spies and plotters against him), and we were faced with a visit-to-visit hunt for a nanny for Quinton's trips to Burt's, an endeavor which continues sporadically to this day.

The tabloids have suggested that my insistence on a nanny when Quinton is with his dad is somehow linked to questions about Burt's sexuality, which is absolutely, categorically not true. My concerns (and this is part of the court record) are about substance abuse and the unpredictable behavior that accompanies it.

As Geoff and I contemplated the wisdom of becoming further involved, in addition to our worries about Quinton, we knew we faced many court dates ahead and the probability of more tabloid headlines as well. As uncomfortable as I am under that kind of scrutiny, I understand it; it is part of what I do for work.

It is not, however, part of what Geoff does. He is a private man and a respected attorney working in a conservative, traditional firm that has no need or desire for a *Hard Copy* camera crew hanging around in its lobby. As it was, once we went public as a couple, the firm needed to take extra security precautions, screening the phone to head off press inquiries to his secretary and his colleagues and monitoring the traffic at the receptionist's desk when reporters or photographers appeared.

Geoff didn't want to be perceived as having taken advantage of me; I didn't want to be perceived as anything but calm and in control. More than anything we wanted peace and quiet and some kind of serenity. As Deidra said to me once, "Maybe it's not so good to have fireworks all the time, Mom—because with constant fireworks, there's always the possibility of danger."

As Geoff resolved his other relationship, he also sought advice from a close friend who was a lawyer, invoking the attorney-client privilege of confidentiality as they discussed the tangle of ethical and personal concerns that arose out of his becoming involved with me.

While he was working this out, I talked with Dr. Sharon and Quinton's therapist. When, I asked, would it be all right for my son to know that Geoff was special to me? When would it be appropriate for him to see affection between us? I went by the book and let the experts guide me on this one.

As Quinton began to sense the change in the relationship between Geoff and me, he seemed to warm to it. There are many people who make up his world, who have been in his life since the beginning, and who provide his security—his family has never been just me, or just Burt and me, and so he's quite used to sharing me. He's not afraid of people, either. He doesn't cling to me, and he's very confident. And his capacity for love is limitless. The first time he saw Geoff and me kiss each other, he rushed over to us and said, "Do that again." And when we did, he put his mouth up to ours, giggling all the while, and made it a three-way kiss.

That October, Geoff and I went out in public for the first time, to a formal charity event. Around the same time, I was contacted by *People* magazine, saying they were going to do a story about us, offering me the chance to cooperate—or not—with them. I was hesitant at first, because *People* had run two other cover stories that year on the Burt-and-Loni divorce wars and had printed quotes (and bad information) from the *Enquirer* stories, especially the Terry Warren one. It had been one of those "he says, she says" deals, in spite of the fact that I hadn't said anything.

But Geoff and I eventually decided that this might be a more pleasant experience; at the very least we would be on the record for real. So there we were, in November 1993, smiling for all the world to see on the cover of *People*.

I wasn't unhappy about the piece—it did, after all, portray me as more cheerful than I had been in some time and getting on with my life, which was certainly true. But after it was published—and the tabloids began to put their own particular spin on our relationship—things became very strange indeed for Geoff.

He began hearing The Big Question from coworkers, old girlfriends, cousins: When is the wedding? He got fan letters from strange women and phone calls from one end of the country to the other, from people he hadn't heard from in years and people he'd never even met. Anyone who had access to a *Martindale-Hubbell Law Directory* could figure out how to contact him; women started calling him, asking him to handle their divorces.

In his office people stared at him as he walked through the halls; others he barely knew felt perfectly free to ask him the most embarrassing questions about his personal life, often on the assumption that the garbage in the tabloids was true. When he walked into a room, conversations abruptly stopped. On Mondays he was quizzed about his weekends; on Fridays he was invited to Saturday night parties, by colleagues who until now had rarely even greeted him in the elevator. For someone who likes to play his cards close to his chest (he had been in naval intelligence during Vietnam), the sideshow was achingly uncomfortable.

A senior attorney from his firm warned him that his relationship with me was a potential conflict of interest and could put not only his job but his entire career in jeopardy. Because the firm—and Geoff in particular—had represented me in the cosmetics matter, they now wanted me to sign a document (which I did) acknowledging the conflict and recommending that I seek independent legal advice.

We had hoped that the love that was growing between us, and the joy it brought, would be a matter primarily for ourselves and our families. That it would also call into question his ethics and professionalism—both of which had always been above reproach—was not just irritating but sad, and completely unfair to Geoff.

I wouldn't have blamed him if he'd gone underground or decided that I—and the three-ring circus that seemed to accompany me—was simply too much bother for a sane man. The height of ridiculousness came when I started getting phone calls every few days from Scott Jackson, relaying "confidential information" that had supposedly come from a private investigator and that Burt thought it was in my "best interests" to know.

First Scott told me that they had indisputable evidence that Geoff was gay. "Light in the loafers" was Burt's term. And then, a few days later, Scott said they'd discovered that Geoff was keeping a couple of starlets on the side, paying for their apartments, visiting them for sexual favors. When I failed to respond to that "revelation" with anything more than laughter, Scott came back with the terrible news that Geoff was being kept by a wealthy Hollywood wife. By the time we heard this last one, my entire household was in hysterics. We were absolutely sure that the next batch of "indisputable evidence" would contain an accusation that Geoff was actually an extraterrestrial.

In the meantime Geoff had been attending the weekly taping of *Nurses* on Friday, arriving from the office around five and staying until we were done. The first couple of times he came, he sat in the audience, but soon he watched from backstage.

Taping days were always the longest for everyone, of course, because we started at the normal time in the morning, rehearsing and blocking scenes and working with the technical crew, and then in the evening we did two performances of that week's episode, for two different audiences.

By the time Geoff and I got home, I had been in full battle regalia—high-fashion costume, hair and makeup, and heels—since early that morning, and my toes usually felt like someone had been pounding on them with a croquet mallet. Geoff would make me sit down and kick off my shoes, and while we sipped champagne and discussed the latest bizarre crisis, he would rub my feet until the pain was gone.

One night I said, "I don't know what I ever did to deserve this kind of lovely treatment."

"Sweetheart, I'll give you a month's recovery time for every year you were with him," Geoff said. "And after that we're going to begin to put it all behind us and live a life together on our own terms."

I've been asked—challenged, almost—why the relationship with Geoff happened so fast, especially after a long (by Hollywood standards) marriage and a fairly traumatic breakup. I guess I was expected to go into mourning. Or hiding. The only response I can give is that I could have waited another whole lifetime and not found a man as right for me as Geoff is. It either happens again or it doesn't. To deny it because of some arbitrary time frame would have been foolish.

After the *People* cover, the stories began that we were engaged. But we have no plans to marry and never have had. We've just been a couple, together, moving along one day at a time, into a commitment that is defined only by us and by no one else. He is my partner and my dearest companion.

Chapter 19

One inadvertent gift that resulted from the betrayal of my marriage was the end of my lifelong belief in the Prince Charming myth. And about time, too. I still treasure my Snow White collection, of course, and there's still a part of my heart that will always long for the man my father was, or perhaps for the role that he played in my life. But I learned the hard way that just as I no longer have to save anyone, neither do I have to *be* saved.

However, that doesn't mean I won't read fairy tales to my granddaughter, and it doesn't mean I've made a "never again" vow about love. If you want to be alive and live in a real world, if you want to have any emotions at all in your life, you must willingly, knowingly, repeatedly set yourself up for things possibly not ending up "happily ever after." If you choose to love anyone—children, lovers, spouses, parents, friends—there's always the chance that you might lose them or that they might do something that will hurt you. The alternative—to walk away from risk and pain and possibility—never appealed to me in the slightest. I can't imagine "retiring" from love.

Thanksgiving of 1993, my house was very full of love indeed. Assembled around the holiday table were my sister, Andrea, her husband, Steve, and their son, Erik; Deedee, Charlie, and McKenzie; Charlie's parents, Chuck and Gail Hoffman; Jeanne Jensen, Linda, her son (and my godson), Cary, and her sister, Patty; my friend Christopher Lawrence; and Geoff and his mother, Ginny. And Deedee's father, Bruce Hasselberg.

Geoff, who loves to cook (and the more people to cook for, the better he likes it), was master chef to the whole clan that day, and there was a tremendous closeness among all of us. We had a great deal to be thankful for.

Earlier, when I asked Geoff if it was all right that we had invited Bruce, he grinned and said, "Well, after all, it has been twenty-nine years since you two were together. Now, if it had only been twenty-six, I might have a problem with it."

In the morning, before her father arrived, Deedee said, "This will be the first holiday I will spend with both my parents together in my whole life." And when Deidra and I went together to greet Bruce at the door, he put his arms around both of us, saying, "I'm so glad to be here with my girls."

Quinton was at Burt's overnight, so Bruce spent the night in Q.'s bunk bed. The next morning I came into the kitchen to overhear Bruce telling Geoff what a lucky man he was to have me, what a wonderful woman I was, what a good mother.

I backed up so they wouldn't see me, thinking what a gift I had just received from Bruce, after twenty-nine years and so much sorrow between us. And now we would play with our grandchild all Thanksgiving weekend, in peace and affection. I wondered how many years it would be before Burt and I would come to that, or indeed, if we ever would.

Nineteen ninety-four got off to a rough start. To begin with, the Northridge earthquake caused such destruction and loss of life, and it wasn't a headline about a distant place—it happened in my "neighborhood." All tragedies are heartbreaking, no matter where they occur, but this one, so close to home, was especially distressing to me. As if I needed to be reminded just how close, Jeanne Jensen, Linda, and Cary lived with us for six weeks, because their home was completely wrecked. The quake and its aftermath underlined not just the fragility of human life, but the very undependability of the ground we stood on.

The first quake I was ever in occurred when I was married to Ross and we lived in Van Nuys. As the house began to move, he ran into the dining room and stood with his arms outstretched in front of our brand-new hutch, as though he could somehow keep the glassware and china from shattering. He couldn't, of course. That's when we learned the invaluable lesson that stuff is just stuff.

The night—or rather, the predawn morning—that the Northridge quake hit, I was still in the rented Bel Air house, and Quinton had spent the night with Burt. Although Geoff and I had become lovers, we never lived together in that house, and he never spent the night in the house when Quinton was home. But that night, thank God, Geoff was with me.

I wear earplugs when I go to bed, because I'm a very light sleeper and hear every little noise. Over the years I've gotten accustomed to the ground occasionally shaking—if you've lived here awhile, you pretty much have to do that, the mild quakes happen so often. You sort of half wake, wait a second or two to see if it's worse than normal, and then roll over and go back to sleep.

Geoff says he was awake when it started. He'd gotten up to go to the bathroom, and he noticed that the cats were acting weird, jumping around, making little squeaking noises. And then it started to really rumble. I didn't hear it, of course. But he did, and he threw himself over me because he thought the mirrored wall above the headboard was about to come crashing down on my head.

A major quake, and this was certainly that, sounds like a fully loaded freight train roaring not past but *through* your house. I was about half conscious, vaguely aware that he was holding me, and shaking, and then that the whole place was shaking. I knew it was a quake but because of the earplugs had no idea of the magnitude of the sound Geoff was hearing. What that sound signaled, of course, was the simultaneous structural breakup beneath the ground and above it.

When the quake subsided, I took the earplugs out, and Geoff

said, "We have to get the flashlights and look around. You have no idea what just happened here."

It was still dark, so with the aplomb of a quake veteran, I said, "It didn't seem that bad, honey. Why don't we just go back to sleep and take a look in the morning."

"No, Loni," he said, and I was frightened at how serious his voice was. "You didn't hear what I heard. I'm telling you, it was a big one."

And indeed, as we slowly picked our way through the house with the flashlights, we were stunned at what we saw. The house had sustained a great deal of damage. Every floor, every room, was covered with broken glass. The pressure pipe on the large upstairs water heater had burst, and gallons of hot water were spewing all over the place. A whole cabinet of Lalique crystal had hit the floor. In the kitchen, every cupboard had opened up, and the remains of all the dishes and glasses blanketed every inch of the floor. The pantry was one solid, gooey mess of foodstuffs. And there were large cracks in the ceiling and walls and in the foundation.

As we went from room to room, my hands got sweaty, and I started to shake. "I cannot believe that I might have rolled over and gone back to sleep after this," I said. I had never known the role that sound played in fear.

I had one phone in my bathroom that wasn't hooked up to our electrical security system—I've always had one, ever since my mother's illness. I was frantic about Q., so I tried to call Burt immediately but couldn't get through—his phones were all connected to his system, which went out when the quake hit. I managed to call Dee and Charlie in Tahoe, and Geoff reached his mom in Pennsylvania, to let them know we were OK, just minutes before all the lines in the city went down.

It was still dark outside, and with the electricity out all over L.A.—so no radio, no TV—there was no way of knowing how far-reaching the quake had been. The house, which was high on Mulholland Drive, had a panoramic view, and when we looked down into the San Fernando Valley, we didn't see a single light, not one, until the emergency vehicles hit the highways.

Soon we could see the glow from fires, where the gas lines had burst.

We took the flashlights out to the car to try the cell phone—— which didn't work—and perhaps hear something on the radio. It wasn't until sunrise that we could look out over the valley and see that it was still there. A cloud of eerie orange dust hung in the sky, as though someone had stepped out of heaven and shaken a giant carpet. It looked postapocalyptic.

Burt got Quinton safely back to me around eight-thirty that morning. He was unharmed and amazingly unfrightened. Because the earthquake had happened to him at his dad's house, it never occurred to him to be afraid anyplace else in the city. For the next few days, each time an aftershock would roll the ground under us (try to imagine an ocean swell, only solid), he'd just say, "Oh, that was a good one," and then happily go back to whatever he had been doing.

In May I received the news that *Nurses* had been canceled. My response to the cancellation was mixed. I hadn't been a longtime part of the show, and I hadn't created the character. But I liked the people I worked with tremendously—they had been exceedingly kind to me, and patient with all the drama that my being there had entailed—and I was sad not to be in touch with them anymore. Most of all, though, it was work. And I needed work.

However, I was completely astonished when *Evening Shade* was canceled. In spite of the stories of the scenes and the bad behavior, I didn't think that things would go that far. I had believed and hoped that Burt would somehow manage to do a course correction before he took the show down, and many talented, respected professionals with it. They were on the *Cheers/ Mary Tyler Moore* track—I don't think there was any question in the industry that the show itself (and then the syndication reruns) could've gone on for years.

He still doesn't take responsibility for his role in the series' demise; he sees it as having been taken away from him because he left me. "I lost my wife, I lost my series," he says. But of course, I didn't get lost—I got thrown away.

No matter what the myths have been about my spendthrift ways, Burt and I always had separate finances and separate credit ratings. I have paid my own way since I was nineteen, and while with Burt, I kept my own business managers and spent my own money. He never gave me any spending money, although the court records state that Pam Seals regularly received an allowance. I paid the nannies, I paid for all Quinton's clothes, I paid for the adoption, I paid for the moves, I paid for Quinton's and my travel. Not until the last four months we were together did I ever have an allowance or a credit card from Burt (and no, I didn't max it out), and that was because *Nurses* hadn't yet begun, and I needed help with household expenses.

I paid for my own clothes, too, although contrary to rumor there were never any ten-thousand-dollar dresses at all, let alone any that were worn once and given to charity. It's true I love clothes and shoes—on any given day my car could probably find its way to Neiman Marcus all by itself. And I've always been careful about not duplicating what I wear in public. In this business, if you wear the same gown twice, that picture invariably gets taken and published, with a caption underneath accusing you of being either careless or clueless. I remember, once, a tabloid ran two pictures of me side by side, one taken with Ross, the other a year later with Gary. SAME DRESS, DIFFERENT MEN, read the headline.

I know some people don't approve of the way I look. There's a theory that if you're a serious woman, then dressing up—the glamour stuff, the gowns, the sling pumps, the hair and makeup—shouldn't be an important part of your life. But there are so many different parts of being a woman, and they should all be appreciated and celebrated. After all, little girls like to play dress *up*—they don't play dress *down*.

I think the cosmetics industry, the clothing industry, and the whole supermodel craze wouldn't be at such a fever pitch if most women didn't feel exactly the same way. A lot of them apologize for it, and that's too bad. Haven't we at last, as women, come to a place where we can do and be and wear what suits us, without apology?

I sewed my own clothes, and many of Deidra's, until I was in *WKRP.* Although I don't do that anymore, I do work closely with my designer, Robert Turturice. We've been collaborating for years, and very rarely do we put together a dress that's just a dress. Usually it's several pieces that combine in different ways, that can be taken apart and put together again and again and look completely different each time. I've recycled gowns for ten years, with changes: a different top, a different sleeve, a different wrap or belt, a different length. Everything I've got has been redone more than a couple of times. If that's a lie, may my mom, the famous Maxini Kallini and her Sewing Machini, come and haunt me in the night!

During the discovery process of the divorce, we found that Burt had made thirty-eight million dollars during the five years we had been married, which totally bowled me over. Technically I was entitled to half—and probably could have asked for a share of the estimated fifty million dollars he had made during the six and a half years we lived together before we were married as well. But I didn't want that; besides, according to his accountants, all of it—and more—had somehow disappeared. When the lawyers asked me what I wanted in the settlement, I said, "I want a home. I *had* a home once, and I sold it, because he asked me to. I want Quinton well provided for, and I want a home for us."

I had put all of the money from the sale of my Alomar house into Burt's houses—into Carolwood, into remodeling the house in North Carolina, and into Valhalla. Before we were together, his houses were just places on the map that he collected. And then threw stuff into. Nothing was created, put together. When I began to make homes of them, building a world around him, he liked it. "Look what the Countess has done to the castle," he would brag.

And so the house I live in now is my settlement. I received support during the first eight months we were separated, while I got my feet back on the ground, and then waived any alimony thereafter. I receive child support for Quinton, which stops when he's eighteen. Burt refinanced Valhalla to make the down payment on my house; his payments to me each month are equivalent to my mortgage payments.

In spite of the bicoastal battalions of lawyers, it seemed to take forever to resolve the settlement. The final arrangements—the interim support, the house, and the child support—were ultimately negotiated not by my lawyers or Burt's, but by Geoff, who had become increasingly frustrated not just by *my* frustration, but by the legal bills that were piling up in the face of what was either Burt's paranoid obstinacy or his sheer ignorance of his own affairs. Geoff and Scott Jackson, Burt's assistant, worked back and forth over the phone for months to finally get us to an agreement we both could sign.

In the meantime I had only weeks to find a place to live; the lease was running out on the Mulholland house. We had to be out by the first of June 1994, and people had already begun coming by to look at it. One night at dinner, Geoff cheerfully reported that while I was gone that day, he had given the guided tour of the house to Warren Beatty and Annette Bening.

When I first began house-shopping, I talked to the real estate agent who had sold the Alomar house for me, since she knew my taste. And when I walked into *this* house and saw the marble staircase and the two-story library with its sliding ladder, I just laughed softly to myself and thought, oh, Mom, if only you could be here.

As I went through the house that first day, I knew it was mine. And when Linda Jensen saw it, she said, "This looks like Alomar, only all grown up." When I went home that night, I couldn't sleep. I already knew where I was going to hang the pictures.

"Stop decorating the house before you own it," Geoff teased.

It had been built with great love and skill by a contractor, Joe Scardino, who had lived in it himself with his wife, whose name is also Jo. The foundation is built on bedrock, not on sand or landfill, and in the Northridge quake the house sustained only a few hairline cracks. It's a very special place, and we almost got involved in a bidding war, but the Scardinos decided to sell to me because, they said, they wanted to think of us all living in it after they left.

There's a bright and sunny kitchen big enough to accommodate my whole extended family, with a breakfast room that looks out over the swimming pool and the valley beyond it. There are formal living and dining rooms, with space to spare for my piano. There are four fireplaces, and French windows with leaded glass that offer a glorious view from every room and let sunshine in everywhere.

Just off the kitchen is a large family room, the center of Quinton's social life, complete with my jukebox, a pool table, a fireplace, and a big television. All the family bedrooms are upstairs—there's a room for everyone (after the earthquake, Sybil moved in with us, too), and we're all on the same floor. The master bedroom has his-and-hers bath- and dressing rooms and a fireplace. And that fireplace (this is so magical to me) goes through to my pink marble bathroom, complete with a sunken tub (with a view) and a twinkling crystal chandelier overhead.

The day Geoff, Quinton, Sybil, and I moved into the house, we moved in as a family, and being here is a culmination of all my dreams for my life ever since I was a little girl. It is the place I was always coming to, even though I didn't know it. No matter what happens outside, I know that inside is a haven. And every day, someone says, "I love this house." Quinton will bring his friends here when he's a teenager; maybe he'll bring his dates to this house. When McKenzie visits, she goes up the stairs behind Quinton, and then, like every toddler who ever was, comes sliding gently down again, bouncing on her bottom, one step at a time.

I knew I had made the right decision the night my son-in-law said to me, "Mom, ever since I've known you, you've lived in a lot of mansions. And this is the home all of them were trying to be."

It was nearly six months after I left Florida before Burt and I spoke without lawyers present. Our first conversations were brief and cautious ones about Quinton—where he would spend the holidays, how his school vacations would be divided up. The first time Q. was to spend Christmas with Burt, he announced flat out that if I didn't drive him there myself, he wouldn't go at all.

When we arrived, Burt came out to greet me, and we awkwardly hugged each other. "See, Quinton," said Burt. "We all like each other." We were rewarded when Quinton skipped into the house ahead of us and didn't look back.

"Geoff, Geoff, Geoff, that's all I hear," said Burt, watching him go. "You know, Loni, I can make a paper airplane, too."

As he walked me to the car, I said, "Presumably you went away to get happy. Are you happy?"

He shook his head no.

"But now you have the woman you wanted," I said.

"No," he said. "Now I have the woman I need."

We've had other meetings since, of course, good and bad, and courtroom battles over money and custody. He's occasionally late with payments. And he says he cannot find some of my things—furniture, paintings, some jewelry—that were in the Florida house. They belonged to me before I met him, so he doesn't think they're important.

I do have a piece of *Evening Shade*—after he pays back that four million to CBS and if the syndication ever makes any money. But they sold the series at a terrible loss, and I know I'll never see it.

The anger surfaces, of course, and the sheer frustration that once we had a marriage, and now all we seem to share are headlines and joint custody of many high-priced attorneys. We've never been able to get through a conversation about why he did what he did to me. In fact, it's never been clear that he believes he did anything to me, but rather has decided that *I* did something to *him*. Whatever the circumstances, Burt sees himself as the injured party.

Sometime after the 1993 holidays, my friend Sharon Sanders, who takes her daughter Chase to the same gymnastics class that Quinton attends, ran into Burt, who had brought Q. to class.

"I'll never get over the shock of Loni serving me divorce papers," he said to her, shaking his head and looking very sad.

Sharon called me after this conversation, asking, "Has he re-written history or something? Does he really believe that's the way it all happened?"

As the first day of the child support hearing in early December of 1994 ended with no resolution, it was clear we had to try to do something to bring at least the contentious legal-document part of our lives to a close. And so it was that on that second day of that hearing, Burt and I found ourselves at last out of the glare of the courtroom cameras and talking quietly in the judge's chambers.

"Burt, please look at me," I said.

"No," he said, looking down at the floor. "I can't. Or I'll cry."

I flashed back to our first magical New Year's Eve, when we flew over the holiday lights on the Intracoastal. He wouldn't look at me then, either.

"B.R.," I said, "you have to look at me, or else we won't be able to settle this."

So he looked at me. And he did cry. And slowly, minute by minute, we talked out our agreement, told the lawyers what we were going to do for Quinton, and resolved it ourselves.

We knew the cameras were just outside the courthouse door. He asked me to walk out there with him, and we would give them a statement together. It seemed little enough for me to do in exchange for what I hoped would be the end of the public battle. In a way, I guess, he got what he'd demanded in the sixteen-page letter, although Quinton, thankfully, was in school.

As we walked out of the courthouse, Burt grabbed my hand. He was shaking like a leaf in the wind. "You talk, please," he said.

When I stepped forward to speak to the reporters and he remained behind, it was the *first* time, in all our years together, that I had ever stepped ahead of him. I felt stronger than I had in months, completely independent and completely sure of myself. I can do this, I thought calmly.

It wasn't until after I'd spoken, explaining that we had come to a mutual agreement to do what was best for Quinton, that Burt began to relax and made a wisecrack or two. And just as we wished the reporters a Merry Christmas and turned away, he took my shoulders and kissed me. It was a total shock. And I felt something. Not adoration, not love. Protective, maybe, or parental. Almost as if he were my child.

We left the hearing in our separate cars. It was late afternoon. All I wanted to do was go home, kick off my shoes, and think, maybe, about Christmas. When I opened the door, I was surprised to find Geoff there ahead of me, home from the office much earlier than usual.

"You just relax for a while, sweetheart," he said quietly. "I'm making you dinner. If you want to talk, we'll talk. If you don't want to talk, well, that's OK, too."

I could hear Quinton down the hall in his room, chattering away at Sybil. I walked down there and visited with them awhile, sitting on the floor while my son cheerfully told me about his day. And then I walked back to the kitchen to watch as Geoff fixed dinner and to give him the details about my own day, about how Burt and I had come to our agreement.

As I sat at the counter sipping a cool glass of water, I wondered idly if there was anything sexier than a man who moves around a kitchen like he knows what he's doing. I felt such a sense of peace and comfort, as though I had been in this house, listening to the voices of these people I loved, for always. I suddenly realized that the coming Christmas would be the first one in our new home.

That night I asked Quinton to sit and watch the television news with me. It was the first and only time he's seen any of the TV coverage about the end of the marriage, and I wanted him to see his daddy and me when we came out of the courthouse together and spoke to the reporters together about our desire to reach an agreement for our son's sake.

Because he is my son's father, I want Burt to be healthy, to find a way to battle his demons successfully, to do the work he does so well, and to have a partner who will not only enrich his life, but will be a nourishing part of Quinton's life as well. I have no way of knowing if he has that now. I can only pray that he does.

Some days I look in amazement at the ups and downs and up-agains of my life, and I wonder how I've made it this far. I thank God, of course, for my parents and the example they set, and I thank my family and friends for their love and kindness. But I'm also grateful for the completely serendipitous timing of my birth date, which gave me automatic membership in the obnoxious and creative army called Baby Boomers. Because as painful and messy as this time in history has been, it has also been a great—well, OK, a *challenging*—time to be a woman. Especially a woman who likes to bend a rule now and again.

I've been fortunate to come up through the entertainment industry with an entire generation of women who have constantly redefined the cultural perception of what a viable, sexy woman is. Candice Bergen, Susan Sarandon, Cicely Tyson, Cybill Shepherd, Jaclyn Smith, Goldie Hawn, Meryl Streep, Sally Field, Tina Turner, Susan Saint James, Diana Ross, Deidre Hall, Farrah Fawcett, Liza Minnelli—the list is rich, inspiring, and wonderfully long. When Jessica Lange won the Oscar for *Blue Sky* in 1995, I practically leaped out of my chair with glee, and I suspect I wasn't the only one.

First they told us in this business that an actress was all through at thirty. Then we pushed the barrier to forty. Now it's fifty and still being pushed. When Liza Minnelli's hip failed her at forty-eight—when the years of dancing and kicking took their toll—she didn't retire from kicking. She said, "Give me another hip!" And she kept on moving.

We know about nutrition, we know about fitness, and we know that when we're taking care of ourselves, it shows. But, oh, it's a drag to do, especially in hard times. Stress and grief will make you sick—yet there is no life that has no grief. Maybe all husbands don't have hidden mistresses, maybe the IRS doesn't come after everybody, maybe some people's parents simply die of old age. But sooner or later the dark days come to everyone, and when they do, I believe that it's what we do about it *physically* that will get us through it spiritually and mentally.

For years all my fighting and energy was spent on someone else and on a marriage that, it turned out, I was in all by myself. Now that I don't have to do that anymore, I have all this energy left over, for love and for life. I whiz through my workouts with Magic Mike, because I'm not distracted when I'm there. And where it used to take me two hours to get ready to go someplace (because the first hour was spent with B.R., helping him put himself together), now I'm frequently ready ahead of everybody else, downstairs, impatiently tapping my toe, ready, as my son would say, to get going.

And on those days when the only thing that will get me out of a funk is cranking up Little Richard on the jukebox and bopping around the room, Quinton (who plays great air guitar) and Geoff are right there, bopping along with me. We all know that the only way to heal a heart and keep it strong is to keep on moving.

All our lives women are told that vanity is a sin. And in fact, the kind of vanity that becomes obsessive, that excludes people and real life, *is* a sin, because literally, it's life-denying, not life-affirming. But I won't apologize for the kind of vanity that keeps me healthy and happy and extends the benefits of that health and happiness to my colleagues, my friends, and my family.

The way I feel about plastic surgery and cosmetic treatments is that I don't want to look twenty years younger or deny who I am at this point in my life. I *like* this time in my life, and I'm glad to be here. I just want to look like I've had a good night's sleep or a nice vacation. Since I want to be a working actress until they carry me away, I've always said that I intend to live long enough to have everything lifted.

When I was twenty-six, I had breast reduction surgery, in Minnesota. I had been experiencing terrible backaches and shoulder aches. With a little rib cage and almost no hips and these amazingly disproportionate breasts, I looked like those granny cartoons in *Playboy,* with her boobs to her knees. I was in a community dressing room in the theater then, and I was self-conscious about the way I looked and felt. But the best defense is a good offense, I'll never have to hear the big-boobs jokes, I decided, if I'm the one who tells them first.

It was my gynecologist who recommended the surgery, as a health procedure. I was young, and I healed quickly. I had more energy. I literally stood up straighter. It was my first experience with plastic surgery, and it was a very positive one.

In 1985—the year of my mother's dying, the year that Burt was most critically ill with TMJ and his drug problems—I had my eyes done. I had spent months on end crying and not sleeping, and when I looked into the mirror, I saw carry-on luggage where my eyes used to be. No, this won't do, I thought. And I went to the surgeon. We're only given one life and one body. This is the way I feel about mine.

Is my life perfect? No, of course not. I have bills to pay. It takes longer to learn lines these days. Quinton acts up, Deedee and I have misunderstandings, Geoff has to work late, I don't see my sister often enough—she and Steve live in Alaska now, and I have a phone bill that resembles the national debt.

And in early winter of 1995, I lost another old friend to cancer: Doug McClure, with his boyish face and his wide cowboy grin, who managed to be a friend to both Burt and me during our bad days. I have a video of our gang's last Christmas party together in 1992, and there is Doug, mugging maniacally into the camera and doing his brilliant Burt Lancaster imitation. I hate the disease that killed him, as it did my parents and Patty Fuller and Bill Bixby and Bert Convy, and I'm proud of the work I continue to do on behalf of cancer research and treatment.

But there are amazing days to sweeten the sorrow. Geoff and I go to Quinton's soccer and T-ball games and watch as he swings a mean golf club. He's learning to read, and more often than not his friends are at our house, bouncing around and making various messes. When Deedee and Charlie come down from Tahoe with McKenzie, she toddles around behind Quinton as though the sun rose and set on his head. With luck I will be Gramma to more like her in the years to come.

I've stayed in therapy, continuing to learn about my patterns and ways to change them. I always loved the excitement of a dangerous man, and it's happened to me every single time—the danger at the beginning and the inevitable crash. And I always thought that it wasn't about me, it was about them. But of course, it *was* about me—I picked them. *I* picked them. Geoff's not dangerous (although I suspect crossing him in court may be), he's *strong*. I'm grateful that at last I've learned to recognize the difference.

And I'm working—a TV movie, with more to come, and a butterflies-in-the-stomach musical comedy stint as Lorelei Lee in *Gentlemen Prefer Blondes,* traveling in July 1995 on the Kenley Players summer circuit in Ohio. When I began singing the score around the house, Quinton wrinkled up his nose one day and said, "Mom, you sing pretty good. I think you could probably do that for work."

He said it in exactly the same tone of voice he once said, "Mom, you're pretty funny sometimes. Maybe you could get a job on TV." Everyone's a critic.

There were friends who went away in the bad times and stayed away. Then, recently, some came back. They apologized, of course, and I very politely accepted. But the others—the network of loving family and friends that has circled around me and helped me move into this next phase of my life—are and continue to be more generous than I ever could have wished. Their names are legion, and they run again and again through these pages. Every time I thought I was alone, there someone would be, with a hand to hold, a shoulder to lean on, a joke with a punch line that lifted me back into real life. And when Ross met with Geoff and me for cocktails in New York in the fall of 1994, we all toasted each other with genuine affection and respect and a sense of "having made it through."

I had dinner recently with Tim and Daphne Reid, and as we reminisced about *WKRP,* they reiterated something that Hugh and Charters Wilson had said to me soon after Burt and I separated: "We're glad we got you back," almost as though I had been away on a long interplanetary trip and only recently returned to earth.

One of the most amazing gifts has been the reaction of people I *don't* know—people in the streets of New York and Los Angeles, or in Branson, Missouri, or in airports from one end of the country to the other. Old, young, men, women, they come up to me and touch my hand or my shoulder. "Are you all right?" they ask. "We're rooting for you." In the first few months after Burt and I separated, people would sometimes have tears in their eyes when they spoke to me, and I would find myself comforting them. Good heavens, I'd think, this isn't right that they should be so worried for me.

"Thank you, but I'm fine," I'd say, patting them gently. "No, really, everything is getting better every day, and I'm going to be just fine." The more I said it, the better I got. And I didn't do it alone.

Those strangers, along with my friends and family, have helped me believe that this book, and the story it tells, might be of help to someone, just as the telling of it has been of help to me. I want my children, and their children, and the children that come after them, to know that family, faith, and a good laugh can get us through almost anything.

Geoff and Quinton and I spent Christmas of 1994 in Tahoe with Deedee's family. There was a blanket of new snow on everything, and the town twinkled with little white lights. On Christmas Eve, as we sat in church and listened to the choir and I looked at the children's faces, I suddenly ached for my parents. The candles, the carols, the way it smelled—everything felt the same as it did when I was with them. And I was surprised to find that I felt envy. For Deidra's life, for my sister Andrea's life. They got what I thought I'd have, I said to myself. Why am I the odd woman out?

Then Geoff reached over and took my hand. And I remembered —when all is said and done, I have the life I wanted.

On New Year's Eve 1994 a celebrity psychic made her

predictions for the coming year, and one of them was that by the end of 1995, Burt and I would reconcile. I hope nobody put their money on that one: This is the same psychic, after all, who some years ago predicted that I would marry Rock Hudson, go back to being a brunette, and start performing Shakespeare.

Last spring I went to the Kentucky Derby, something I've wanted to do all my life, but I never could find the time (or a willing date) to make the trip. The night before, Geoff and I went to a ball, where I sashayed across the floor in a Nolan Miller dress spilling with silk roses. The next day, beneath the shade of my big picture hat—one like my mother might've worn—I watched the beautiful horses run. I was so completely happy in that moment that I stood up on my chair, with Geoff holding me to keep me from toppling over, and I cheered right along with the rest of the crowd.

A few days later, I dreamed of being in a big hat shop, and each time I took down a hat to try it on, it changed into another, better hat. The only way that dream could've been better was if it had been about shoes.

There was a time I thought I'd lost everything. Here's what I actually lost: bicoastal homes and household staffs; private jets; too many cars; a glamorous life; a public face; busy-ness; naïveté; fear.

Here's what I found: wisdom; strength; Geoff; courage to try new things, to take risks; a new closeness to my daughter, as we raise our children together just as we raised ourselves together. And I found *time*—to think, to read to myself, to read to the kids in Quinton's class, and to go on field trips with them and watch them look in wonder at the big, scary world around them. I guess what I really found was myself.

And just for the record: I am not now, nor have I ever been, anybody's victim. I am, and am quite happy to be, the high-heeled, bottle-blonde, ex–Sunday school teacher, fifth or sixth cousin (twice removed on my mother's side, or was it my father's?) of all the strong and funny ladies, both in and out of show

business, who have made me laugh and given me hope throughout my whole life.

Just in case I haven't said it before, thank you so much—it's
nice to *be* back.

— *not the end* —

Index

Index